GATHERING

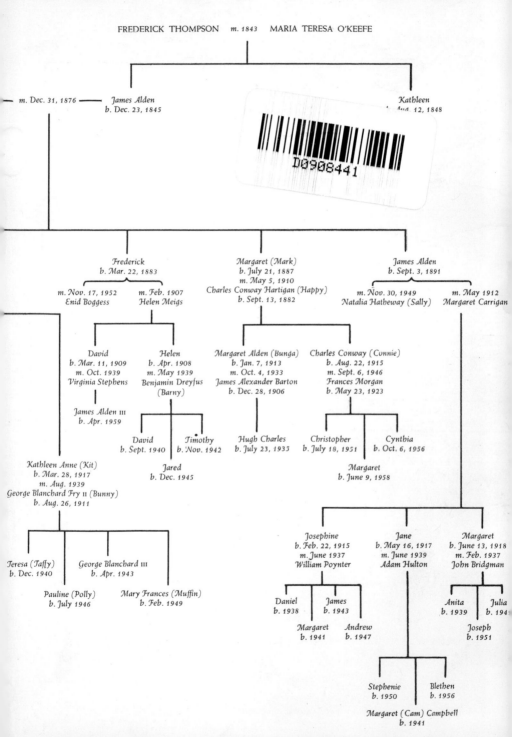

FREDERICK THOMPSON m. 1843 MARIA TERESA O'KEEFE

m. Dec. 31, 1876 —— James Alden
b. Dec. 23, 1845

Kathleen
b. Aug. 12, 1848

Frederick
b. Mar. 22, 1883

m. Nov. 17, 1952
Enid Boggess

m. Feb. 1907
Helen Meigs

Margaret (Mark)
b. July 21, 1887
m. May 5, 1910
Charles Conway Hartigan (Happy)
b. Sept. 13, 1882

James Alden
b. Sept. 3, 1891

m. Nov. 30, 1949
Natalia Hatheway (Sally)

m. May 1912
Margaret Carrigan

David
b. Mar. 11, 1909
m. Oct. 1939
Virginia Stephens

Helen
b. Apr. 1908
m. May 1939
Benjamin Dreyfus
(Barny)

Margaret Alden (Bunga)
b. Jan. 7, 1913
m. Oct. 4, 1933
James Alexander Barton
b. Dec. 28, 1906

Charles Conway (Connie)
b. Aug. 22, 1915
m. Sept. 6, 1946
Frances Morgan
b. May 23, 1923

James Alden III
b. Apr. 1959

David
b. Sept. 1940

Timothy
b. Nov. 1942

Hugh Charles
b. July 23, 1935

Christopher
b. July 18, 1951

Cynthia
b. Oct. 6, 1956

Jared
b. Dec. 1945

Margaret
b. June 9, 1958

Kathleen Anne (Kit)
b. Mar. 28, 1917
m. Aug. 1939
George Blanchard Fry II (Bunny)
b. Aug. 26, 1911

Josephine
b. Feb. 22, 1915
m. June 1937
William Poynter

Jane
b. May 16, 1917
m. June 1939
Adam Hulton

Margaret
b. June 13, 1918
m. Feb. 1937
John Bridgman

Teresa (Taffy)
b. Dec. 1940

George Blanchard III
b. Apr. 1943

Daniel
b. 1938

James
b. 1943

Anita
b. 1939

Julia
b. 194

Pauline (Polly)
b. July 1946

Mary Frances (Muffin)
b. Feb. 1949

Margaret
b. 1941

Andrew
b. 1947

Joseph
b. 1951

Stephenie
b. 1950

Blethen
b. 1956

Margaret (Cam) Campbell
b. 1941

Family Gathering

by Kathleen Norris

Family Gathering

KATHLEEN NORRIS

Doubleday & Company, Inc., Garden City, New York

Library of Congress Catalog Card Number 59–12638

Family Gathering

It was a great adventure, in 1891, for my mother and father to move us all to Mill Valley, once the great Throckmorton ranch, recently platted into building lots scattered on the steep slopes of Tamalpais mountain and on the mountain chain stretching on the east and west to enclose the valley. For my father was the sole support of five unusually healthy and hungry children, his frail and clinging little sister Kitty, his wife with her fixed ideas of "niceness," which included fresh table-cloths daily, butter made into balls, children's under-linen changed three times weekly, and, of course, a cook in the kitchen and a young girl to help with beds, child care, and the Monday wash.

Added to these responsibilities was some regular and some emergency help for my mother's family, and the usual suburban outlay for commuters' tickets, carfare, club, lunches, and so on. He bought a surrey and an old horse named Hatrack; he bought a cow my mother really loved, Dolly; he bought an incubator for my brother Joe to manage so that we might always have chicken for Sunday lunch. Just how this was done on the salary paid the manager of a small private bank it

9

is hard to understand now, but he did it, and was always optimistic, content, and ready with Sunday plans for long walks and picnics in Muir Woods over the hill some four miles away. We were always aware of his presence when he was in the house or anywhere about, for his interest in a thousand small things was vigorous and he usually wanted to share it with one of us.

He would read me a passage from Byron or Macaulay, under his green light in the study that was merely an alcove off the big homey sitting room, or he would call Teresa from her absorption in Gayley's *Classic Myths* to come and tell her poor old father that she loved him. Often when my mother finished some brilliant piano performance he would murmur, "Thanks, Jo. Wonderful!" without stopping his reading. Both older sons crossed the Bay with him on their way to school in San Francisco every morning, and as for the smaller children, they built block houses and walked chessmen about his feet, under his table, unrebuked.

Phrases of my father's making have lived long after him. Once when in the discontented teens I was bewailing the fact, with that faculty all teen-agers have for boring their hearers insufferably, that I was not as good-looking as my sister, mother, or aunts, my father said staunchly, "Well, even if it's so, we can't all be handsome. But I've always felt that a handsome man has only a twenty-minute start on me!" I've remembered this at many a dinner table when a Hollywood beauty happened to be at my host's left.

At another time some members of the home circle accused me of exaggeration. "Let her alone!" said Dad. "Any good story deserves a top hat and a stick!"

And in defense of home hospitalities he quoted his Irish grandfather: "No man was ever carried to the poorhouse on his dining-room table!"

My aunt played solitaire and knit endless jackets and petticoats for that indeterminate group known as "the poor." My mother's contribution to the long winter evenings was, of course, her music. She never touched the piano in the daytime, though it must have been a sore temptation to her. She had been educated by the Notre Dame nuns in Marysville, one of the truly pioneer settlements, a hundred miles north of San Francisco, at the fork of the Plumas and the Yuba rivers. Her talent had been in constant demand, in her youth, at church and school entertainments, and she had been flattered by being asked to play the middle-program numbers in an entertainment by a professional singer—Rosina Vokes, Parepa-Rosa, or the irresistible Lotta Crabtree, I've forgotten which. She and Aunt Kitty, then unknown to each other, had attended all their concerts in a bygone day, and naturally felt that no singers had equaled them since.

My maternal grandmother, Margaret Sexton, was born in St. Louis, Missouri; her early memories were of her grandfather's farm outside of Memphis, Tennessee, where young colts were running under big trees and where she spent most of her time.

She was a tall, gracious woman with regular features, a heavy coronet of braided hair, and a mildly mournful disposition. There must have been some gaiety in early years, for she and four other girls elected, or were required, to be inoculated with smallpox virus, and made a sort of holiday house party of it, enduring a light run of the disease rather than face the horrors of mutilation. They removed themselves to somebody's plantation, where house servants left their trays on a balcony, "and, dear me, how Milly and Betsey and Loveday and I did laugh!" my grandmother observed.

But life subdued her—or, rather, my raging redheaded grandfather did. She didn't want any more trouble, after her thorough breaking in with this tyrant. She yielded everything, explained everything, apologized for everything. She shielded her sons, and bravely lied about them. "Pa" was for a while daring, and fortunate in his ventures; for years they were prosperous, and then suddenly all his friends were phenomenally rich and nothing Pa touched turned out right. Maddened, he risked all he had, and borrowed more and lost that, and remained to the end of his life in a state of rage at the mystery of it.

A wandering Irish actor two years older than she, he had married her when she was seventeen, and they had joined other young adventurers in "St. Joe," buying wagons and stock to set forth for the golden West.

The groom, Paul Lansing Moroney, had come to

America from London, where he was born, with his father, a teacher of letters and church history in a New York State school, near Troy. Young Paul was about twelve; he remembered and used to tell us of the burning summer heat that struck his father down and left him to shift for himself in the first summer. He took up, in Dickensian fashion, with a troupe of traveling players and met my extremely pretty grandmother when she was visiting cousins in Memphis. Her parents making no objection, which seems odd, she and the young thespian carried out their plan, joining the madhouse that was St. Joe in July 1852. Grandmother was eighteen on the roaring, rocketing fourth of that month.

There are many American scenes in the past that I would like to have known; conspicuously, all those tremendous hours of July fourth in Independence Hall in Philadelphia, in the year of Our Lord 1776. But other hours sound equally thrilling, like those in St. Joseph, Missouri, when the young pair met other adventurers there, and gathered in the dusty, irregular streets, among the ramshackle sheds and saloons and shops and houses, to equip the wagons for the long trek. Wagons, for all families had two, one for everyday living, and one loaded with the essential furnishings of the new home, wherever it might be. Grain, seeds, tools, ropes, canvases, chairs and tables and beds, all were stored in the second wagon; linen and china, books, hogsheads of brown sugar, hogsheads of white flour, knives and cooking pots, and personal treasures like the album of family daguerreotypes, Grandma's paisley shawl, and sheet music of popular songs, like "Bright Things Can Never Die," "Brother's Fainting at the Door," and "The Brave Newfoundland Dog." Aunt Margaret used to sing this last with great effect, wringing desperate hands as "Carlo, wave-stemmer, deep-diver, life-saver," was cast into the dark and stormy ocean. And a hundred years later a family boat, merrily cruising the waters of San Francisco Bay, was registered as *Carlo,* in the brave dog's memory.

The little Missouri town must have boiled with youthful energy and rung with youthful voices. Men were leading cattle to and fro, tied horses were wheeling and jingling harness at odd poles and porch railings. Advice was probably as free as the air about them. Take a this and a that, if you don't take anything else. Don't believe anyone who tells you different. You ain't going to keep them girls in hoopskirts, air ye? Soap, honey, we women have got to do some washing. How old are you, eighteen last week? You don't look that. He says we're late now, we're going to get into the snows. It was Ma's; it was about the purtiest thing she ever had, and she give it to me. I'm fixin' to git my bucket fixed.

Sunset streaming through the thick heavy leaves of the village trees; darkness and feeble candlelight coming through the open wagon curtains, little fires smoking everywhere, and a hush over the noise of the day, except for a horse's whinny and a fretful child somewhere battling bedtime. A circled group seeing the Bradford party off. See you in California! I don't know's you will, the way that off ox is actin'. Good-by, Mamie,

I can't tell you the Cinderella story tonight. God bless you, folks.

And in a great outburst of dust the creaking wagons —six or ten—go lumbering toward the sunset, Ma on the front seat beside Pa, with the baby in her lap, the other children grouped at the parted rear curtains, waving back at the companions they have so enjoyed in the beginning of this ravishing adventure. And presently under the wagon great bunches of inflammable brush and kindlings would be tied, and water buckets would swing and splash, and perhaps Pop would letter on the dust-caked canvas hood of the wagon, "Bradford Family," or "J. Billings, Paris, Maine. California or bust."

The slow progress of the oxen dragged my grandparents' party through a real tragedy. A two-year-old boy was missing one morning, when they rested under some trees, out on the long, barren prairies, and the mother, with a four-year-old beside her, and another baby coming, joined the all-day search for little Harry. But Harry was not found, and at dusk they had to move on. Water was scarce, Indian attacks a very real danger, and the comparative cool of the night hours the only thing that made progress bearable at all. Harry's mother, for years afterward, used to meet incoming teams with the anxious plea about a little boy lost, just so high, in a blue apron . . .

It was no use. But she wouldn't let the new baby be named Harry; no, nor the one after that.

My grandparents shared the complacency that to this day San Franciscans feel in this exploit, for on the way they had passed many fertile valleys and mountain meadows tempting to dirty and tired and bewildered women, who must have entreated their dusty and bearded escorts to call it a day, unyoke the oxen, and settle down. But all America's history would have been strangely curtailed if some of these westbound wagons had not gone wearily, haggardly on, leaving death, hunger, fear behind them when they saw at last the shining blue of the Pacific. My grandfather was twenty-one and my grandmother three years younger when they arrived in San Francisco, she several months advanced in pregnancy. Exactly why this gallant, Irish-born young husband decided to sail immediately to South America on a freighter, I never heard. But proof of this further journey lies in a photograph of Grandfather, erect in frock coat and beaver hat, standing before some park statue in Chile that long hung in our dining room.

My mother was born before he returned. Whether the eighteen-year-old wife wept when he went away, whether she tried to dissuade him, we never learned. The probability is that some chance-made acquaintance on the trip West had heard of fabulous fortunes to be made in the Andes. Or perhaps the fact that the godown my grandfather bought in San Francisco burned down within the week sent him after further fortunes. He left my grandmother with his brother John, and John's wife, in a one-room shed furnished only with several hogsheads of gunpowder and some barrels of cube sugar in dark blue paper, salvaged from the grocery. Upon the sale of these commodities the married life of the pair was launched.

My quiet, long-suffering grandmother must have accepted this decision as she accepted everything. They afterward settled in Marysville, as farmers, and she bore thirteen sons and daughters, seven of whom lived to maturity, a pretty good survival average for that time.

Silt from the slow-moving Plumas buried the river farms as years went by, and there were damaging floods to complete the ruin. My grandfather moved his family to San Francisco, prospered, risked everything, lost everything in the sensational stock market collapse in the seventies, and took to managing the old Occidental Hotel in Montgomery Street. My mother was his oldest child, his pride and his darling; "Joey" had a seal coat and muff; Joey had a concert piano. When the bad times came and he moved the whole family to Arizona, to open the Continental Hotel in Tucson, Joey was already married.

My only memory of this grandfather is of a choleric old man with white and ferocious mustachios, glinting blue eyes, and a peaches-and-cream complexion. He sometimes took Joe and me downtown when we were very small, to exhibit us proudly to his cronies in hotel lobbies, and to point out to us the valuable properties that he either had once owned or could have bought for a song.

My other grandmother was a spirited, tall, and well-built Irish girl, the youngest of a family of orphans, supported by a dairy, somewhere near Cork. When she was seventeen her two oldest brothers, who were her guardians, appointed a certain distant kinsman, John O'Sullivan, to be her husband. John was just home from the sea, and Maria Teresa O'Keefe had no recollection of having met him, but marriages were often arranged in this fashion a hundred years ago, and on a certain day she was duly introduced to John, duly married in one of the churches of Cork, and—possibly surprisedly—apprised of the fact that as the captain must sail immediately she was to bid him good-by, join a large clan in drinking to his good health, and promise to join him in the Sandwich Islands some months later. All of which she did, but when she and a harum-scarum maid known to history as Kattie reached the islands, the Hawaii of today, after a hideous trip of wild seas, wormy hardtack, tipped decks continually awash, and the demise of a few less sturdy fellow passengers, John O'Sullivan and his ship failed them. No word was heard of them then or ever.

Maria Teresa rose to the occasion. She wrote to the Pope and to Lloyd's of London, forwarding her letters God alone knows how, and from the first duly received, after a little more than a year, permission to consider herself free when half the usually required seven years

18

had elapsed, since the union never had been consummated; and from the latter a confirmation of her worst fears, if indeed this spirited lady, now besieged by suitors, had really feared anything at all. And in three and a half years she married one Frederick Rand Thompson, Boston-born, and apparently sent to this outflung post to relieve the general pressure and anxiety he had afforded a strait-laced and self-respecting family.

His portrait, a Copley or a counterfeit Copley, hangs in the sitting room of his youngest grandson, in Mill Valley. It shows, at the age of seventeen years—an age at which, apparently, our ancestors began to stir like worms in a cocoon and burst forth in unimaginable deeds of derring-do—a handsome, big-featured, high-colored face, a heavy wave of black, plumy hair, a Roman nose he was to bequeath to more than one unappreciative female descendant, and a beautiful, sensitive, full-lipped mouth ready to burst into laughter. Laughter still sounds in the legend that lives on in Hawaii; how dashing were the horses he rode (where did they come from?), how sudden his wit, as he acted as auctioneer when cargoes of rum and sugar and English cottons were anchored below Diamond Head; how hot the temper that led him either to interfere in a fight with knives or to be a principal in it. Anyway his was a young and violent death.

Maria Teresa took Jimmy, aged five, and Kitty, aged three, home to Ireland by way of China, lingering there for some months with the family of the English consul, one McBaine, loitering comfortably home across Rus-

sia, declining an offer of a third marriage, here and
there, and finally landing at the old home—Snugboro
Dairy, on the outskirts of Cork. Here Kitty danced a
Hawaiian dance for her Irish kin, followed with a good
stamping number from Russia, and won them all by
adding, of her own volition, a Celtic "come-ye-hither."
Young Jim had his seventh birthday in London, on the
way back to the islands, and saw little boys sweeping
the crossings, and no big bunches of bananas hanging
anywhere, and felt homesick. They had two years in
Boston, then back to Hawaii they went, and my grandmother successfully opened a boardinghouse, and ran
it for some ten years, and then came up to California
and opened another on Stockton and Bush streets in
San Francisco and made a great success of that. Jimmy
was left behind, presumably to complete his education,
but he presently followed and took a spirited part in the
life of the new city. He met my grandfather Moroney
when both he and that fiery redhead were in court. My
father was there to explain why he had led a riot of
"Twenty-one-sters" on the news of Lincoln's death, and
my grandfather to justify his refusal to hang mourning
symbols on his home for the same reason. Not too cheerful a beginning for their future relationship, but my
young tall redheaded mother came into the temporary
jail, to walk home with her outraged Pa, and my father
selected his future wife at that moment. Later, both
being popular young people in the rather small group
of the "Irishtocracy," they were asked, still not introduced, to become godparents of a friend's baby, and my

father sought out the grand old Italian Jesuit, Father Varsi, a prince by hereditary right, a saint on his own, to ask if godparentship was any bar to marriage.

Maria Teresa took seriously the profession of boardinghouse keeping; she went down the hill to early Mass every morning, stopped with her egg ring at the market, and sent boys running back to the house with laden baskets. Over and over again the boys returned to fill them, and finally she went home, at nine o'clock, to sit rosy and triumphant at the breakfast table, with her bonnet strings loosened and her adored Kitty chattering across the table.

Then two wooden tubs of hot water were brought in, and all the silver carefully washed, with Kitty drying, after which it was stored in the sideboard; the silver never went downstairs.

With ten years of this sort of hard work behind her, my grandmother planned a sabbatical year. She and Kitty visited their kinsfolk in Ireland, sailed for London, and there the dream ended. Maria Teresa was impregnated deep with cancer, the then incurable disease; she must go to a Paris convent hospital, and spend the last two months of her life quietly, near the chapel, always with her hand in Kitty's. My father met his sister at the New York dock some months later and did not recognize the bent little white-haired figure, smothered in crepe, that crept down the gangplank. I tried to put Aunt Kitty into a book called *Miss Harriet Townshend*, but I had to weaken and give her the happy marriage that the real Kitty never had; she crept under the wings of my gentle generous mother and for the rest of her life lived in the reflected glory of "Jo's creets," her abbreviation of "creatures."

At the very end, dying on the day they moved her into a hospital with nothing wrong except the asthma that had bothered her for years, she said to her old friend, the nurse, as she had so often said to us, her greatest word of praise: "You're a kind creet." And winding her lapis lazuli rosary firmly about her little hands, she went to sleep.

We were born in a seven-room, two-story brick house, far down on Jones Street, only a few minutes' walk from the shores of the Bay. The house had iron balconies and a garden, and smelled of eucalyptus, verbena, nasturtiums, and the good salt sea.

This was a simpler day. It was a day of bustles, calling cards, *The Mikado*, smoky stoves, burned oatmeal at breakfast, *Dotty Dimple* and *Dotty's Cousin Prudy*, night prayers in "Mother's room," and much use of the words "duty, genteel, obedience, respect, truth-telling." Troublemaking by children was not analyzed or considered seriously; children in the eighties had no inhibitions, no fixations, no neuroses or possibly harmful "conditioning." When they were good they were praised and rewarded with marshmallows or shoofly crackers. When they were bad—or even suspected of evil-doing— they were spanked, quite often unjustly. Their calm, unprotesting endurance of injustices in the nursery was perhaps a good training for larger injustices on wider scales, later on.

No telephones, motorcars, radios, or television sets disturbed the even tenor of my mother's day. She moved, the supreme authority, about her home, and worked quite honestly beside her servants at the herculean tasks of the time. The tasks included the washing of mammoth heaps of laundry, in a household of women who wore petticoats and underpetticoats, children who had to have two and three changes of clothing daily, and didy-size babies. There were damask napkins all round at every meal, eight or nine long tablecloths every week. All these were washed by hand-rubbing on a corrugated tin board with yellow soap in hard blocks. After this treatment they were seethed in an oval tin boiler, punched at intervals with a broomstick. They were then rinsed and run through a wringer's rubber wheels, afterward pinned on long lines in the sun, or in the damp laundry room if the weather was wet or wintry.

Another household task was the incessant cooking. The range was topped by a long sheet of iron, pierced, over the fire end, with a great removable ring itself composed of five lesser rings. All along the length of the stove pots must be incessantly bubbling: slow-cooking food, beans and soups and corn-meal mush, and perhaps three varieties of bread in the process of raising. A stone crock of yeast, murderously plunging and smoldering like a fire pit on a volcanic mountain, sent up sighing bubbles, and in a grease pot rested sticks wound

23

with dark rags. Besides the washing and cooking there
was the setting and clearing of tables, the handling of
dishes messy or clean, the polishing of silver, the push-
ing of brooms and dusters, and the unending straightening of the children's nursery and bedrooms.

Yet it all got done, daily, and my mother could sit
peacefully in the afternoons at some chosen spot in the
garden or porch, a great basket of mending and darning
beside her, and await the awakening of babies from
naps or the tempestuous return of children from school.
That was where we always found her, and consternation ruled the entire household if she wasn't there.
Small children come from school exhausted, pencil dust
on hands and faces, sweat on small necks, tears very
near, hunger destroying them. Before the Mill Valley
days Joe and I walked a long city mile from our first
school, clinging close to German Lizzie when we passed
the crazy woman's door, out from which chicken feathers and curses sometimes blew, but otherwise free to
play an enchanting game of hide-and-seek in doorways,
in marvelous store spaces filled with lumber and grain
and sunlight and chickens, push open old ladies' formidable brick gates, enter empty cottages, and scale the
stairs that ran right up the center of the steeper streets.

But however exhilarating the game, we arrived home
broken in mind, soul, and body, and wept while we related the day's crises and the cruelties of our school-
mates and teachers.

My mother listened, distributed soda crackers and
milk—not today's hygienic biscuit and orange juice; no-

24

body had ever heard of orange juice—and perhaps presently reminded us that we had left our back-yard empty-box castles unfinished, or that there were new crayons in the playroom.

She was a loving mother. She thought we were wonderful. She used to like to get all five of us into her lap and arms and kiss us indiscriminately. But this didn't mean that she was not a disciplinarian, or failed to apportion appropriate punishments, when spanking days were over. You could be banished to your room, deprived of desserts, obliged to apologize to Lizzie, to cast your special box of candy into the general supply, birthday or no birthday. After the age of five, corporal punishment was no longer administered. As for my father, he never touched a child or punished anyone, yet he had from us all instant obedience, respect, and the deep love that we feel when we talk of him today, sixty years after his death. He was so sensible, so willing to explain, so anxious for us to be happy, so generous in entertaining us, that we always considered that he was on our side of any crisis.

My mother was extremely religious; she and my father had married with old-fashioned seriousness, old-fashioned vows, and they never lost consciousness of them. We were raised in the Roman Catholic faith, urged to pray our way out of any tantrum, any revengeful fury, any panic. We all prayed when Teresa's tiny cat devoured an inch-long pink scrap of newborn mouse —found by chance, with his immediate relatives, in a bedroom slipper. The surviving mice were cast out into

25

the wilderness of the empty lot next door, and we worried all day lest Dad, when he came home, should censure the gluttonous kitten, perhaps banish her.

Teresa, aged four, and lisping almost to the point of unintelligibility, heroically raced ahead of us to meet my father, as he walked from the cable car on Union Street, with her frenzied defense: "Micky eated a mouth, but it wath her thooty, it wath her thooty!"

My father, picking up the apologist, agreed that perhaps it was a little cat's duty to eat a mouse, and Teresa half strangled him in the bliss of relief. Many a failure in the family circle has since been justified by the use of that potent word.

Our schooling was erratic; my father's main concerns were the moral rather than the intellectual side of our development, and the care of our eyes. We were not allowed to bring any schoolwork home, and he would inquire suspiciously, if he saw one of us reading, "You're not studying, are you?" The effect of this was to make of Teresa and Joe passionate if stealthy students. As for me, after two sessions in the Mill Valley ungraded school the harassed teacher had turned over to me her six youngest pupils and I ran a little school of my own. This was in my twelfth year; two of my pupils, Otto, eight, and Hans, seven, were destined to become famous San Francisco eye doctors. It was Otto Barkan who gave me my first eyeglasses, about 1930, and who looked bewilderedly at me with a tentative "Isn't it Miss Thompson?" Both little boys had naturally considered me middle-aged.

Lizzie was with us twenty years. She was supercon-
scientious, and her confessions, made punctually every
week, after seven days' slavery in a large household,
used to hold the priest's attention for an hour. We knew,
for we had to wait for her. Our own approach to the
matter was more casual; in fact I once won my mother's
interest by complacently reporting that Father Varsi,
who had been selected as my first spiritual director, had
opened the grating and spoken to me.

"He doesn't usually?" my mother asked, aghast.

"He doesn't even push back the little door."

"Ha," murmured my mother. And I imagine the small
girl reciting her misdeeds in darkness and solitude was
somehow helped to a realer knowledge of the Sacrament
after that.

Lizzie's conscientiousness took the form of rigid obedience to my mother's always gentle commands. Joe and
I decided long afterward that one day Mother must
have said casually, seeing her older two off for their
afternoon exercise, "Keep them walking, Lizzie. It's
chilly."

From that moment, for the few years we remained in
the city, Lizzie kept us walking. She walked us through
the long granaries along the water front, where the
ships lowered sails and dropped anchors, and the Bay
waters slapped and chuckled at the piers. She walked
us through Chinatown, and the pigtailed Orientals bestowed on us sugar cane or lichee nuts. We watched the
crates of ducks and tanks of frogs and fish, we smelled
the pungent smells, we toiled up the steep stony heights

27

of Nob Hill. Lizzie walked us out to the sand hills, visited crippled little patients she knew in the Children's Hospital, walked us two miles home. When Lizzie was given directions she followed directions, and our orders were to stay with Lizzie.

Everything was easier for her and for my mother when we went to Mill Valley. My father's two-acre lot, containing a score of magnificent oaks and redwoods, cost him three hundred and twenty-five dollars. The plans for a five-bedroom house, with an immense chimney and fireplace, came to fourteen hundred dollars. My mother winced. "Is that a lot, M'soo?" asked this Victorian lady.

Never quite at home with the familiar diminutive "Jim," she had called him "Monsieur" during their early married life, and after a while he was "M'soo" to his sister, her sisters, every adult member of the group. To outsiders in her conversation he was always "Mr. Thompson."

For a long time Mill Valley's population was something like a hundred in summer, half that in winter. It was all ours, we ranged free, riding on the milk wagons that came down from the Portuguese ranch on the ridge, riding on the primitive bulldozers and trucks, horse-powered, of course, as men broke through new roads and newcomers put up experimental tents, and wandering about in a state of bliss known only to children on vacation mornings. We had few associates, and needed few. One boy, whose father had been in school with my father in faraway Boston, lived down the road, and Spinney was like a brother. One small girl, "Tee's Ellen," came over from the city sometimes, and the beauty of Ellen's older sister, the lovely Miss Mollie, caused me great anguish. For her I suffered the first violent pangs of adoration.

We were five and had been six, a small brother having died in the magnificent beauty of his third year; brown-eyed, gold-headed, he had been my mother's wonder child. She never spoke his name after the brief three days that marked his passing, but it was likely that another son's birth, in early Mill Valley days, did something to round out her boasted half dozen and fill her heart. Jim was an entirely different child from his grave little brother, but he was wholly satisfactory, and she had three girls and three boys again.

Our oldest was Joe, an electrical engineer from his teens, almost from the time Edison harnessed electricity. Joe it was who almost persuaded my father to let us have a telephone, about 1898, but my mother's quiet pronouncement on the new machine was quite justified: "No, no telephone, our friends are not the sort of persons who would use a telephone." But we had electric light, in the last years in the Valley. Eight-candlepower bulbs dangled from the center of every ceiling. We had lamps and candles, too, as more reliable, and anyway, all electricity was turned off, in faraway San Rafael, at midnight. Gas globes that sprayed upward while corresponding electric globes sprayed downward from sitting-room fixtures were common then; they are museum pieces now. But we had never had gas in the house.

I came next to Joe, little more than a year younger; then the lovely Teresa, a blue-eyed Irish type, with rich gold baby curls that framed the most honest, most engaging, serious little face that ever a child wore. Complete strangers stopped my mother when this doll-like little beauty walked beside her. I had been troublesome, getting myself poisoned—I trust not deliberately—by a "trained nurse" who came when my mother was ill. But accidental or not, I was worrisome to raise; they clipped my hair short, and for a time sent me daily to a slaughterhouse to drink warm ox blood, and tied blue silk veils over my eyes to keep away bright sunshine.

Teresa and I were always together in school, but I never took full courses; I could pick and choose, because of illness and my time as a volunteer teacher. We were together out of school, too, for Joe was going across the Bay with my father for schooling now. Fred was several years younger, and Margaret and Jim like a second family, for the child who was lost came after Fred.

Teresa and I roomed together, rose from paper dolls and "flower ladies" to sharing poetry, pressing wild flowers, and at last going without Lizzie on long Saturday expeditions. We were expected to take the small children along with us, for a picnic lunch, and many a heavenly day we spent up on the ridge, under the blown small oaks and madroña trees, dreaming and reading and talking of our future.

Fred was eager, active, ambitious, the boy in the family's eyes "most likely to succeed." And Fred today lives the life most men would like to lead, after many active years. His home is an old sea captain's oceanside farmhouse, with a deep canyon rising up to redwoods at the mountain summit, an old orchard where deer roam every evening, his dog, his library walls, his fireplace, his grandsons and, best of all, the close companionship of the rarely cultured woman he loves; if this is not success at seventy, what is?

On Saturday picnics Margaret, the fifth child—early given the nickname Mark—would climb a sprawling great oak, the only giant tree on the hill, and stretch like some little woodland animal on a swaying branch high over our heads; Jim, and the inevitable small boy pal, usually "Os," amused themselves for hours with no reference to their seniors.

We took books along always; the unspeakable calamity would have been to find ourselves without books. We memorized selections from Tennyson, and I polished the recitation of Aldrich's "At the Russian Court," and Bret Harte's "Flynn of Virginia"; for girls were expected to recite for the entertainment of guests in those days, and I secretly enjoyed it.

Teresa and I read Mrs. Gaskell's *Charlotte Brontë* and Mrs. Craven's *Sister's Story*, Elizabeth Phelps Ward's *Gates Ajar*, and *Stepping Heavenward* by Elizabeth Prentiss. We had a somewhat grudged favorite here and there among the aligned works of Scott, Thackeray, Bulwer-Lytton, and both Kingsleys, but Dickens we knew by heart, and *Cranford,* all the Kirk Monroe series of "Dorymates" and "Campmates," *Marjorie Fleming, Helen's Babies, Lorna Doone,* Grahame's

Dream Days—all were grist to our mill. My father gave me, salvaged from my grandmother's boardinghouse, six formidable volumes of Miss Strickland's *Lives of the Queens of England,* and Joanna of Navarre and Eleanor of Aquitaine became as sisters to me. We also devoured wholesale the lives of various saints, old religious controversies, St. Augustine, and Father Faber. Newman's *Apologia* was worn to rags.

We read Marion Crawford, and how we all read Kipling, quoted Kipling, wailed for more Kipling! No writer today means to his readers what Kipling meant to us sixty years ago.

Jim, who lived with his wife and children in the old Mill Valley home for many years after the rest of us were scattered and gone, came upon a little line-a-day diary of my mother's some ten years ago. It had been overlooked in a carton of old papers hidden under one of the beams of the unfloored attic. With his small-boy memories of her, and the diary's help, he put together a touching little book he called *The Scenes of My Childhood.* It is out of print now, but I hope it will someday be revived, for the diary gives a picture of a long-lost day, and the tribute to the father and mother he barely remembered is a poignant one, poignantly worded.

One noticeable note from it is my mother's regret that a good cook is leaving her: "Germaine automatically discharges herself by asking a raise to eighteen dollars a month." Another astounding feature is the carefully noted meals that this burdened pair, the unassisted father and supporter of eight persons and himself, and the mother of six exacting children, could set forth for the entertainment of dinner guests who came from San Francisco quite frequently. At least twice a month these events occurred, and often, if music or a whist game was in question, the guests stayed overnight, and breakfast and lunch the following day are noted. These meals were served in courses; the two I cite came to six courses each, unless one adds cheese, crackers, and a finishing cup of coffee as a seventh.

In June 1898, at a dinner for ten, there was tomato soup, deviled crab with rice croquettes, chicken terrapin, filet of beef from the Bohemian Club, browned potatoes, onions à la Josselyn, asparagus mayonnaise, coffee ice cream, marbled cake, Neufchâtel cheese, crackers, coffee, and the appropriate wines. There were ten at table. "Children early supper on porch," was the way Aunt Kitty and I handled them.

Another dinner, a few weeks later, listed a light beef soup with meat balls, sweetbreads sautés with wine sauce, saddle of mutton, roast potatoes, corn fritters, purée of artichokes mayonnaise, rice cream with strawberry sauce, cornstarch cake, pineapple cheese, olives, almonds, pickled walnuts, ginger. And the modest finish: "black coffee in demi-tasse cups."

The calories involved seemed to me even less appalling than the labor. Germaine was a good husky Lilloise peasant; Aunt Kitty, Mother, Teresa, and I did what we could. But how we all managed it is a mystery to me still. Germaine did all the waiting on table; perhaps some of us helped her with the dishwashing. And my mother was charming, amused, listening, superintending, and showing no trace of strain at the head of her own table. She had a quiet wit, too. Once when my father brought home two unexpected guests she said to them, upon leaving the table after the meal—a not too impressive one—"You dined tonight with M'soo. Some night perhaps you will dine with me?" But she never apologized.

On another occasion some gushing guest asked a certain old general who was a close friend of the family, "Ah, but weren't you scared when you saw the actual guns?" and the General smilingly echoed, "Scared?" "A dictionary to the General, Teresa," said my mother.

In the winter of 1899, when I was nineteen and Teresa sixteen, an arrangement was made by which half the family should live in San Francisco half the week, with everyone coming home for weekends. My mother was not quite her serene self this winter, because Joe had accepted a job in Astoria, Oregon. Mother sadly missed her first-born, all the more because she said little or nothing of the first break in the family ranks.

Mother agreed to spend part of the time in the city, hoping to shuttle us back and forth in detachments; now his two older daughters and Aunt Kitty taking care of Dad during the week, then Mother and the smaller children coming over to keep him company, while we kept the fires burning at home. In the end we all fitted ourselves into an apartment just a little too small, and unless the weather was exceptionally fine didn't do all the packing up and moving of food and clothes that week-ends in the Valley entailed.

My mother and aunt picked up old friendships in the city where both had been girls a generation earlier, deep in dancing and theatricals, and had applauded Jenny Lind and Parepa-Rosa in concerts, and gasped at Booth's *Hamlet*. There was talk, unspeakably dreadful to me, of my making my social bow at a tea, and attending the Greenways, and my mother and grandmother conferred over a dress that was to be all ruffles for my first ball. My father was dubious about this, offering mildly that, as I knew none of the belles and beaux of the hour and did not dance, I might have a rather dull time. But Mother and Aunt Kitty protested briskly that once I heard the musicians tuning up I would be inspired to get right out and dance with the others. I knew in my heart that an evening of agony was ahead. My secret dream had been to go out to the Children's Hospital on the sand hills and study nursing.

But before even the first of the season's dances took place events that changed our lives had occurred, and my youth was gone forever. My touch upon life had never been a light one; my instinct had always been to seek out the children in any general gathering, any church picnic or bazaar, and see to their conduct and their meals; any boy who essayed friendship had met only embarrassment from me; I did not know the German word *Backfisch* then, but if I had I would have known that it described me. Teresa had already had a quite serious offer—of marriage or perhaps merely of friendship—from a recently graduated young medical student. But as he approached only my father, and my father had advised him to let such matters wait, and told Teresa that she need not worry about it, we made it a matter of some laughter and some arch references to Alaska, to which the discarded admirer had gone with the gold rush.

Two members of the Bohemian Club of whom the club was proud were Humphrey Stewart, a musician and composer, and Daniel O'Connell, a delightful Irishman whose verses flowed as smoothly as the river Shannon. It was O'Connell who wrote the libretto for the opera *Bluff King Hal,* and Stewart who wrote the music, and as both were of a high order, it has since seemed mysterious to me that *Bluff King Hal* had for only two weeks an enthusiastic reception in San Francisco, and then nothing else at all. The music is infinitely more haunting and the words more brilliant than another San Francisco opera, *Natoma* (written much later by Joseph Redding, also a prominent Bohemian, and Victor Herbert), which was given quite a magnificent performance at the Metropolitan Opera House in New York.

As the wife of a former president of the club, my mother attended the opening production of *Bluff King Hal,* escorted by my father and Aunt Kitty. To our excitement the morning papers stated that Mrs. Thompson, "in a Worth model of check black and white taffeta," had ornamented a stage box. The dress actually had been made by her mother as part of her trousseau; she rarely wore it; she rarely had had occasion to wear it.

But by the time the line was in print the wearer of the black and white taffeta was ill. Perhaps she had stood too long in the drafty lobby of the Baldwin Theater. Or perhaps the slow grieving for Joe, her laughmaker, her adored cap and bells, went deeper than we thought. She had never been particularly strong, often subject to the grinding headaches of the Victorian lady, headaches that could be so easily handled now but that meant several days' suffering and rest in bed for her.

She called us in the night; my father went for a doctor, and I did what I could with hot-water bottles and cold bandages. The next day we had a nurse in attendance, and I managed a strangely silent house. I remember that Mark, Jim, and I went down to the shore of the Bay and watched slow barges come through the Gate, and one liner under full sail. In the sober afternoon foghorns were blowing, little stones clinking as they were dragged up and down by the tides. While we watched, a man went down the pier and flung a tied sack into the water, and presently to our horror a cat came swimming steadily in to shore, with a dripping kitten in her mouth. Mark's little red petticoat was wrapped about the kitten, but the mother went back into the cold winter water and brought another kitten out. A third time the cat disappeared under the lapping, rippling little waves, and that time she did not come back.

We carried the kittens home, stopping at a barbershop in Union Street because my father had asked at breakfast that Jim's hair be trimmed. The barber gave him a slick part and a damp heavy wave across his forehead; my father brushed it for him in a more youthful way afterward.

It all comes back. The dim quiet afternoon, the man with the bag, the cats, the barber, and our return home —a home now filled with shadows, whispering, noiseless quiet shifting forms. My grandmother sat in a big chair by the dining-room fire. She appeared entirely unable to realize what was happening, speaking and looking at us vaguely when we talked to her.

My mother was darkly flushed and perfectly quiet, deep in the bed. They had stopped the pain that had gnawed at her in the night, anyway. I knelt beside her with her rosary, her hot hand moved over mine. Teresa brought her some soup. The younger ones came in.

Six days of this, and then Joe was back from Astoria, and it was the last day. My father came home from the bank early in the afternoon; he sat in a big armchair by the window in her room, but when we prayed he knelt down with us. She opened her eyes once to whisper, "Good friends, M'soo?" their little formula for any moment of misunderstanding in their early married days. My father managed to answer hoarsely, "Good friends, Jo!" and she sank back, her hand, wound in its blue rosary, in his. Her eyes were again shut. Joe stayed kneeling; when he got up from his knees the nurse gently guided us all out of the room.

Family Gathering

The strangeness of it! But it was only words then, meaningless words. Everyone went on as usual, but to us all it was as if at any moment she might be back among us. What it was to my father no one ever knew. Her funeral was the day before Thanksgiving, and my father wanted to go back to the Mill Valley house afterward. But it seemed so cold, so changed, that it was like a strange place.

Joe had gone back to his job, Teresa was ill with loneliness and a heavy cold; it was all wrong, it didn't help. It was my quiet little aunt who persuaded him that we must go back to the city, the children go to their schools. "We must help each other, Jim," she said faintly. He went mildly enough.

Members of his club would drop in on us during the next weeks, not staying long, not saying much. He was immensely appreciative of everything anyone did, and Christmas came nearer and my aunt and I tried forlornly to plan some way through it.

Then, a week before Christmas, the doorbell rang and I found a tall truck driver standing outside, looking apologetically at me. He said he had brought the "old man" home. Old man! Father? The next day was to be my father's fifty-third birthday. My father was getting down from the truck, the two heavy horses standing still. The driver explained to me that this "old man" had called on his wife, praised his very small children, refused tea, sat in their little kitchen like a man bewildered for a while, and finally had been brought home by the returned husband and father. I asked him where he lived, and it was in the little brick house on Jones Street with the iron balconies and the painted doorknobs that had "come around the Horn." The house in which the married life of "Joey" and "M'soo" began.

That night my father dined with us—at least he took his place at the table, but he did not eat. He drank more than one cup of tea, listened to the usual daily talk from Aunt Kitty and me as to the children's activities and anything else that would break the dreaded, noticeable silences. An old friend, his doctor, Louis Deane, had come in to play chess with him, but halfway through the meal my father said he thought he would go to bed, we others were please to stay where we were. The doctor went with him to his room. Later I met the doctor in the hall; he was sending for another doctor, he could get only a very weak pulse. I went in and talked to my father, got him some chopped ice, tried to give my aunt some warning of the terrible foreboding I felt. My father lay quiet, his eyes shut. The children came in to kiss him good night, and Fred said suddenly, "Give her our love, will you, Dad?" My aunt knelt in the shadows; Teresa, who had been ill, knelt beside her.

At about eleven my father opened his eyes and spoke clearly.

"She couldn't keep her anniversary without me," he said simply. He did not speak again.

We went back to Mill Valley for a few confused, cold winter days, when the empty house seemed like a barn. And it was then decided that we could not live there; the cost of commutation to the city for the three of us who must be breadwinners would more than cover a city rent, schools were much too far away for the children to manage, and long lonesome days in the old house would be too hard on Aunt Kitty.

Energetically we went to house hunting, and finally found in San Francisco a thirty-dollar rent that was attractive. I know now that if we had gone "south of Market" we could have secured something for half the price, but we never thought of looking in any neighborhood but the ones to which we were accustomed, the ones in which our friends lived. The place had a glorious view; the handsome house that the widow of Robert Louis Stevenson was building was right on the corner; Aunt Margaret and my grandmother agreed that it would be perfectly suitable "when young men come to see the girls."

Our flat was perched on Hyde Street Hill, between Union and Filbert. From our rear windows we could look down on the shabby fringes of the lower city, the water front with its long warehouses that were still called godowns in my father's early days, the glorious, ever changing waters in the Bay, with Tamalpais rear-ing her familiar outline on the north, and the long slopes of Berkeley's hills in the distance. Alcatraz—not then the "Rock"—and Angel Island, never dreaming of a "Treasure Island" fame, were in the foreground; in short, it was our own old-and dear picture of our own city, and the years we lived on Hyde Street were made happier because we had it.

There were the conventional double parlors whose windows gave a rather dull view of cable cars and a reservoir. The front room was to be the parlor, with Mark's couch in it; but with the folding doors open it rapidly became a bedroom, Teresa and myself sharing the rear room. Then came the boys' room, with a window on a shaft, then Aunt Kitty's room, getting a southeastern exposure and the same fine view the dining room had. For this flat was a "duplex," years before the name was given two-story flats, and our big dining room with four great windows was belowstairs. The kitchen and a big basement were pushed into the hillside, and there was a narrow cell of a "servant's" room, fitted up for Fred. Pictures and curtains duly went up, groceries were moved in.

Our fright subsided and the first weeks of responsibility were exhilarating; we could do it! We could pay the rent and manage schools and guidance and new shoes for the young. Teresa and I firmly enforced the Saturday baths, spent Saturday afternoons matching socks and ironing table napkins and handkerchiefs. The small girl and boy fell into line and did their homework at the end of the kitchen table with all the decorum of their adored Nesbit "Would-Be-Goods."

There were no quarrels among us. Walkers on a tight-rope do not quarrel. There never had been any in my mother's day, and there never have been. This is what the grammar torturers of the past generations used to call "a simple declarative sentence."

In a book by Erle Stanley Gardner now on my bed-side stand, he describes the household of a Jewish rabbi whose ministrations, help, advice in a city slum kept him busy for all his daytime hours and often into the night. But he was "gentle," and his wife was gentle, and their children were gentle, obedient, merry, intelligent.

Such a household is heaven on earth, and it is a goal that can be reached, and indeed is reached in many and many a home. To rob children of such priceless posses-sions as the love of and for their parents, and for each other, is a cruelty that makes all other efforts at cul-ture and education futile. We had heavy handicaps, as young persons, and we made many mistakes, some of commission, most of omission, from sheer ignorance and inexperience. But we never had a quarrel.

After the first rush of novelty and the feeling of in-dependence and responsibility—both like a bracing sea breeze to me—had somewhat worn off, sober realization set in, and we felt our first real grief. We knew then that Aunt Kitty had been stunned with sorrow; and we had not sensed it; she had reached the age of fifty, she knew what we had lost, and perhaps glimpsed, with all the horror and apprehension of the woman who has been protected all her life, the struggle ahead. "They seemed so young!" she would say to me pitifully. But one's parents never seem young.

What we did realize, as the hard months hammered along, was what we had meant to them, and they to us, how we had relied on them and how little we knew of the world. The idea of a downtown job was abhorrent to me; to be shut up in an office for an entire month for the paltry wage of two ten-dollar gold pieces was all out of proportion. I could not conceive of myself getting in the least interested in sordid business; it would be drudgery from the first minute to the last. And who could ever guess when that last would come!

Joe returned from the Astoria assignment and got a position with one of the first of the electric companies, a small company that specialized in the first X-ray equipment. A small electric automobile had been left there for repairs, and Joe was one of the first to drive a Stanley steamer and bring all the little boys in Chinatown running out when he clanged the bell. The car belonged to one Charles Fair, brother of Mrs. Virginia Vanderbilt and Mrs. Theresa Oelrichs of New York. Another car was later to be Charles Fair's tomb, on a steep road in France, with a chauffeur at his ear shouting an unavailing *"Arrêtez, monsieur! Arrêtez!"* which probably meant absolutely nothing to Charles Fair. Joe used to say regretfully that if he had been the driver a low warning, "Go easy here, Charley," would perhaps have saved three lives. The Fair will case became famous, the question being who had died first, wife or husband, when both had been crushed together. It was this case that placed on the books the statute that in such a situation a man must be presumed to have survived his wife.

Joe, Aunt Kitty, and I must have had some serious talks about our prospects, but I do not remember that they were ever apprehensive. My first offer of a job had come from the magnificent old owner and manager of the city's finest dry-goods establishment, the White House. Raphael Weill, perhaps in his sixties then, was beloved by the entire city, and has left his name on one of our high schools, and also upon certain epicurean dishes still served in Paris restaurants. He had been my father's friend, and if I had been wiser and older I would have thanked God for his interest and help. I had a week in the ladies' wear department of the White House, under famous "Mrs. Mack," and made but one sale, of two Fiske, Clark and Flagg shirtwaists. The name comes back to me, after sixty years. I wonder if they are still being made? I loved salesmanship and Mrs. Mack expressed regret when she kissed me good-by.

The prospect of "one of poor dear Jo's" daughters becoming a common, vulgar saleswoman, brought into contact with supercilious society women all day, had absolutely floored my aunt Margaret and my grandmother. Aunt Kitty, still in a state of shock, merely listened dreamily to the conversation; one blow more or less made no impression. And I was quite foolish enough to give up a better-paying job for employment in the wholesale hardware business. Incidentally, one of the managers and owners of this establishment was the older brother of the gangling noisy cello-playing wild Irishman to whom my affections were pledged. My aunt and grandmother could lean back, breathing more easily; I was to be immured in an office, mezzanine to be sure, and partly visible, through glass walls, to the rapacious men below, but still not subject to approach from every Tom, Dick, and Harry. Approach from these three probably would have been exactly to my taste.

Joe was paid sixty dollars a month, I was paid twenty, and Teresa five plus her transportation for helping with the children in a Sausalito kindergarten. We lived on this gross income of eighty-five dollars for more than a year, and lived well.

Presently Fred took the step that all boys of fourteen would take if they dared. He quietly left school and found himself a job, proposing thenceforth to contribute to home expenses. Even in retrospect Fred seems our most self-possessed and integrated member, definite and downright from his very childhood. Inasmuch as the said job had been secured right under my eyes, with the wholesale hardware firm where I worked myself, and he and I could walk together to work, coming home on the Hyde Street car at night, it was conceded that this was a workable arrangement, and Fred never went to school again. Except, it might be observed, to the very arduous school of his own choosing—a regulated course of the study of engineering, shipbuilding, chandlery, Spanish, and classical literature. At this age he decided to give up candy, as an act of self-denial likely to harden his resistance against other temptations, possibly alcoholic, to be anticipated in the future. And it was in this connection that Fred quoted a slightly altered Goldsmith, in reference to himself: "the ruined spendthrift, now no longer proud, claimed truancy, and had his claims allowed." And in a moment of fraternal argument he silenced Jim with "The devil damn thee black, thou cream-faced loon, where gottest thou that goose-look?" But it was nine-year-old Jim, studying chess moves under Teresa's direction, who murmured, "Fain would I rise but that I fear to fall!"

I reported for work on the first Monday of 1900. As I had never progressed beyond simple basic addition, subtraction, multiplication, and division, the dark secrets of bookkeeping floored me instantly, and for weeks I sat numb at a desk, wondering what I was expected to do with the invoices that mounted up steadily at my left hand. They came from Miss Gleason, who had penciled upon them such mysteries as "16–10–10," or "37," or even "41."

"Per cent discounts," said Anne Adelaide Gleason, my friend then and my friend today, herself rapidly solving a few and passing them on to Miss Dean on my right.

"Instead of taking them off we find it simpler to put them on," said the office ogre, issuing forth from his cubicle to wonder why I was holding up a whole line of girls.

"Put them on? Yes, sir."

"Simply multiply by the difference. Do you understand that?"

"I guess so." I worked out the price of twenty fishing rods at four different discounts. "Could it come out seventy million?"

"Susan!" They called me Susan out of admiration of one "Susan Thompson and Her Pickaninnies" who had recently come to the Orpheum Theater. "Susan, this whole place isn't worth seventy million! These are to be sold to a few old farmers up in Davisville! Now look, before you take the discount off they only add up to thirty-one dollars, honey. They've got to come out less than that, don't they?"

"Do they?"

"Well, listen——" Miss Gleason was endlessly patient. And after a while some knot cracked in my brain, with all the force of a splitting atom, and the stack of bills went down and down, and I struggled up out of blank fogs and began to enjoy odorous sandwiches out of a paper bag at noon, and airings outside the girls' dressing room high up on the roof. Names began to fit people, and work to be manageable, and the escape at night into the dusky, home-turning city, and the shout of welcome at home all made life bearable.

Night after night we sat down seven, and night after night the eager talk entirely obliterated any deficiencies in the variety or richness of the food. No European peasants ever rang more changes in combinations of the less aristocratic vegetables, rice, potatoes, cereals, apples, bread. Minestrone almost as thick as a stew composed many a meal, and sheets of corn bread or quick biscuit were every-night items. No odd crust of bread or stale roll was overlooked; on Friday nights—fish night to Catholics—we had a great tureen full of them, toasted and swimming in hot milk. Roasts and broiling meats were out, but every Sunday there was a special dinner, and Christmas Day, 1900, dreaded by Aunt Kitty and me as the anniversary of my father's funeral, turned out to be crowded, gay, touching, exhausting, and generally satisfactory. This was due to Teresa.

Teresa had watched from our high dining-room windows the lives of various children in what was a rather squalid region below—a region of shanties made of corrugated iron, fences that had once been wire mattresses, nibbling goats, lines of straggling garments flapping in the winter winds. Teresa had gone down to make friends among them and had returned with the brilliant idea that we should give a Christmas party, distributing among them the luxury toys we might, with luck, collect from our own friends' nurseries.

This idea resulted in a landslide of velocipedes, doll buggies, blackboards, and coasters. A box arrived holding six beautifully dressed big dolls, sent by "two old sisters across the street"; we never discovered who they were, but the dolls stand to their eternal account somewhere. Our basement was like a toyshop when after weeks of mending and painting the toys stood good as new, and our forty guests were augmented by mothers and aunts to the point of suffocation. But the ice cream supplied by the never failing O'Sullivans was plentiful, neighbors had sent in cakes and cookies that far outlasted the event, and the first dreaded Christmas passed in a blaze of glory and an exhaustion so complete that there was no room for anything that night but cleaning up, weary congratulations, and sleep.

Exactly what kept us afloat it is hard, at this distance, to discern, although estimates of living expenses in 1900 are absurd to the point of utter incredibility when placed beside the figures of today. On our earnings of less than one hundred and ten dollars a month (and it was even less than that for the first two years of the century) we never missed a meal, we never missed presents on birthdays and Christmases, we lived a highly exciting and satisfying life.

Our grievous fault was abounding ambition. Nothing was ever in the ideal state it was presently going to be or ever anywhere near our goals. But we kept at them day and night. We did our own Christmas cards with colored inks and varied verses. We drew endless designs of dream houses, usually placing them on peaks running out over the Pacific, and going into details of mullioned windows, derived from Mrs. Molesworth's books, and Dutch half doors. My own fancy was to write illustrated verses to literary idols in the East, and most of them responded in kind.

The great and shining star of American letters at the moment was William Dean Howells, who answered my infant muse with a sketch of the sun sinking behind the Golden Gate, and the words "There's your promise!" I reminded him of this some years later, at a luncheon, but he had forgotten it. President Teddy sent me his picture, Richard Harding Davis and Charles Dana Gibson and delightful Peter Dunne obliged. One of the most charming was a picture from Cecil O'Neill, whom I supposed to be a man, whose sketch and poem in answer to my letter Joe had framed for me, but whose postscript rather horrified my aunt: "Come on to New York, we need your sort."

Presently we had floods of books, for after two years at the hardware store I went into the old Mechanics Library on Post Street, and Teresa got her first real job in the new, arty, enchanting bookshop of Paul Elder and Morgan Sheppard, only a block up the street. It was rare for me to take home less than three volumes, and Teresa could always choose what she would, providing the covers were kept immaculate. Everyone was reading *The Helmet of Navarre, Dorothy Vernon of Haddon Hall,* Jack London's blazing success, *The Call of the Wild,* and first among them all, to our thinking, William De Morgan's great novels, *Joseph Vance* and *Alice-for-Short.* These last remain worth-while reading even today, when so many others are forgotten. We actually bought these secondhand from the library; it was good to own them.

Early hot April Sundays and golden September mornings we took our lunch, stopped for Mass somewhere, and went out to build a fire on the five-mile stretch of ocean beach below the Cliff House. We walked over to the "blue Eddy" car and got "dummy" seats, savoring to the utmost every instant of the holiday. These months were the balmiest of the year, although July and August might have some clear warm weather. But in summer the "trade winds" so beloved of our forefathers whined in gritty whirls of dust and chaff and floods of cold sunshine over the city, and the foghorns droned all morning long. November and February were supreme picnic months, and mornings then might find us under the oaks at Paradise Cove, cheerfully eying the grim walls of San Quentin Prison, or up in the Sausalito graveyard. Joe and I had had a handsome heavy block of granite placed over our parents' graves, where it stands in an abandoned cemetery to this day. We put simply the two names together with the words "United in life, by death they were not divided," cut into the stone beneath. We had no idea what this tribute would cost and it turned out to be two thirds of our inheritance, scuttling almost completely the sum left when the estate was settled.

The number of good times we had was astonishing. Every weekend had its opportunities, or if it had not, we made them. A friend of Joe's had a lumber barge, and often some twenty of his friends were bidden to spend the day on it, being towed up to Richardson Bay to swim, build a fire, and lunch on shore. Or our younger members were carried away by kindly friends, and we could walk over Sausalito's hills to Jolly's Beach, out in the salt air for all the daylight hours, emptying the overloaded luncheon basket the Campbells had packed, and dragging home exhausted to the music of Clay's harmonica. Then there was a pickup supper with everyone interested in his own appetite exclusively, and an hour of singing about the piano. We sang Scotch songs out of faded old books, and "Bill Bailey," and "In the Good Old Summer Time," and a thousand more.

Of course our days had their deprivations, scarcely noticed, and their humiliations, which ate into our very souls like caustic. To be encouraged to ask for a favor and then refused it is an experience all impoverished friends of all comfortably rich persons know.

"You taught me first to beg, and now . . . you teach me how a beggar should be answered," says Shakespeare's Portia. But it is not only the poor who feel life's endless snubs; they are no respecters of persons.

There was the Christmas gift of a creamy tweed coat that somebody sent Teresa, and Teresa gave me. The face of the clerk in the store where we tried to exchange it for a larger size remains with me still. He said, "This has been worn, madam," and then folded it, put it in its box, and handed it to us with a bow, calmly aware that the matter was entirely out of his hands.

There was my own long-enduring smart over the love affair that wouldn't fall into line, the crashing agony of finding the important name in the social columns of the newspapers; he was attending the Greenways, he was in private theatricals at one of the Tahoe Lake country places; he was going to a Spreckles fancy-dress party. There was Joe's quiet mention of the fact that Elizabeth, the girl of girls, was in town, from Oregon, and how he would have liked to take her to a show and to Zinkand's afterward. She came to dinner instead, and the inevitable spilled glass of milk made straight for her lap, and conversation was stiff, flurried by anxiety over the meal, Joe too conscious of wanting her to like us, and Aunt Kitty trying to conceal a natural consternation that any girl alive should threaten our jealous possession of Joe. Teresa was absent.

Teresa, like Fred, had taken a step her parents, if living, would probably have prevented. She wanted to become a nun, and to a close friend who also wanted to become a nun she belittled the mere teaching and nursing orders and leaped for the heights. Alice Meynell's *Letter of a Girl* and Francis Thompson's *Dread of Height*, which she had long ago committed to memory, held no menace for Teresa. Teresa joyfully went to embrace the heroic labors of the Little Sisters of the Poor, taking my heart along with her, incidentally. The loneliness she left behind her was a foretaste of the utter silence that was one day to separate us. This venture failed. She was to try again years later.

But I was reaching for freedom, too, and after five years of various jobs I followed the advice of an old friend of my own people, Henry Morse Stephens, well-known lecturer and historian, and went over to the University of California to take a course in "daily themes" with Professor Chauncey Wetmore Wells and to find means of support while a student there. It was simple to establish myself in the household of a young instruc-

tor whose even younger wife and small sons welcomed
an experienced baby sitter and cook. Board and room
were considered ample pay for these services, and I augmented them by sitting two hours every afternoon with
small practicing children at the piano.

To me the campus atmosphere was intoxicating. I
loved gaunt great Hearst Hall, which one fine old California lady had given to the girl students; loved community sings in the amphitheater on Sunday afternoons.
In the classrooms—I took only composition and two
afternoons a week in conversation French—I had two
ecstatic moments. One was when the professor read a
paper aloud to the class, observing merely at the finish,
"We appear to have a writer among us." Another was
when I went to tea with him and his wife, and he quite
seriously assured me of his confidence in my work. This
brief experience of college life had many more wonderful moments and many starry soft Berkeley nights when
I walked for hours on the hills and looked across to San
Francisco's lights. I had no associates, no young wardrobe, no undergraduate entertainment, no identity, really, for no one suspected whose heart leaped with sheer
joy when one paper after another was noted.

At Christmas I had to go home; Aunt Kitty was ill,
and Teresa, back again in her old place in the bookstore,
somewhat sobered by a frustrating experience with the
convent venture, could not handle the domestic situation alone. So I went back, and the greatest earthquake
in Western history gained power somewhere deep in the
earth, and the brief first weeks of 1906 went by to April.

On April first we moved back to Mill Valley, not to live there but to get the old house in order for a summer rental. On April eighteenth the apartment in Hyde Street was burned to the ground, and with it went much irreplaceable family treasure. The lower half of the city, the part that was at water level, was one great waste and rubble, with a few twisted cable-car tracks lying on the wide ashy spaces that had once been streets. We lost the oriental shawls that had been among our treasures, my Irish grandmother's little letter-seal of a shamrock and a thistle, with the rose carved away, the little bog-oak ring by which she gauged eggs in the market, the diary that my other grandmother's mother had written of the years before and during the Civil War, and countless photographs and scrapbooks that would have helped to rebuild the city's past, for us at least, small as they were in actual value. But there was no talk of loss in those rehabilitation days; everyone was rather in a mood of exultation at being alive at all.

To us, in Mill Valley, with plenty of water available, with a big stove that Joe had built in the center of the garden from the fallen bricks of the chimney, and with dairy products practically donated from the farms up in the hills, it was holiday. Everyone came to us, and life was one magnificent house party—or, rather, garden party—no one dared go into the houses.

Family Gathering

We brought mattresses out, and slept in a row on the porch, and stared up at the beautiful spring sky, and planned our futures. Soot drifted over from burning San Francisco; boats of all sorts took San Franciscans anywhere they could go to find shelter. But nobody was allowed to enter the city; the boats went back empty. Snipers were discouraged by being put to scraping still warm bricks on the piles of ruins; the two-sheet newspapers, published on Oakland presses, were composed of frantic personals. "George and Rose are with Grandma in Stockton, has anyone seen Pa and Harry?" "Jerry Johnson family, get to us at Park Avenue house in Alameda when you can." "Has anyone seen two-year-old blond baby, yellow hair, calls himself Dappy?" "Dan, Phil and I have chance to get to Chicago, will join Theodore."

Oranges and cherries were piled high on open wagons in the wrecked city and sold to orderly queues; bakery bread was warm and spongy and burned sometimes, but plentiful. Trains arriving in the Bay cities brought cases of food, rushed into the area as early as midmorning, two days after the shake, from north, east, and south, with medicines and ice for invalids and babies. America was on the job; nobody went hungry.

One pretty young refugee was an office associate of mine, Linda Johnson, nicknamed "Jack." Jack arrived in Mill Valley simply clad in a nightgown and raincoat, but my sisters helped with her wardrobe, and we all discussed the advisability of her going to Los Angeles to be immediately married. She was engaged, and loved the man, but was dubious about his job; nickelodeons had not reached the dignity of a lifework then. Our verdict was for the marriage and she duly entrained for the south and was married to David Wark Griffith.

Six of us wrote earthquake stories and rushed them to Eastern magazines. Five were taken; mine returned. George Sterling, Jimmy Hopper, John Fleming Wilson, Julia Heyneman, Bruce Porter, all received flat little envelopes with pink slips in them; my envelope had the old dull, heavy, familiar feeling. Julia Heyneman was an artist, but her true love was letters; later she went to London and painted in the studio of the great John Sargent, and sent me a memorable cable. Bruce Porter was to marry the daughter of William James one day, and John Fleming Wilson presently went to New York, where his story, "The Man Who Came Back," was made into a successful play. Carmel-by-the-Sea still boasts of Sterling and Hopper. They all had their share of those happy hopeful days in the garden, after the earthquake.

It was a deep blow to me that my efforts should be rejected when the Eastern magazines were so obviously eager for earthquake material, but after the summer months, when everyone's affairs were beginning to take shape again, and when the Mill Valley house was regarded as a sort of Gretna Green, my prospects brightened suddenly; I got a job with the Red Cross in the city, and it led to my getting a better job on a morning newspaper. The Red Cross had undertaken the colossal work of rehabilitation. Mine was the job of recommending this applicant for a sewing machine and that one for new eyeglasses, visiting the camps where lines of square two-room cottages had risen up by hundreds, without water, without plumbing, but decently painted a dark green. Among the refugees I picked up little human-interest stories and left them at the *Call* office. And the *Call* printed them, as part of the immense volume of earthquake literature, of which nobody could get enough. And in September, catching me and my contributions redhanded, the city editor offered me the "graveyard"—i.e., the social column. Two half columns a day, and four pictures and four columns on Thursday for the Sunday paper.

Wild with hope, I enlisted the entire family, and everyone else of whom I dared ask favors, and owing to their combined sleuthing, a column took shape, a second column, a third. I began to breathe.

Teresa, demurely handling old books to restock libraries, kept her ears open. Mark, visiting down the Peninsula and at Mare Island, gleaned hints. Aunt Kitty and Aunt Margaret came forth from their shells and contributed backgrounds; this debutante's mother was a Glendenning, that leader of the smart set had been born Mollie Peyster. I kept lists, walked miles, telephoned endlessly, and the social editors of the other four papers were friends, who prompted and corrected with a loyalty never met anywhere else.

This job was the turning point for which I had been waiting. But I never had dreamed that the turning point could be a job, a detested slavery in the vulgar haunts downtown. The turning point for all the heroines of Victorian fiction was marriage; the one obsession of the Victorian mother was to get the girls married. Seven daughters meant seven agonies, seven crises attended by discouragement and hurt feelings, as M'ma lured the elderly doctor and the beardless young curate into her toils, displayed Henrietta's music and Charlotte's pretty drawings, rebuked the indifferent brother who would not bring eligible men home for a visit. To go back to Mrs. Bennet and the adorable Elizabeth is to be shamed and sorry for the helplessness and dependence of the crinolined young ladies sketching under the elms of the park.

It was a revelation to me that work, downtown work among men, could be an intoxicating delight; it was good to wake up in the stillness of midmorning and look forward to it, and good to creep cold and tired to sleep at midnight still rejoicing.

Aunt Kitty merely stipulated that I must never enter the Press Club, a haunt filled, she firmly believed, with spittoons, bars, tobacco smoke, and unscrupulous males. After some months she relented about this, but my grandmother never did, and continued in her loving and anxious regret that now Jo's girls never would marry.

Once I felt myself at home in the city room of the *Call*, a new life opened for me. For the first time I realized, like a great burst of light, that the work one wanted to do was better than any leisure, cure for any heartache, disposed once and for all of any sense of drudgery or injustice, and was the secret of the true savoring of existence.

The *Call's* city room occupied two angles of a square frame of rooms built about an elevator shaft and the usual triple angle of stairways. It was, of course, always smoky, hot, and, in our case, scented by strong soaps, for there were little washbasins along the inner walls, embellished with drooping damp towels on rollers. Here many members of the staff performed casual ablutions, drying their refreshed scarlet faces on the roller, combing their wet heads, and turning back beaming and fresh several times in the length of one day. Our newspaper day began at four or five o'clock and lasted until the paper went to bed at midnight, but my task included much rushing about all afternoon among the handsome homes of the city, to follow up the calendar of parties, gather details of engagements, get descriptions of decorations, and possibly glean here and there those odd hints of gossip that are so much more important to a social column than mere facts.

After a few months of the *Call*, the *Examiner*, temporarily located down in the ashy, desolate stretches of the lower city, offered me a salary of exactly three golden half eagles every week, a breath-taking raise, and I worked until I went East to be married under the rule of "Cobbie," the great city editor who trained a small army of writers and is fondly remembered by them to this day. The full name, of course, is Edmond Coblentz.

Never in my more than two years of this work did I

come anywhere near the threat of libelous procedure, but I did have my troubles, sometimes for writing too much and sometimes, surprisingly, for writing too little. In one case, when I was reporting a week's convention of women's clubs, I modestly slipped in a reference to one speaker's hearty recommendation of—it may have been birth control, or it may have been telling the children the facts. I think the latter, for if I was a little shaky on that particular point, on the former subject, owing to Aunt Kitty's rigorous chaperonage, I could have ventured no intelligent report at all. It was a scary and bewildering experience to find my story blown up to front-page prominence the following morning, to meet my aunt's horrified comments, and to be sharply challenged by the offended club. Just why had I stated, the club's spokeswoman demanded during a hot half hour in the office of the editor in chief, that "several ladies, disgusted with the talk," had swept from the hall? Who were they? Would I produce them? I could only stammer that I thought—I supposed——

Well, what the speaker had said would sound mild enough now, and I might well find myself in the clubwomen's camp, but the episode was a painful one, all the more because my office associates chose to assume big-brotherly, not to say avuncular, airs, and elaborately curtail their speech, for fear of offending my reportorial innocence.

But except for the occasional panics that are an inescapable part of newspaper work, all was glory. The late morning hours, the chats over a noon breakfast with

Aunt Kitty, the afternoon chase through the windy, gray summer streets, or the glowing sunshine of February and March, were only a prelude to the entry into the beloved atmosphere of the city room, with the desk-to-desk gossip, the telephone messages, and the mail. Then the important feeling of settling down to the late afternoon grind, hammering away at a defective typewriter as dusk shut down over the city and the business blocks one by one became darkened and silent. After a while the city editor began to give me unimportant interviews, special women's stories, oddities in women's news. I went out on a tugboat to interview the concubine of a visiting Chinese dignity, who loftily described the moral misgivings of our fire-chastened city as mere "lubbish." I rode a big horse around the ring in a rodeo; I affected feeble-mindedness and was taken by one of the older newspaper women to be committed and take a good look at the interior of the state hospital—this, it was pointed out to me at the dinner table, was a chancy thing to risk. But with Victor Hugo's fearful description of an octopus in mind I would not go down in a diver's suit.

When a beautiful young actress came to San Francisco and went into sanctuary in a small hospital someone in the city office got wind of it, and that she was about to divorce the New York theatrical potentate Daniel Frohman. I was given the seemingly hopeless task of covering the story. My newspaper and I were exactly the two things she had come three thousand miles to avoid.

The superintendent of the hospital repulsed me coldly. She had never heard of Margaret Illington or Mrs. Daniel Frohman, either. She was sorry. Good morning. I lingered. "She said she'd be here," I murmured, as one bewildered. Finally I took out my card, that card that honestly said, "Representing the *Examiner*." Upon it I scribbled, "Margaret dear. They won't let me in. Hope you are better. Kathleen."

To the suspicious uniform at the desk I offered this card, "in case Mrs. Frohman does come in." Under her dark gaze I sat down in the waiting room and reached for a *Black Cat* or a *Smart Set* or whatever magazine was available. And three minutes later she was still cold but faintly apologetic beside me. Would I please follow her?

In a dream I was ushered into lovely Margaret Illington's sickroom; in a dream I sat beside her and heard her say that life in the Frohman atmosphere was too exacting for her—I think there were critical sisters or a mother-in-law involved—in a dream I shared her lunch. And at three o'clock with my scoop, a signed photograph, and a good-by kiss I floated on clouds of ether downtown in a drenching rain, waded through mud to the temporary shack that housed the newspaper in a devastated area, and went into the glorious atmosphere of wet clothing, tobacco smoke, printer's ink, and india-rubber that is the city room.

Yes, I had seen her. Really. And she wanted to divorce Frohman and marry a certain Major Bowes, and darn his socks, and live an obscure and happy domestic life. And that was the "darning sock" story that flashed all over the headlines everywhere. Major Bowes was later radio's first talent scout.

Every newspaper reporter has one scoop of which to boast. The trick in later years is to get yours into the conversation before the others do.

Your true reporter envies no one. She may interview the heir to a million today, visit the yacht of some other darling of fortune tomorrow, listen to the happy babble of the screen's latest idol, as she lounges among pillows and with a flash of diamonds upon her unaristocratic little hand shakes from a hundred-dollar cobweb of a handkerchief a hundred-dollar scent. The big rather dowdy woman with the wet coat and pad of yellow scribbling paper sees nothing in these material advantages; they do not lead to the city room. She is here in this magnificent hotel suite, or this yacht, or this railway station, on business, and it is a great business.

"You're a reporter?" says dimples, eyelashes, diamonds, mink coat, money, and adulation. "Yes, and you wish you were!" says the interviewer, in her heart. She loves the disorderly group at the downtown suppers; the heavily breaded, greasy veal cutlets that were lying limp and pink in the window fifteen minutes earlier; the shop talk.

Each issue of the paper is a crisis; three hundred and

sixty-five crises every year, and no two the same. There's no business like press business; no pride like the pride that the simple badge, worn under one's coat collar, engenders in the human heart. One glides through expectant crowds, enters guarded doorways with just a nod to the police, and attends select social functions with none of the terrible misgivings that assail the unknown girl—fears of being a wallflower, pitied by the dowagers, ignored by the dancers.

Colonel James Benét was in command at the Benicia Arsenal now, and young William Rose Benét a graduate of Yale, was at home, Laura home from Vassar, and small Stephen over in San Rafael at school. Our welcome at the spacious headquarters at Benicia, which had been built right after Civil War days, with narrow windows and deep window sills, enormous rooms, a classic doorway, was inexhaustible; Teresa and Mark were much at home there before Aunt Kitty and I went up for a visit, and Frances Rose Benét, "Mother Bun," who was to play so great a part in Teresa's life, presented us at this time with a tiny gold key in a tiny quilted box: the key "to the Benéts' hearts forever."

Colonel Benét used to lament half seriously that, with all three of his children developing poetic gifts, the financial future of the family looked rather dim. But in the games we played in the high-ceiled old parlor in Benicia he showed where they got some of their extraordinary gift, not only for rhymes but for references, quotations, familiarity with every book that ever saw covers, and some that did not.

Once when Teresa, Bill, Mother Bun, Laura, small Stephen, and I had decided to try our hand at Petrarchian sonnets, the Colonel, laying down his book, offered some advice.

"You can't go wrong if you begin with 'What time they' or 'As one who,'" he told us. Sometimes I used to feel that he would have been happier himself as a writer. But this Spanish family had been two hundred years in St. Augustine, and always in the services, and he followed suit. Billy was the first of eight generations ever to vote.

Meanwhile a cousin of my father, Rear Admiral Harry Lyon, U.S.N., had been moved to the command at Mare Island. He and his gracious, full-blown, beautiful Argentinian wife had immediately written us, had followed their letter with a visit to us in Mill Valley, and had opened the Mare Island headquarters to us all. Teresa and I adored the place, Aunt Kitty liked endless reminiscences of the family in Boston with all its ramifications, and Mark, getting up toward a delectable sixteen, liked the general atmosphere of a naval post and the dances in the old sail loft.

So life suddenly became gracious and gay; Teresa loved her work in Paul Elder's old-book room, I was in a continual state of smug complacency over my own prowess, both of the older brothers were married, both parents of babies, and our compact little household of three women and one schoolboy presented no difficulties whatsoever. It often amused me, years ago, when women of my own or the preceding generation loudly proclaimed themselves martyrs because "I simply haven't had anyone in the kitchen for two weeks." To them as to my mother that was a state of insuperable difficulty. But their great-granddaughters raise families of three and four children without any regular domestic help, and manage considerable outside activities as well. "No dishes!" breathed one of them recently as we sat down at a first sumptuous meal on the *United States.*

"But look at the modern kitchen equipment and the gadgets and the frozen things!" my generation defends itself. "Housekeeping today is nothing!"

Which of course isn't true. It would be interesting to estimate the tonnage that American housewives handle each year in hard-to-open packages, cartons, cellophane wrappers, strings tough enough to hold dreadnoughts tight to the dock, cans and can openers, cardboard boxes and silver foil. If this gross weight does not balance the old jobs of shelling peas, hulling strawberries, and peeling potatoes something is wrong with the scales!

L ife might have gone on on those terms indefinitely, for me. I liked to wake up in the silence of the late morning hours, reach for my paper, and check my particular contribution to its contents, wander out at noon to follow up whatever threads of news, social or otherwise, had come my way. With Aunt Kitty's knowledge of San Francisco's beginnings, Teresa's listening post in the city's most popular bookstore, and a score of friends who made themselves volunteer aides, my column held its own, and when on Thursday I had to fill a whole newspaper page with pictures and news of the upper set I was never at a loss for material.

Then came another guidepost at another crossways. Some kindly debutante having given me a hint that her chum, Molly McRowan, was about to announce her engagement, I duly went out, by blowy streets and cable car, to the McRowan house. Molly I had known since she was a small child; she was now a giddy, pretty madcap of an eighteen-year-old who had just made her bow to San Francisco society. The young man I did not know, but like everyone else I knew of him, and that his brother, untimely dead, had been one of the nation's most promising literary lights.

A splendid life-size photograph of this man decorated Miss McRowan's bedside table, and she told me in a joyous stammer, for she stammered and lisped very engagingly, that she was going to be married and soon, despite parental conditions of a long engagement. I went back to the office with the scoop, but according to strict rules I had to get the young man's confirmation. He worked in the office of a magazine, the *Sunset*. I telephoned there.

His confirmation of the scoop came in a series of shouts. Miss Molly was a mighty nice girl, but she'd been engaged to some six or seven fellows in turn, and he wasn't among them. Could he come down and see me? I said there was no necessity for that; he had denied the engagement, that was enough. In half an hour Molly's father called me; it was merely a girl's mistake, he said. She was barely eighteen, she was not engaged to anyone. That was that.

That was in February 1908. A few weeks later, on March third, I went somewhat reluctantly to the regular weekly meeting of the very smart, very exclusive post-earthquake Skating Club. I had several times attended their meetings and was rather bored by them. Also the fleet, under the aegis of Rear Admirals Schley and Sampson, was slowly making its way up the coast, and I had been rendered ecstatic by being selected to go as far down the coast as Monterey to cover some of the feminine facets of the occasion: what the head officers' wives were wearing and saying.

But there might be an engagement announced tonight. Miss Maude Payne and Duval Moore were about ready to tell the good news, and we wanted it first. So with wet feet, a tired back, damp hair, and one of Cousin Leila Lyon's coats, recently made over to me, I went out to the Panhandle in a steady downpour.

Hardly within the door, I was grasped and turned about by Molly McRowan, laughing, and towing a tall dark man by the hand, and as enthusiastic about her "thillineth" in announcing her engagement to "Charley" as she had been over the engagement itself. "Miss Thompson, Charley Norris." The tall dark man then sat beside me, told me the names of the skaters I couldn't

identify, and, the rain being over, walked with me back
to the office. Car lines stopped at midnight.

M y affairs of the heart had been limited to
one, although, like any other hearty, contented, absorbed young woman in the business world, I had had my share of those nebulous
attentions that indicated interest on the part of men
quite as badly off financially as I was myself, and from
ten to thirty years older. I also moved in a vigorous
group that favored long Sunday walks, meals on wind-
blown beaches, days spent in badly handled small boats
on the rocking Bay, and romance healthily in abeyance.
Fifty years later I have been now and then surprised
to learn that among the young males of the party there
were several enamored of my charms. But this, I have
come to perceive, is only kindly old-man talk. At all
events, they gave no indication of their feelings for me
at the time.

Where my feelings were honestly engaged was in the
prospect of one more regulation marriage among the
"Irishtocracy, and pick of the Celtic Shovelry," as my
brother once called it. A descendant of distinguished
dairy farmers named O'Keefe, of County Cork in Ireland, it was natural for me to pick a young giant named
Jack, with a background quite as Irish as my own. Our
most ambitious plans were merely dated "sometime or
other," and included a chicken farm in the Petaluma

71

neighborhood of California; a farm that would blow with the white feathers of pedigreed Minorcas all the year through, and echo to the voices of tall girls with buckteeth and giants of shockheaded boys with skins as brown and tough as leather, and wild yells of laughter that would shake the chandeliers of the nearest town.

But my prospective chicken farmer vanished among the islands of the South Seas and settled on a hemp ranch at Cebu. My answers to letters were dispatched with revealing promptitude, but there were longer and longer intervals between the answers, and finally one brief and regretful suggestion that the whole thing had been a mistake.

It was on the wet Sunday when this letter arrived that dark, vigorous young Charles Gilman Norris made his first call, reminding me that I had met him at the skating rink a few days earlier. He said he had come to leave a book, one of his brother Frank's, and reproached me with the fact that I had said I had a sailing engagement that day. Was I avoiding him?

This preposterous idea, on a second meeting, made me laugh, even with reddened eyes; his second forceful question was directed to them—to the wet eyes. Not to disturb Aunt Kitty, I drew him into the hallway and said hurriedly that I would explain some other time. I said I had had a letter that disturbed me.

"Here, let's walk," he said, holding the coat he had taken from the hall rack. "You can tell me walking."

The rain had stopped. San Francisco was mistily

smiling all over her seven times seven hills. We walked fast and long, part of the time through a cemetery, where we read things off stones. We liked the same books. He knew Teresa, in the bookstore. He knew Fred. We made an engagement to walk out to the cliff on the next Sunday, with a packed lunch. We made an earlier date to see the fleet come in. And now he said, in a sentence I was to hear one thousand and ten times in the years to come: "We eat!"

"We eat at my house," I said, hearing, to my own surprise, that my voice was quite cheerful.

"You can't do that," he said, halting.

"My aunt said to."

"The little lady who came out to say, 'Don't get your feet wet'?"

"Yes. Aunt Kitty. She said, 'Bring him back to dinner if you like.'"

"She'll cook it?"

"Teresa's there. Mark will set the table."

"Your brother?"

"My little sister."

"They won't. Honest, will they?"

"Of course they will."

"Well I'll be darned. She said ask me to dinner." He mused upon it. It was tender; it said, "I like him," and he had had little enough of tenderness in his life. Girls, yes, and parties, and the Greenway and Cinderella cotillions, but not the home variety of warmth and closeness.

Long afterward he told me that his mother had more

73

than once assured him that no one could ever love him. It had bred in him a genuine fear that it might be true. His mother herself confirmed it when she told me one day that "Doctor," as she called him, had cost her so much during her struggle to bring him to birth that she had not wanted to look at him. Asked for a name for the baby, who was not expected to live, she had murmured her physician's name, "Dr. Charles Gilman Smith," and a hastily summoned clergyman had given the poor baby all four names in the confusion of the moment.

The next day I went off to follow with twenty other reporters the navy's slow movement up the coast, but when the fleet entered San Francisco Harbor I sat on one of San Francisco's grassy hills, and Molly's ex-fiancé was again at my side. And thenceforth, mixed into my professional career, which had been so complete and absorbing without him, the shadow of this dark young man fell unbrokenly. He came in to have a cup of coffee with Aunt Kitty and me at noon, and walked with me to my first assignment, whatever it was, and one night we went to dinner at one of the makeshift restaurants that the great fire had driven out to Filmore Street, the Louvre, and became engaged over that Western delicacy known as an oyster loaf.

And if I had had long and humiliating experiences with a lover who employed none of the fine arts of courtship, this vehement man went to the other extreme. He had amused my younger brother while I was following the fleet, and bestowed upon him many small gifts, and his satisfaction in discovering any little thing of which my aunt or Teresa or especially myself stood in need was almost pathetic. No, it was actually pathetic; like David's housekeeper, he had always wanted someone he could love.

No week was to go by, for the following thirty-six years, without its gifts. During that first week Cigi gave me my first fountain pen, brought staples to mend a loop in the wire fence in the back yard, sent two handkerchiefs to the office half an hour after he had noticed that I had a cold, and presented me with a glass of stuffed olives, and a ring once belonging to his brother Frank. His instant impulse was to give one something; handsome things when he could, but anything and everything when his funds were low. He did most terribly want to lend me rent money; I explained that overhead in our house was sacred, always set aside before we so much as went to the bakery for bread.

This so broke him up that when our engagement was a recognized fact I did once plead financial strain, borrowed a small sum, and repaid it with extravagant thanks. Our plans were a vague agreeable dream as far as I was concerned, for at twenty-eight, I did not feel myself free to marry, nor particularly susceptible to the suggestion of it. But it was delightful to share the extravagant ideas of this agreeable boyish person who had taken my breath away when I spoke of New York City as the Mecca of all my dreams by saying simply, "Well, let's live there the way Frank and Jeannette did." New York to him was just another place, where he had

75

lived after graduation from college. To me no unattempted peak in the Himalayas ever seemed less attainable.

But soon he was offered a job on the *American Magazine* and at this opportune moment we had an offer for the Mill Valley house, an offer that gave each one of us exactly three hundred dollars. For a twelve-room country house surrounded by redwoods and only fifty minutes' train trip from the city, a little more than twenty-one hundred dollars did not seem too bad a price; each of us retired to a corner to gnaw upon his portion, like lions in a zoo.

Mark and Teresa put theirs aside, to be most useful within a few years; in Mark's case for wedding plans, in Teresa's to be added to Aunt Kitty's and Jim's as a backlog, when she went abroad. Aunt Kitty banked hers in good Boston fashion. Joe's of course was timely pump-priming for the shaky little Pacific Electric Manufacturing Company he had started, and as Fred was then in Germantown, with the Bethlehem Steel Company, or in Mexico working on agricultural problems, or perhaps only in downtown Los Angeles outfitting merchant vessels, his was probably sunk in the problems of a wife and a small child.

My dowry made it possible for me to marry. I had never foreseen any such solution to the problem, and with a joyous heart I prepared to join Cigi in New York, leaving San Francisco with his mother in April.

Everyone in the family worked on my clothes, Aunt Kitty hemming the wedding dress cut from a whole piece of pongee embroidered in little chrysanthemums in the same shade; the coat was cream-colored fine serge with kimono sleeves. Aunt Margaret wound heavy black satin about me for an evening gown, and the above-mentioned old saint of the White House, Raphael Weill, personally picked my going-away suit, and stated that the price of it was twenty-five dollars. This caused the saleslady a severe shock; but her protest was swept away by the fatherly "Yes. This will be nice," as he crushed the sales price from view. "She will get good wear from this." And she did. The dark straight skirt and long jacket of dark, soft flexible tweed were hung up respectfully at the ranch, twelve years later.

Cigi's mother had secured herself a drawing room on the train; I was near her in what the children used to call "the aisle." This was my first overnight trip on any railway, and each instant of it was momentous to me. My august companion had selected the very slowest of rolling stock; we had to get out at stations for our meals, and the seats were cushioned in red velvet. Twenty minutes were allowed for luncheon and breakfast, thirty for dinner. On long tables in the station restaurants every imaginable edible was placed: prunes, sliced ham, hard-boiled eggs, layer cake, doughnuts, bologna sausage, apple pie. Girls slanted cups of hot coffee toward one, landed them right side up; men lighted cigars. Then back to the hot train for more marveling at the mystery of the mighty Rockies, the plains, and the gradual thickening of cities and towns that meant we were drawing into Chicago. Here we had luncheon and a drive—for there were four or five hours to fill—and here it was that my future mother-in-law pointed out a pinnacled, towered, and balconied house on the lake and uttered the desperate words: "Clysmic in my children's nursery!"

Cigi was the only survivor of her seven children. Four died as infants; Lester, the middle child of her three sons, lived to a princely, gravely intelligent twelve years, lingering through the slow angelic weeks that frequently marked children's deaths in the last century, and leaving her alone with the companion she called "B.F." and the scampish Cigi, then aged six. Frank, who had flunked out of the University of California at Berkeley, was at Harvard, studying composition but determined to be an artist.

In their pain and loneliness over the small boy's loss Gertrude and B. F. Norris, with Frank and Cigi, sailed to France, and she kept both boys in Paris for a year. Frank at seventeen worked at the académie Julien on the left bank; Cigi, ten years younger, in a black alpaca apron went to an elementary school. Frank wanted to become an illustrator, preferably of his own tales, tales that involved medieval armor and jousting; his first fiction was written mainly for the opportunity to illustrate it. But his first attempt at writing showed him where his work lay.

It was about four o'clock in the afternoon when we dragged over the Jersey flats toward the Hudson River and the "skyscrapers" that towered to heaven then and are such forgotten dwarfs now. And here was Cigi, racing along beside the train and greeting us with "Mother, how in the name of all that's decent did you pick out this special train!" and "Katy, I love the hat!"

It was true—Broadway and the Flatiron Building, the editorial rooms of the *American Magazine,* and Central Park, and the vestry of the dim, shabby, enormous Paulist Church on Fifty-seventh Street where we were married on April 30, 1909. Cigi's mother, who was by this time in a rather deplorable state of exhaustion, wished the event to be small and quiet. Our only witnesses were Albert Boyden, vice-president of the *American* and Cigi's best man, my aunt Mary, very fluffy and lovely with an ostrich-feather boa that blew about in the spring wind, and my father's cousin, Rear Admiral Harry Lyon, who had come up from Washington to see that the bride was delivered in all dignity into her husband's keeping.

We had a wedding supper at Delmonico's. I remember creamed chicken, ginger ale, and French pastries, and that our invalid was afterward escorted to her room in the old Park Avenue Hotel, down on Thirty-second and Fourth, where she revived surprisingly and sat with us in the fountain court for some time, recalling other marriages in her own family, and assuring us that we would find life in New York hard, because of the extremes of weather, unknown to Californians. She also spoke of the terrible menace to small children, the "second summer." And finally when we escorted her to her room, read us several of Kipling's poems.

Our first apartment was situated on East Seventy-sixth Street in New York City. We took possession of it late in the evening of our wedding day. As all our luggage and oddly assorted possessions had been placed carefully in the apartment on the preceding afternoon, by ourselves, everything was ready and we could walk to our new home.

We discussed my new mother-in-law as we walked, for she had somewhat upset our plans. We had intended to go that night to a summer place in Massachusetts, Cataumet, for our honeymoon; although it was early in the season a hospitable cousin of mine had assured me that we could be comfortable there, and invited us to come on for a Boston visit when we felt inclined.

But the magnificent senior Mrs. Norris—she was never by any slip or chance to be called "old"—had expressed at our wedding supper such distress at being abandoned, convinced that at any moment she might become seriously ill, that we agreed to put off our trip. We had further agreed to go to see her the following day and to dine with her every evening during the remainder of her stay. We dutifully reviewed the tragic circumstances of her life and decided that she must be our first consideration.

Our flat, which occupied the entire third floor of an old brownstone house, consisted of two good-sized rooms and a neck of narrow small ones: the kitchen, bathroom, and a large closet all in line. The front room had two tall windows looking down upon Seventy-sixth Street, the long narrow rear room had a bay window giving upon the familiar city view of fenced narrow back yards, trees, and the rear elevation of exactly similar brownstones with their backs turned to us. Never having seen anything like this before, among the hilly and irregular dwellings and architectural flights of San Francisco, I was fascinated by the opportunity for intimate study of my neighbors' lives.

Our rooms were furnished, and in no mean fashion. We had sublet from a modestly successful writer of that day, Geraldine Bonner, whose father had known my father as a fellow Bohemian in San Francisco. Our landlady was a spirited little person named Joy, who had traveled in Europe and picked up some beautiful furniture there; our tables, chairs, highboy and bed had once adorned the palace of Ludwig of Bavaria. As Miss Bonner's personal effects were very fine, too, we had to give everything museum care, and that hot first Eastern summer, for me, is associated with the smell of glue and varnish and the anxiety of replacing bits of veneer and inlay as they fell from their age-old positions.

Cigi had drawn two weeks' pay in advance, he had no holiday; our next check would arrive on May fifteenth. Our rent was thirty-five dollars a month, and for the following year we sternly set aside half that sum from each pay check for rent. Cigi's salary was exactly thirteen hundred dollars a year.

I wish I could look back across a long half century

and take a dispassionate outsider's view of that serenely confident couple, rejoicing in a dream come true after a year of delays, obstructions, difficulties. Here we were, really and truly, in New York itself!

Excitements there were in plenty. The city was our dooryard, and we explored it. Free tickets, for the opera, even for first nights, were forthcoming on the strength of Cigi's status as the "dramatic editor" of the magazine. I don't remember that the *American* particularly favored the drama, but it did now and then feature an unusually successful play or performer, and we were never refused seats—sometimes rather high upstairs, sometimes in a stage box. The uncertainty of our luck added to the thrill.

Our first play was Maude Adams in *What Every Woman Knows;* my mother-in-law accompanied us on this occasion and disapproved of the star as having "no presence." As Gertrude Doggett, Cigi's mother had played ingénue parts with the great Lester Wallack, in such plays as *Diplomacy, The Lady of Lyons, Jim, the Penman,* and *Rosedale.*

But Maude Adams had come to San Francisco a few years earlier with *Quality Street* and *L'Aiglon,* and had had the city at her feet. Cigi and I blindly adored her. We saw another play, *The Fourth Estate,* before Mrs. Norris left for California.

It was exactly two weeks after our marriage that we saw Cigi's mother off in a flurry of lost baggage checks, forgotten essentials, wrong train gates, wrong sleeper, hurrying clock.

Family Gathering

We walked to Bryant Park back of the Public Library and sat on a bench in the May shade, silent in the deep content of being alone. With gasps of relief we could congratulate each other upon a visit successfully ended. Our life together officially began at that moment. We had both been confused by the ramified needs of the situation: not to hurt her feelings, not to outrage each other's rights by changing plans incessantly, to be patient and long-suffering under unnecessary waits and delays, not to telegraph recklessly open signals over her only too suspicious head, not to waste the few moments we had alone in apologies and explanations.

The fourteen days had thereby been fully occupied, and the fourteen evenings, even the first one, had been more peacefully if still somewhat bewilderingly filled by the thing she loved best in the world to do, and did best: reading aloud to an appreciative audience. We were that audience. In the fourteen days of her stay I was her sole companion, and we explored the city together; every night Cigi and I dined with her, very careful not to open unsympathetic subjects or to hurt her feelings, and constantly required to explain what we had said or had not said. And after dinner she read to us, in her hotel room. In that time she read us all of Frank Norris' *Pit* and *McTeague*, Kipling's *Boots*, and *The Lay of the Mary Gloucester*, and much of Noyes and Francis Thompson, and as far in Browning's *Ring and the Book* as Caponsacchi.

And whatever I imply about this redoubtable, frustrated, passionate woman as a woman, at least I may

83

pay tribute to her great gift. She was a reader; there are no women readers now, but I remember Aunt Kitty speaking of Charlotte Cushman and Fanny Kemble as giving her more pleasure from reading than from any play, and Gertrude Norris was of their kind. Her voice, her manner, her entire aspect had power, tenderness, variation as she read.

When Pompilia "ba-a-a-ed out her thanks," or when the ocean began to swell through the broken timbers of the *Mary Gloucester*, its old lamps rocked in their sockets, and its old timbers gave way, one heard those poems read as Browning and Kipling themselves never heard them.

So she read to us, and even marked out during the day what she intended to read at night, and while it did not seem to us quite the orthodox fashion in which to spend a honeymoon, it kept her absorbed and satisfied, and when she did finally leave for California we could exhaustedly assure each other that we had nothing to regret.

When we were at last free to make our own plans, we agreed upon a budget. It was one of the odd accidents of my life that, having had a hard training in actual—if happy and carefree—poverty, I should marry a man from San Francisco society whose ideas were quite as stringent as my own. In both of us was rooted a good, healthy terror of debt;

we agreed that, whatever worries might be ahead of us, upon us and our love that shadow should never fall. And as a matter of fact it never did.

Cigi was a sort of glorified man-of-all-work on the *American Magazine*, a job that had been given him on the strength of friendships with his wonderful brother Frank, remembered by so many figures in the world of letters in the early century. It was Frank's great enthusiasm for *Sister Carrie* that first brought Theodore Dreiser to the attention of the reading public, and there were many lesser lights to whom his reviews brought encouragement. Frank had been dead seven years when we came to New York, but his memory was still touchingly alive.

The *American Magazine* had started life as *Frank Leslie's Popular Monthly* in 1876; the name was changed in 1905, and in 1906 the *American* was purchased by S. S. McClure's erstwhile partner, John Phillips, and a group of the leading contributors to *McClure's Magazine* who had become dissatisfied with McClure's policies. Albert Boyden, assistant editor, like many of these people, became our lifelong friend. In May he gave us a tea in the spacious apartment he shared with two other bachelors on Gramercy Park South. To this tea came enough literary folk to satisfy my secret dreams of salons and celebrities. Among them were other members of the magazine's staff: Ida M. Tarbell, Ray Stannard Baker, John Siddall (the philosopher of the "Sid Says" feature), Finley Peter Dunne, of "Mr. Dooley" fame, as well as Juliet Wilbor Tompkins, an old friend from California,

Josephine Dodge Daskam, Charles Hanson Towne, Joseph Chase, the painter, and his wife Margaret, Wallace and Will Irwin, and Will's clever wife, Inez Haynes Gillmore, Theodosia Garrison, Franklin Pierce Adams. There were newspaper writers, too, and artists, and a sprinkling of singers and theater folk. Altogether it was a dazzling first look at the city we were to come to love.

All of them were gracious and many of them we were to meet again and again at quiet dinners here and there, Reinald Werrenrath always to sing; Theodosia sometimes to recite for us her bewitching poems.

But at the time of that first tea we were outsiders indeed, and we walked home through the lingering beauty of a May twilight smoldering with vague jealousies and desires. We did not belong; we knew it.

It was a long time before the brilliance of this occasion was equaled; life went on, plain, strenuous, and yet gloriously satisfying and delightful, in the two-and-a-half-room apartment in Seventy-sixth Street, and if time had brought us no more than we had then, it would still have come under the heading of fun and success.

Cigi was a six-footer, with a smooth wave of black hair, black eyes, and a perfect skin. He was clean-shaven at this time but presently developed a small, sharp-pronged mustache that with his round, boyish face soon made him a target for caricaturists at bohemian dinners on the lower East Side. From every table came a menu sketch of my escort. I was tall too, with a heavy mass of reddish hair never correctly dressed, and an indifference to clothes that was to remain with me all my life and in time cause Cigi acute concern. By today's standards we were both overweight.

On those golden spring days of 1909 we walked in the nearby green shady stretches of Central Park, listened to free Sunday concerts, went out to Columbia University to attend organ recitals, watched chess tournaments, tried out Italian and Hungarian dinners at sixty-five and eighty-five cents a plate, and rented a piano so that we might crash through four-hand arrangements of "Die Schöne Meluzine" and "Fingal's Cave." When Cigi was free, after office hours, there never was a moment to spare.

There was a Yiddish theater far down by Canal Street, there was a modest theatrical experiment going on in Cherry Lane, all of whose players were friends, and most of them San Franciscans. Also we visited the Doubledays at Laurel Hill on Long Island, and I wrote letters home on exquisite paper from the guest-room desk.

The Doubledays were simple, friendly people, with a family composed of a collegian son, Nelson, a nephew, Felix, and a daughter, Dorothy, all still in their teens. The master of the rambling, comfortable house had been named "Effendi" by no less an authority than Rudyard Kipling, the three initials of Frank Nelson Doubleday offering a good chance for a pun on letters. And Effendi he was to a wide group of novelists and bookmakers and poets and artists to the end of his life.

Mrs. Doubleday was a serene and lovely person who had herself, a few years earlier, taken an active part in carrying on the work of her husband's new publishing firm. When there was a shortage of books she sat down and wrote books, careful studies of nature and of birds that are reference classics today. And on these the business limped along until the stream of new writers began to filter in, to widen into the largest and busiest of all the publishing houses.

On our twenty-five dollars a week we handled our expenses without strain. Seven dollars a week was my household allowance, and it sufficed. We had no telephone and no daily paper; Cigi brought home two papers from the office every night.

I marketed on Third Avenue, stopping for Mass at the old Church of St. John the Baptist, between Lexington and Third. In the lower church there was a shrine dedicated to St. Ann and packed with crutches, braces, leg irons, and even wax models of hearts, livers, vertebrae. Here in the atmosphere of miracles I said fervent prayers for my brother Joe, recently made proud by the birth of a son, my brother Fred, married to his loyal sweetheart at the supposed hour of his death, in Mexico, but destined to live healthily until this day. Also I prayed for the wonderful Teresa, and for little Mark and Jim, living with Aunt Kitty in San Francisco.

Letters of course flew—no, the term is premature, they made their way back and forth by railroad. Aunt Kitty reported weekly, Teresa oftener than that; the brothers as often as devoted brothers do write, which is practically never. And presently Mark was writing excited letters about coming East with kindly Frances Rose

Benét. Mark, at eighteen, was already wearing Midshipman Charles Conway Hartigan's ring and had quite made up her mind to join the Navy and see the world. "Happy" Hartigan already wore the nickname that was to go with him all his life. The oldest son of a railroad vice-president from Norwich, New York, he had graduated from the Naval Academy at Annapolis a few years before.

Mark came to me while Mrs. Benét went to Carlisle, Pennsylvania, the headquarters for her own family. And Happy, joining us for the last few days of his leave, took us all to see *The Midnight Sons,* with irresistible Blanche Ring as its star, and a mild young comedian named Vernon Castle inconspicuous in the cast.

When the burning-hot weather came it had its own charm for me. Thunderstorms were unknown in northern California, and hot nights were a mere exciting extension of the hours when one could be out and doing things. The hundreds of New England classics upon which we had battened in our earlier years had prepared Mark and me for the seasonal changes; Celia Thaxter, Sara Orne Jewett, Elizabeth Stuart Phelps, Miss Warner of the *Wide, Wide World,* Thomas Bailey Aldrich, the serials of Trowbridge and Howard Pyle in *St. Nicholas,* and William Dean Howells' *A Boy's Town* had long ago set the stage.

Curiously, the hot summer weather rarely disturbs a Californian in the first year. Its novelty is distracting, its real beauty of leafy outdoor meals and starry nights carrying one through; the general inclination to collapse with a pitcher of iced tea and a book comes later. The beauty of deep waving foliage, roof gardens, and shady streets is all new. Cool little outdoor supper retreats were scattered all along the streets, and on Sundays we often got to Coney Island at six in the morning for a swim, came back for church and breakfast, and were ready for the afternoon concert in the park before the first crowd got to the beach. We picnicked sometimes on benches down by the old Aquarium, watching the boats come and go, or sat watching the tennis in Van Cortlandt Park. On one occasion we ate sandwiches while leaning on the parapet of the Statue of Liberty herself, down the harbor, and we made it a point to investigate every elevated car line from one end to the other.

Immigration from Europe was a simpler matter then than it is now, and one of the sights both Cigi and I always remembered was the day on Ellis Island when a ship came in bringing some three thousand men and women, strange, uneasy, weary and disheveled from the crowded trip. They were tired people who faced the long delays, patiently shawled women and bundled children, curious, sheep-faced men who filed past authority—authority for identity, health, references, and sureties. Large buns holding slices of smoked fish and mugs of milky, sweetened tea were distributed that day. This looked plain enough fare but it disappeared with significant rapidity. The immigrants were scared, bewildered, homesick, but first of all hungry.

And it was good to see their sudden alacrity as the last barrier was cleared, the welcoming door of America thrown open, the long-ago dream come true. Rough men with four-day beards rejoined their families with quickened step, bundles were raised, children's mufflers tied, women's discouraged faces lighted with great hopeful smiles. Little boats were tethered on the dancing water, ready to take them the last short step to the equally eager crowds behind the light fences that crossed the city dock, and there were cries of "Anna! There they are! Mama! It's New York, Wilhelm!"

I had never known anything like the freedom and the thrill this city supplied. That first year is not only glamorous to a backward glance, it was glamorous in its own moment and we knew it.

The mere fact of living in New York was enough for me. I loved the look of the words, written on my letters, I loved the huddled basement shops and the crowded subways.

The discovery of an opposed point of view presently arose to surprise and disconcert us. My anticipation of life in bohemian New York—that is to say, joyous, impecunious, creative New York—was gathered from occasional experiences of it in San Francisco. Not many experiences, for my working hours were night hours. But there had been nights when a select few gathered in somebody's studio over the old Bush Street Market, to feast on shiny salad, red wine, French bread, and sausages. Or some half dozen of us, often with Joe in the party, would wander down to Solari's or Coppa's restaurant in the Italian quarter, to see perhaps a long-haired young man on a ladder thrillingly adding charcoal sketches to the portraits on the walls, to devour antipasto and minestrone and afterward wander through the odorous sights and sounds of Chinatown, slip into the temple for an awed moment of incense and chanting and the ringing of gongs, or into the theater, where the rustle of the audience chewing pine nuts and sunflower seeds punctuated any interval in the play, and the property man wandered through even the most poignant scenes calmly changing the position of chairs or banners.

And if San Francisco could afford us these shredded glimpses of the *rive gauche,* what might not be expected of fabled Greenwich Village, far down near Washington Square and Christopher Street?

We stood modestly out of the way of the famous staff of the *American* and its contributors, but first tastes of the Village were my delight. I loved the crazy crisscross of streets, the carefully chosen rowdy names of little basement restaurants, the red tablecloths, red wines, unkempt locks, and dirty feet in dirty sandals. It thrilled me to see heavy-browed men and lanky girls in smocks —men and girls who had had stories taken by *The Black Cat* and *Argosy*—deeply absorbed in games of chess, and not knowing that admirers were pointing them out! The sidewalks were cluttered with cabbage leaves, push-carts, and girls—girls on the point of crying, talking in urgent undertones to slouched young men who were looking the other way. When an actual policeman came in to investigate L'Estomac du Chat one night I was in ecstasies, and on another occasion sang two stanzas of "The Wearing of the Green" on St. Patrick's night, to prolonged applause.

It was bewildering to discover that none of this appealed to Cigi at all. His idea of married happiness was not a large drafty studio with unfinished canvases stacked about—neither of us painted, he pointed out—bearded old models picked up on the water front, meals redolent of garlic, and children with charcoal-streaked faces being reared in an atmosphere of paint and putty.

Bewilderedly, I stored this dream of myself as a sort of highly conventional and well-behaved Trilby, and confined myself to occasional company dinners, cooked by myself. Our finances dictated an economical dinner, and as it was sure-fire I rarely varied it. A chicken soup made from odds and ends of chicken scraps from a First Avenue market is, as David Copperfield puts it, "no great debauch," a chicken curry and rice deep in condiments can thriftily follow, and a salad glistening with olive oil, with hot crackers and cheese, have one expensive item only. And for years Joe sent me a gallon of olive oil from California as a birthday reminder.

Abandoning Greenwich Village to its smoke-wreathed cellars, its beads and dangling locks and rattling pianos, its celebrities absorbed in chess and indifferent to fame, its lovers whose feelings punctually got out of control and ended in sidewalk altercation, we confined our amusements to the public parks and skating pools and concerts and ball games again.

We went up to Goshen when the first snow fell, for Thanksgiving, and to my eyes my first sight of this miracle, my delirium of delight, inspired one of the children to ask her mother in a guarded whisper if that California lady had been shut up all her life.

We were the guests on that never-to-be-forgotten occasion of Mr. and Mrs. John Phillips. Theirs was a rambling colonial house surrounded by mighty leafless trees and filled with highboys, Revere silver, braided rugs, rocking chairs, wardrobes with dim mirrors, Pembroke tables, and horsehair sofas. It was also filled with delicious children, storybook children daring in their own field of profound conversation and riotous behavior, but with old-fashioned manners where the grownups were concerned. There was a grandmother in the family; aunts came and went, books were everywhere; all was perfection.

Of course, besides these satisfying contents, the house also brimmed with beautiful odors of pies and turkey, round brown cookies, square-cut corn bread. We had a glorious sleigh ride, a spill, a call upon a dim little old cousin in a dim low-ceiled old room to which all visitors must make pilgrimage or break a proud old heart. And to New England I said in my surfeited heart, "I knew you would be just what I thought you'd be!"

Good news of the clan at home came steadily; Aunt Kitty wrote, "These creets spoil me." Fred and Helen were expecting a second baby, Mark gallantly helping Teresa through the Christmas rush at the bookstore, and visiting Mare Island and San Mateo friends for weekends, and Jim earning his first money checking umbrellas at Paul Elder's. Joe's switchgear shed was meanwhile continually threatened with extinction, but the circuit breakers and transformers somehow staggered on from split to split on thin ice, and the day came when Joe wrote me that he and Jim didn't have to go to the general-delivery window at the post office any more on Sundays in the almost always vain hope that a check had come through that would enable them to pay the rent.

And all this time Cigi was suffering agonies of anxiety lest my feeling for my own people should rise and wreck our life.

"I married you. I didn't marry Aunt Kitty and Joe," he would feebly contend.

He had a deep-rooted passion of possession where the few persons he really loved were concerned. It was not that pleasant early-marriage emotion that so flatters a young wife and permits her to boast to her friends of George's fury at the "poor innocent soldier who picked up my umbrella," or to gasp ecstatically, when being shaken breathless under ferocious reproaches, that Willie Whitesides never meant a single thing to her and that their meeting was pure accident.

No, Cigi's need to be loved, to be first, ran far deeper

than that, and among the inevitable surprises of our first year together was my discovery that even my adored family came under the ban of his uneasiness. He told me that his mother's life had been haunted by relatives, his father's peace of mind destroyed, and that he had a horror of "things-in-law."

Much disturbed, I wrote this guardedly to Teresa, and had an answer on a note of laughter.

"Don't be an idiot, Katy, and scare the poor boy to death. He'll like us all when he knows us. Don't keep reading our letters to him, or let him know you write me every day."

And that crisis was handled once and for all.

Thanksgiving was barely past when the amazing letter came from Teresa. Her long faithful labors at Paul Elder's bookshop, her eager interest in half the great libraries of San Francisco and the Peninsula, were to be interrupted by a marvelous holiday. She and the lovely friend she called "my Ellen" were going abroad for four miraculous months! Mostly to be in London, where Ellen had a sister-in-law with a spacious brick house in Lansdowne Road, but to Paris, too, and to Rome. "Oh, Katy, Katy," said the ecstatic letter, "aren't we the luckiest people!"

"My Ellen" was Ellen Eugenia O'Sullivan, of the pioneer San Francisco family. She was the youngest of some dozen brothers and sisters, all delightful, and one,

Cornelius Denis, the adored "Neely" of the whole city, was famous. Denis had cultivated a magnificent voice in Europe (incidentally had heard an unknown John McCormack sing at an Irish festival and had encouraged the lad) and had won for his wife the daughter of another San Francisco pioneer family, an artist in her own right, Elizabeth Curtis. Denis and Bess had divided a romantic life between London and San Francisco. Early in the century Denis toured America, playing the singing heroes of the old Dion Boucicault plays, *Arrah-na-Pogue* and *Shawn the Post*. His death a few years earlier was a sad curtailment of an established career; his widow and her sons and daughter continued to make their home in London, and his portrait by John Sargent lives on in the family as a guarded treasure.

So it was to "Aunt Bess" that Teresa and her Ellen were going, and the anticipation of meeting them, in Hoboken, and getting my arms around the shabby, joyous little figure of Teresa made my first New York Christmas one deep wild expectation. It was a good Christmas. Cigi gave me astonishing things, considering his available means: a sweater and a set of mixing bowls and a worsted scarf for early Mass. On Christmas Eve I gave him a delicious dinner of chicken and homemade pie and gravy.

That is, it looked as if it might be gravy, served in a silver gravy boat with a silver ladle. But it was actually three small checks, saved for some two months with an effort at secrecy that had all but strangled me. Their sum total was thirty-seven dollars for three brief sketches,

97

and fifty dollars as a bonus, for the one that the readers of the *Evening Telegram* had voted the best of the week. Eighty-seven dollars right out of the blue!

One of the papers that Cigi brought home to me at night was the *Evening Telegram,* and I had noted that in every weekday issue the *Telegram* published little stories of three to four thousand words apiece. I had tried my hand at these stories on a rented typewriter whose letters *a* and *p* slipped their moorings occasionally—but then three dollars a month rent wasn't bad! —and although the printed acceptances seemed to me a mere practical joke, and I anticipated somebody's eventual attempt to return the stories and get the checks back, I concealed the whole matter on the one trembling chance that the kindly praise might be honest, the checks genuine.

Up our three flights of stairs a young man from the *Telegram* did duly come, and with a sick heart I identified myself as the "Jane Ireland" of the stories. The nom de plume had been adopted in a too scrupulous effort not to identify myself with my late illustrious brother-in-law. This, in a city of almost six million persons, was perhaps being a trifle too nice, but Frank Norris himself had written first under the medieval title of "Francis Norreys"; a pen name always seems a protection, to a beginner.

Cigi's reception of this Christmas surprise went far beyond my expectation. He was incredulous, exultant, and then brooding. He was still pondering over the possibilities of the situation as we walked downtown over virgin snow on Christmas Day, for a lunch at Childs' and the excitement of seeing Nance O'Neill in *The Lily*. And walking home, for bus fares were a consideration overlooked by our budget, he burst forth with a brief prediction of what our situation would be if I would go on writing. If I would go on writing! How my feet touched the ground after that I don't know. It was one moment that ought to be in every woman's life, when her man is proud and a little bewildered at a new development in her, and they plan together as a team.

The happy Christmas did wonders to put us into serene spirits, and when it actually was Teresa, in a shabby familiar suit and my old coat, running eagerly up the tracks to go half laughing and half crying into my arms, her second great hug, from Cigi, was equally enthusiastic. The truth was, she had won him long before this, during our brief courtship, and he told me apologetically on that very first night that he had forgotten how nice she was.

Ellen got a welcome as warm from me, and I have a memory of Cigi, with a throwback to his French childhood, kissing her hand. Whether he did or not, we were all wildly happy, and the three days before the *Kronprinzessin Cecelie* sailed were wonderful ones for Teresa and me. For Ellen as well as Teresa this was a first trip outside the boundaries of California, and everything enchanted them—most of all, perhaps, the great ship and the great dock with the river water rocking about it and the sound of the boat's low hoarse whistles as the escort tugs got ready to nose her out of harbor.

Teresa's position was that of guest; Ellen was responsible for the practical side of the party. It was a trip that was to color and change all of Teresa's life, but no such thought affected either of the happy girls who hung over the rail and waved good-by. Delights unimaginable lay ahead, and their wildest dreams of fun and independence came true: wandering through little French wayside fairs, roaming through Paris galleries, kneeling with fast-beating hearts for an audience with the Pope. And always back to Aunt Bess in London to touch base.

One event took place in the London weeks that was of immense satisfaction to me. It stemmed from a visit made to San Francisco some years before by the rare and fine and famous English poet, Alice Meynell. It was when I was working as a desk clerk in the old Mechanics Library in Post Street, and Teresa was a saleswoman in Paul Elder's bookshop up the street, a block away.

Mrs. Meynell was brought into the library by her friend Agnes Tobin, a member of the old San Francisco clan and a poet in her own right. Agnes had translated Petrarch's sonnets into English, and a very beautiful job she made of it. Mrs. Meynell's poem, *A Shepherdess of Sheep,* was dedicated to the Celtic purity and unworldliness of Agnes Tobin.

But at the time I knew nothing of the art of either poet. When Alice Meynell came to my desk in the library and put down a volume of poetry I stamped it automatically, taking a good look at what I mentally called the dowdy elegance of this unknown lady, the impressive homeliness of her face, the deep fringe of curled hair over her intellectual brow. In an exquisite low voice she asked as she touched the book, "Do you perhaps know it?"

It was Dante's *Divine Comedy*. I said, with a gulp of agonized shyness, that I did. My grandmother had it, a large, heavy, gilt-edged gift book, lying on her parlor table, and Joe and I, as small children artlessly coloring Doré's illustrations with crayons one rainy day, had found ourselves in trouble.

"We have it with the Doré illustrations," I said. The Englishwoman's face brightened, and she talked of it for a moment with Agnes, then turned to me and said something in Italian. A small male drudge who toiled about among the arcades of the library, and who was at the moment piling books at my feet, said in a hoarse whisper, "That means the sun lookin' through a glass winder." Thus armed, I could enter the conversation with a mildly doubtful "Like a ray of sun through glass?" and of course the poet was pleased at this sign of understanding, and wrote the phrase for me, and they went away and I forgot about them instantly.

Some days later there was a note for me from Mrs. Meynell: "My dear Miss Thompson, Knowing your very deep interest in the Pre-Raphaelites, I am anxious to continue, if only for a few minutes, our talk of Thursday. Will you come to share a cup of tea with Agnes Tobin and myself tomorrow afternoon at five? Cordially, Alice Meynell."

To this I answered, on my best Christmas paper, that I regretted that I had promised to take my sister and brother to the Chutes on the following afternoon, because it was my brother's birthday. A few days later Teresa came home from a holiday week with friends across the Bay to hear me ask amusedly at dinner:

"Does anyone know I have a very deep interest in the Pre-Raphaelites?"

Teresa's puzzled look led to puzzled answers, and to heartbreak, of course. The letter was for her! She had had a chance to have tea with one of her idols, and I had spoiled it! For by a strange coincidence Mrs. Meynell had talked to me in the library only a few hours before she had talked to Teresa in the bookshop, not connecting us at all, for Agnes used only our first names. My little sister, who had had few opportunities in her life for such an afternoon, showed nothing but a momentary sense of disappointment, but it went deep.

So deep, with us both, that when she was actually on her way to London I wrote Mrs. Meynell the whole story, and there was a storybook ending. Teresa met her poet and stayed as a guest with the Meynells, especially loving the brood of children immortalized by their mother and by their great admirer, Francis Thompson. And I felt that the episode was indeed *come raggio del sol traluce in vetro.*

Firmly eschewing, by Cigi's stern decree, the lures of the Village with its smocks and bobbed heads and red wine and untrammeled revels of all sorts, we dieted, took long walks, kept early hours. I had much spare time and I looked in a desultory fashion for a not too confining job, because my attention was centered upon a November arrival: the eternally surprising, incomparably commonplace, inexhaustible miracle of expecting a baby.

In an idle hour I wrote a little story of child labor in a cheerful, worthless, affectionate family. For these were the days when the New York papers, and indeed all the Eastern press, were filled with talk of slave wages and sweatshop horrors. They were the days of "willow plumes"—ostrich feathers augmented with filaments cut from other ostrich feathers, and glued on to extend the said feathers into sweeping fountains of beauty. They were exquisite; Cigi, whose first use of any extra money was to present me with some useless luxury, bought me a pale yellow fan which, with my trousseau's one formal gown, a sweeping black satin, set me up completely.

But the picture was different when we learned that mere babies were tying these plumes on the fans and were blinding their precious eyes. When we learned that girls working over in airless, hot, crowded New Jersey lofts were madly pedaling the machines that turned out shirtwaists at thirty-eight cents each to sell for one ninety-eight. When we read of the child labor in Southern factories—factories, in one case, they said, whose windows overlooked the golf course, so that the toiling six- and seven-year-olds could look out and "see the men at play." Often the parents of these children were not working at all—they were too expensive to hire—but they braced the wan little weary breadwinners with coffee and bakery doughnuts, and roused them crying from sleep when the whistles blew. Public indignation, aroused then, finished child labor once and for all.

I obtained three jobs in the following manner. Reading one of the earliest of the pulp magazines, I was struck with its numerous typographical errors—errors in spelling, in repeated or omitted lines, in punctuation, in grammar. Noting exactly forty-one of these in a single issue, I went to the publisher and confronted him with all due humility and civility with the situation. He called Miss Miller; Miss Miller said that she had been on vacation, which was odd because it was March, and that otherwise she would have caught errata. But she agreed that I might well take Miss Smith's place, for Miss Smith was getting married.

Emboldened by this, I went to another publishing house and to a printer's, and was encouraged by definite offers from all three. Which has made me wonder, all through the ensuing years, whether an indiscriminate diet of books, books, books, under the supervision of a discriminating father with a sharp eye for the misuse of words, is not a sort of educational specialty and might not well be added to college curricula. For this was a time of unemployment talk, and then, as now, capable persons were complaining that there simply were no jobs available.

Through the spring of 1910 I was miserably sick for the first morning hours, soddenly sleepy for the next four, and as bright as a button, demanding amusement, when darkness fell. This particular malaise is like no other; it is lightly dismissed as morning sickness, and falsely confused with simple nausea; neither describes it. It is an all-over languor, a shuddering distaste for even the smell of food, a hunger derived from listless chewing upon stale toast or salty ham, and a complete inability to rise to one's feet, count the wash, or go for a good walk around the reservoir.

But through this time we were striking roots in our adopted city and beginning to take a violent interest in its newspapers and columnists, and the men who wrote book reviews. Cigi had known the Irwin brothers, Will and Wallace, in the Bohemian Club in San Francisco, so that friendly contact with this busy and successful pair, and their wives, was natural. Lovely Juliet Wilbor Tompkins, who was turning out thoughtful and delightful American serials as fast as *Munsey's* and other magazines could use them, was an old friend of Frank Norris, and gave us one of our first, delightful, book-talk dinners. She admitted to us that when magazine material was short she quite often filled in, appearing twice in the same issue under different cognomens. Juliet had had a brief marriage with another San Franciscan and old friend of the Norris family, Emery Pottle, who later won recognition in letters in his own right. The staff of the *American* was always hospitable, too, and our social calendar began to fill. When the artist Joseph Cummings Chase, who later was to do crayon portraits of all the great military figures of the First World War, from Foch and Pershing down to—or up to—Sergeant York, engineered Cigi's entrance into the Dutch Treat Club, other doors were opened.

Cigi had first known Joseph and Margaret Chase when they all lived at the boardinghouse of one Mrs. Langdon, on Madison Avenue near Thirty-fifth Street. At that time Cigi had been toiling at the Doubleday plant. "J.C." had a wonderful roomy studio high up in the old Chelsea Hotel on West Twenty-third, and it was there that we had many meetings exactly to my taste, with the stacked canvases, the high skylights, the French bread, glittering salad, the good talk far into the night.

Chase was everybody's friend, handsome, blond, boyish, and he sang delightfully. When serious, it was "Come into the Garden, Maude," when frivolous, it was quite different. One brief song hinting at the love affairs of two great biblical figures finished:

> But when their youth was over,
> And life had lost its charms,
> King Solomon wrote the prophets—
> And King David wrote the Psalms.

Years later Chase was to have a long association with Hunter College, but at this time his was the usual struggle of a young artist to sell illustrations for magazine stories or occasionally paint the portrait of a child. Margaret Chase was a pianist of distinction, and one of the wittiest women I ever knew, but the wit was pungent and slanted, for she had made an impulsive marriage, and she was restless and unsatisfied.

Older than her husband, she had been the dean of a women's college in Massachusetts, a personage, with her own lovely house and complete freedom of choice about where summer vacations should be spent.

Coming to New York with a young, impecunious husband who was in demand everywhere, popular everywhere, and musical only where his own clear, untrained voice was concerned, was a disillusioning awakening. Their first summer was hot, in a small apartment, and Margaret could tell, with a quiet irony, a quiet laugh at herself, of her modeling for J.C., as Diana, with one foot tied to a doorknob, the other in classic flight, and the upraised bow a humble fly swatter. Her ideas of entertainment—matching napkins, capped and aproned maid—were nearer Cigi's than mine, but on these occasions Joe and I achieved something nearer the beads-and-sandals ideal, and those long summer evenings of low lights, star-flooded skylights, songs, and talk make bright the memories of that uncomfortable summer of 1910.

That August Miss Ida Tarbell asked me to come up to her country place in northern New York, and I spent two weeks with her, talking—or, rather, listening to her earnest exposition of political reform and political figures. For she was one of the first of the "muckrakers" and her articles in *McClure's Magazine* made history. But she had a delightfully human side. She lived in a lovely old colonial house and had a good cook, and she sent me home loaded with spoils: roasting chickens, vegetables, great golden peaches the like of which I never thought to see on my own table.

One day she asked me to help her with a wool test. She had bought three small sweaters at a very low price and had found them marked "all wool." Sternly she pronounced that they could not possibly be all wool, and she brewed a strange and potent kettleful of a mixture that would boil pure wool completely out of sight but would betray the spurious cotton filler in a mass of coarse strings in the seething broth.

We stood beside the stove, stirring with sticks and looking our mutual scorn of merchants at each other, finding no words harsh enough for those miscreants who could cheat on children's sweaters. But suddenly the sticks were swirling about in an empty brew, and Miss Tarbell burst into her rare joyous laugh at her own expense.

We drove about the lovely early autumn country, I quite over my morning miseries, and the old horse, Minerva, plodding between the hillside farms. When Minerva split her head on a barbed-wire gate one day a farm hand helped unharness her and we got her down, but he had no appetite for the turkey needle and strong thread with which his wife came running, and I drew the split skin across the terrifying great bared bone of the forehead, and made so good a job of the surgery that the vet, the following day, would not touch it. I have sometimes hinted to one of San Francisco's surgeons that his mother decided his profession that hot afternoon, but with negative reception.

With the first frosts, the first red leaves, health and energy came back to me with a rush and life was glorious again. After Frank was born we moved to a roomy flat on the west side of Ninety-second Street, half a block from the park. We had two fireplaces, big rooms, a dumbwaiter.

Jim came on, at seventeen, to live with us while Teresa was in Europe, and supplied Cigi with a young brother who must miss none of the marvels of the city; a fresh burst of museums, concerts, theaters had set in, interrupted for a short, agonized period when Jim developed a good strong case of measles. I had never had measles, nor of course had the six-month-old Frank.

The measles saga cost me one of the hardest days of my life, for if Frank was my boy, Jim was too, and there seemed to be no place in the city for a good, outbroken dose of measles. Our young doctor, who was to become a very big doctor later, shared my despair. We couldn't go to Mrs. Langdon's boardinghouse, heaven forbid! We might, said Dr. William Caldwell, be quarantined on our fourth floor, with myself nursing both the boys, but I would have to have help, in kitchen and sickroom, because Cigi must immediately leave the house and live elsewhere while the infection lasted. Also, of course, I might come down with measles myself. My quiet little Martinique maid had already left in tears; she had two children of her own in school.

No, said the young doctor sensibly, the quarantine island, out in the East River, was the only place for measles, and for a while I thought I couldn't face it. Send little Jim to a free ward, abandon Jim when he was homesick and ill, and worst of all, when he was quietly convinced that I wouldn't listen to any such plan!

But within the hour he was bundled up and taken down to a disinfectant-smelling city cab marked "N.Y.C. Health Dep't." and just a little hazy with fever, and more than a little scared, he was driven away; Cigi, by this time returned from the office, accompanied him.

When Cigi came home in the early dark I was sitting by the street windows, Frank in my lap, tears on my face, and utter despair in my heart. The deluging rain that Eastern people call the "equinoctial storm" was streaming down, and Cigi's report that he had left Jim snug and comfortable in a hospital bed sounded so false that I immediately suspected it and feared the worst. The truth was that he had been permitted to go only as far as the hospital packet boat, in the river, and over completely tasteless chicken pie and a later lifeless game of Canfield we dragged through a miserable evening.

Next morning at eight o'clock the Port of New York

Authority took over our apartment, and Frank and I fared forth in streaming rain, to anchor at the rest station in the park, where, with the fine woman who had it all to herself this dark day, and had as well a good coal fire, and a table where we shared a luncheon, we passed the hours until six. Then home we went in a red sunset, to find sulphur candles burning in all our rooms and the windows hermetically sealed.

But Cigi's late return brought joy and hope again. He had got to the island and had found Jim cool and comfortable in a clean bright ward with two or three college boys, similarly afflicted, all in charge of lovely young Cecelia O'Connor. Jim's meals had been "swell," his doctor was swell, and Cecelia was supremely swell. Jim had distributed the magazines Cigi brought, and given the candy by common consent to Cecelia, who had little sisters and brothers. He was snug, the fever was down, and it made him sick to remember that I had been crying while I washed and ironed his night clothes the day before.

So that was the way our adopted city put its arms about us in our hour of need, and took care of us, and forever won our hearts. Not too big a city to send a blanket and a cab and a doctor for a sick boy who had no claim upon her whatsoever.

Jim left on a fruit boat for Panama, cured in soul and body of his late malaise, for Cecelia treated her charges seriously, and saw to their spiritual as well as bodily welfare.

Teresa had written me from London of her determination once again to try the religious life, and to join the Carmelites there, but came home from Europe in answer to a peremptory letter from me. I pleaded shamelessly that I needed her far more than a community of Carmelite nuns in London did. I knew what she didn't, that she was not nun material. Even if she had been, that order would not have been a wise choice.

Good nun material ranges from the highest intellectual, cultural, aristocratic level to the simplest rosy-cheeked, holy little housemaid slaving in a city flat. But there are one or two qualities of nature, or character, that any good nun must have. She must be humble and she must be silent. She must hear herself misjudged, hear statements that she knows to be mistaken, apologize for doing what she did not do. She is tried over and over again for the essential qualities. Penalties that may seem to her childish and meaningless may be imposed upon her, and if within her heart true penitence is re-placed by a sort of proud scorn, it is immediately detected by the novice mistress, whose charity toward her novices takes the form of permitting no trace of human weakness to escape her eyes.

Teresa was handicapped by her past. She was some years past the usual age of novice acceptance, perhaps twenty-seven or -eight. She was an American girl who had been very much her own mistress; she had a remarkably retentive mind, and she had read voraciously and widely. Her free and abrupt comments upon various phases of convent life did not seem to her unnatural; she could even infuse a trace of fun into them, and fun, except for the larklike chatter of the normal novices in recreation, has small part in novice training, or indeed in convent life. Grave smiles, happy subdued laughter as Good Mother finds her decorated chair at her feast, and unrestricted childish teasing at the twice-daily recreation—these keep the atmosphere of a convent genuinely sunny. All Catholics know that a nun who has found her vocation is truly the most celestially serene, indeed joyous, creature among living women. In her exquisite poem, *Hawkesyard* (the house of studies for Dominican novices), Sister Mary Benvenuta compares her charges to captive birds in training:

> Here, hooded by His hand, they sit
> Nor fear the due monastic jesses
> That leash them to His wrist, and knit
> Their wills to His, as should befit
> The fledglings of his tendernesses.

But when Teresa amusedly observed to the Superior who reproached her because the card before St. Joseph's statue was upside down, "But he can read upside down, can't he, Mother? He may be looking down from that side," and asked demurely, "Please may I scatter more spilled milk over the refectory floor and wipe it up properly this time?" she was not regarded as entirely orthodox. She told me later that some of the "darlings" in the novitiate who were struggling with eighteen- and nineteen-year-old difficulties in the house of novices couldn't look at her without laughing. "No matter how seriously I looked at them they put their white veils together and simply burst into giggles," said Teresa remorsefully.

Eventually she had a brief and not unkindly session with the Superior. That responsible person asked her frankly if she felt herself fitted for her hard calling. Teresa asked for another trial and was reminded that she had had several trials. Good Mother told her, almost with motherly tears, that she would make a strong good nun, if she would. But she observed that a twenty-eight-year-old will was harder to subdue than the will of a girl ten years younger, and it was for Sister Teresa, before there was any talk of final vows, to make the decision for herself. Good Mother summoned a small portress. The doors that gave straight upon London's streets were open. Teresa knelt for a final blessing and went through that first door, dressing in strange clothes in a small cubicle, in a lonely fifteen minutes, picking up the packed bag that she found beside her.

Ellen had come home alone to San Francisco long before. Aunt Bess was down in the country; it was full summer now, dry and dusty in the great capital. Teresa walked awhile, sat on a coping and watched doves that broke the air with that summer sound of London: coo-yoo, coo-you. Then she found she had some money and bought a bun and a cup of tea, and afterward walked all the way to Lansdowne Road. An elderly maid was there, sleeping in the place as caretaker, and Teresa found clothes of Aunt Bess's that fitted her, wrapped up for return to the convent the tight shirtwaist and dragging skirt in which she had come away, and rested, rested, rested, thinking it all out, for days. Then she went down to Aunt Bess, inexhaustibly kind, to play with the engaging Terence, and cling to the odd and fascinating child who was Biddy, until something of a healing process was accomplished. Then, in a second-class steamer and by second-class passage, she sailed for home, and Frank, the baby of the family, seven months old, went into spasms of ecstasy.

We had had a cable from sensitive, loving Julie Heyneman, a San Francisco artist who was then working in the London studio of the great John Sargent. Just two words, "Teresa out," but nothing in the Magna Carta ever said as much to me. We met her with tears of joy and the baby of the family instantly displayed a maddening preference for his "Goggy" and was given his own special place in her battered heart from that hot, crowded hour on the dock.

Battered she was. But we all went down to a boarding-house in Freeport on Long Island for summer weeks and gradually, as we idled on the beach, sat guarding the crawling baby, and picnicked in the shade of the great trees, the soreness vanished. It was never resentment, it was only self-blame, and Teresa was too healthy a person to dwell long in that uncomfortable country. She could laugh now as she pleased; she could feast upon books, and she could enter—at an imposingly high literary level—upon a tremendously satisfying friendship with young William Rose Benét, just arrived from California, and already working in the offices of the *Century Magazine.* Billy was some two or three years younger than she, and some ages younger in handling the difficult and painful human crises she was meeting. That Teresa ever would marry never occurred even to me, and I was nearest to her. It was unthinkable to her. She planned to take up courses at Columbia and fit herself to teach in some girls' school. Meanwhile she got a job as saleswoman with J. P. Putnam's Sons, her years with Paul Elder's bookstore giving her immediate consideration, and her own truly beautiful person perhaps clinching the matter. Upon first meeting Teresa, I was to think long afterward, discriminating persons might well have paraphrased Francis Thompson's lines about another lady: "flasked in the grape the wine they knew."

So there we were, snugly ensconced in West Ninety-second Street: Cigi working, Teresa giving all her spare time to lightening my care of an infant prodigy, and myself thrilling with such a fulfillment of my own hopes that it was hard to keep my feet on the ground as I wheeled Frank's pram through the park or watched his staggering progress in pursuit of the baby lambs over by the sheepfold.

Cigi had followed up the surprise of the "chicken gravy" with that persistent attempt to market short stories that is almost impossible for the writer of them herself. The return of those long heavy self-addressed envelopes, the first time, the second time, the eleventh time, is calculated to break the spirit of the bravest, and indeed to induce a sort of choking shame, an instinct to conceal the embarrassing failure in the lower drawers of the sideboard or up behind the hatboxes on the closet shelf.

One doesn't want murmured comfort from the home voices, loyal assurances that the story is a million times better than a lot of the stuff they print, and generous loans of money for fresh stamps and fresh self-addressed envelopes. One wants to die of shame. A mother may exhibit a defective child with a heart burning with love and defiance. But she would rather not. She wants to shelter the loved little thing safe away from other eyes than her own. And it is so with the discarded manuscript.

Cigi had no such supersensitiveness. He listed some twenty-eight magazines alphabetically and, having dredged up from some trunk or box two or three stories written by me in the earthquake year, before a job turned up in San Francisco, he sent two of them, called respectively "The Tidemarsh" and "What Happened to Alanna," down the list. The twenty-eight respectfully declined the manuscripts, with no mitigating word of cheer. Cigi was honestly puzzled, but had of course had his own experience on the *American* and also his younger-brother concern when Frank was beginning to write, to guide him. He knew that sometimes a reader makes a mistake, and he started down the line again.

While I had been visiting Miss Tarbell in the preceding summer, he had sent me the breath-taking news that the *Atlantic,* approached a second time, had taken both tales, and I had been set up with a table and a second-hand typewriter, much newer than the rented one, behind the upright piano. We rarely played "Die Schöne Meluzine" now; Frank didn't sleep through duets. The *Atlantic,* with "Tidemarsh" inside it, had been laid on my bed in the languid hospital days after the baby was born. Two or three more stories had been taken before Teresa came back from London, and I was beginning to feel solid ground beneath my feet. Each story drained me dry, but immediately its successor took shape and the cruses of oil brimmed again.

It was during our prosperous busy winter of 1911–12, while William and Teresa were exchanging profound analyses of Donne, Chaucer, St. Augustine, and Alfred Noyes, while we were all going downtown for eighty-five-cent dinners at Zucca's and walking home in cold starlight up Broadway, that *Collier's* offered a two-thousand-dollar prize for a short story. I had just commenced a short story called "Mother," originally planned as humor, the comedy of a fastidious sister's return, after a year's absence, to the pandemonium and poverty of her own home.

But it steadied into seriousness as I wrote, and as the figure of a lovely mother emerged from the tumult and the shouting I found myself analyzing, almost for the first time, the quiet, self-effacing part we take for granted in such mothers, the part of inexhaustible love and service.

Teresa and Cigi came up the stairs together one afternoon some weeks after I had submitted "Mother" in the *Collier's* contest, a rather unusual thing, for her hours were easier than his, and as I looked at them it seemed to me that their expressions were a little unusual, too. It came to me instantly; the *Collier's* awards were announced.

And I not mentioned for one? No. They both said it simply, and Teresa busied herself with the baby's supper while Cigi went to hang up the coats. I went back to the preparation of lamb curry and rice, and saw the kitchen through a blur of tears. Nobody came near me until we all sat down for dinner, and then I had the magazine in my hands and had swallowed the bitter whole of it. Zona Gale was top winner. My name was nowhere.

This was a hard blow, and Teresa and Cigi knew it. But in the end there was compensation. The *American* took the story, and it was one of those fortunate things that hit the tempo of the times. Floods of letters came to me, even before former President Roosevelt gave it his open approval. One of his many forcefully expressed convictions was that "race suicide"—by which he meant family limitation and "birth control"—was destructive to the very existence of the nation. This term and what it implied was quite new at that time. An aunt of mine had hinted to my fifteen-year-old ears long before that there were disgraceful and unlawful steps an over-burdened young mother might take, to cut short too steady a flow of babies, that Frenchwomen were especially culpable, and that we mustn't talk about it. But among my new acquaintances there was more than one woman who, in all friendliness, advised the acceptance of the new doctrine. Better not have babies in New York!

But "T.R." was not among them, and *Mother* expressed his views; he came out in the press with strong praise, and also came in an imposing limousine to call upon me and the baby. And that night at the dinner table we were indeed hilarious and proud. It was somewhere in that happy time of expanding horizons, when a second baby was on the way, and Cigi and I began to talk of living out in the country somewhere, that Teresa showed me a letter written by Abraham Lincoln. It was a love letter, and it came this time from William Rose Benét. And presently it was with deep satisfaction and confidence, as well as amazement, that everyone who loved her accepted the fact that Teresa was going to be married.

We four, escorting the baby, went house hunting in New Jersey, down on Long Island, up in Scarsdale and Pelham. We listed everything that was possible in a small notebook, and spent excited evenings drawing floor plans and comparing notes. Some literary folk we loved, the Burges Johnsons, lived in Port Washington, at the end of one of the Long Island lines, and gradually the charms of Port Washington seemed to eclipse the others, and it was decided that the country home was to be there.

But first, owing to the inexorable laws of New York landlords, we had to wait for our lease on the city flat to expire, and also it was thought advisable to wait for the new baby, in April. Meanwhile, in the lingering spring winds and snows, every Sunday we explored Port Washington or Plandome, and ate prodigious luncheons at Bradley's, down on the shore road. We found the perfect house, found it cost three times too much, found a lovely rambling one that had just been sold, found the tight little bricky one that wouldn't do, found forlorn, rackety places innumerable, which Teresa and I rapturously dreamed of curtaining along the lines of *We Girls*, planting geraniums in the stark flyblown kitchen windows, and planing away the splinters on the stairs, while Cigi coldly calculated that repairs would cost more to patch than a new house would.

Bracing days for Cigi and Teresa and Bill, but tiring for me. The strains of "Alexander's Ragtime Band" that year became for me, as "The Dollar Princess" had two years earlier, forever associated with weakness and sickness; and one afternoon when the others got home ravenous for Sunday supper I went to bed with a dreary procession of rubbish-blown dooryards moving through my inner vision, stairs, odorous upstairs bedrooms, window glimpses through spattered dirt of the always lovely bay. We could get it for eleven thousand—he'd come down—that was the fifteen-thousand one, Katy, with the six-thousand-dollar mortgage—she'd changed her mind, she wasn't going to sell. Was that the one with the two bathrooms—let's look, anyway, it's so darling—let's not. You three go, leave Frank here on the bench with me. Stay with Mom, Topolino. Leave him. All right, take him. Take his graham crackers.

Next day my twin daughters were born, very simply and quickly; six pounds and seven pounds, it seemed safe enough, and I could stagger a rather oddly serious Cigi with a calculation that, at this rate, when we were forty we'd have ten children. His looks, Teresa's face-turning absorption in things out of sight, didn't warn me. Nothing warned me, not even her quiet, cheerful "Let's decide on their precious little names, Katy."

But it came, the creeping terror. It rose over my exultant hour like a tide. It was over—I had three children—with none of the expected agonies—life was brimming my cup again——

Or was it? Not if the expression in Teresa's eyes meant anything, nor the line of Cigi's shoulders as he stood, back to the room, looking out of the window. Not if Dr. Chapin's quiet voice at my bedside was saying what I could hardly sense and yet knew then as if I had always known it. My daughters were gone. There never was to be another child.

We rented a house in Port Washington, an unusual house, as sound as a little fortress, set in a meadow that ran down to a pond, and only a straggling block or two from the station. It had twin bedrooms and twin baths in the south wing, a long drawing room with windows and doors east and west, and a luxury suite upstairs. It had trees about, and scattered friendly neighbors. We loved it, and after us the Sinclair Lewises took it, and after that the Fontaine Foxes, so we felt a friendly proprietary interest in it for many years. After a year of trying out what was then, and may be still, one of the most delightful hamlets of the entire world, we bought a home across the village, on Bayview Avenue. This place stood in a spacious garden, had a garage, even a chicken yard, and when we had had the blinds painted we named it "Green Blinds."

Teresa and Bill presently had a small church vestry wedding, Cigi saving a rather stiff situation by straightening the position of the bride and groom, and the priest as well, with a superstitious recollection that he and I had been aslant at the important moment of the "I do's," and it had had a sinister effect upon our future. Teresa was a very madonna of a bride, Bill collected and definite in responses, and we all went home to breakfast in great spirits, before the Benéts left for South Carolina mountains, where Bill's parents, with Laura and Stephen, were spending a summer vacation. Frank clung to

123

his beloved Goggy and evidently desired to be a member of the wedding but was comforted by the sugar bride and groom from the cake.

By this golden summertime we were members of the Port Washington Beach Club, and Teresa and I had learned to swim. Our youthful years had been spent in a northern California that had not broken out as it has today with thousands of family swimming pools; we had occasionally splashed with brothers at the Lurline Baths or the magnificent Cliff House sport club or museum or whatever they called the mammoth structure with a roof sixty feet above our heads. But the delight of real swimming and boating were reserved for our early married lives, and we lived in the water, and when our first new social advantages developed to include the freedom of beaches out at Sands Point, we were never at a loss for blissful Sunday plans.

J oe came on to New York for the first time that summer to check with his agent in a one-room office in Church Street. Perhaps not a business event to stop the wheels of the city clocks, but to Teresa and me it was deeply satisfying and exciting. We went down to Church Street to approve of the premises, and exchanged proud comments upon it. Joe approved in turn of the Port Washington homes and the baby; he took his business more quietly. His San Francisco plant for the manufacture of transformers and circuit breakers was flourishing modestly, and he had already put out a catalogue under the old first name that had once seemed to me somewhat pretentious: The Pacific Electric Manufacturing Company.

To hear Joe talking electronics with his agent, to see him prosperous and confident, to have him take us to luncheon at the Knickerbocker Hotel, and afterward to mount the top of a sight-seeing bus and drive all over the city—and above all to find him the same amusing, carefree, affectionate brother he always had been—was sheer delight.

When, to the waiter's murmured question as to whether he would like large oysters he answered, "About the size of bedroom slippers," we three, who had steered the topheavy bark of the family's affairs somehow through the long years that had reached this delicious breathing space, laughed together as we always had laughed at good times or bad. At five on that enchanted day it was Cigi's turn to show us the office of the *American,* and then take us to dinner, and then home to Port Washington to awaken Frank and show him off to Uncle Joe. "Time, you thief, who like to get sweets into your list, put that in." This was a happy hour.

There were probably a thousand young engineers in California alone, accepting the challenge of the comparatively new miracle of electricity, and probing its always increasing powers. And in the Union perhaps there were a million Joes, not satisfied with matters as they stood, but eternally inventing little improvements and great, perfecting Edison's beginnings, even as they are to this day.

But to us a vigorous and gifted male, who stood upon his own feet, was a refreshing change from the many stories all about us of the fathers and brothers of those discouraging and poverty-stricken families whose purpose, in idle middle age, is to discourage the rising crop of younger folk and assure them that, no matter how honest and hard-working a man may be, there simply is no market now, under this Administration, for the sort of work they are fitted to do.

O f such was my grandmother's family; my capable, gentle, tireless mother and one younger brother of hers, Frank, were the only exceptions among the six brothers and sisters to the rule of idleness, intermittent employment, philosophic complaint. Frank had married young and had small children of his own; his was a strong and independent nature, and in later years he became a prominent businessman and a very popular member of more than one club.

But two older uncles of ours, and one aunt, displayed no such energy. They had assumed, in youth, all the grievances of the Old South. Many of their friends were refugees from the miseries of the postwar period, ladies to whom the word "genteel" aptly applied, who lurked behind Nottingham lace curtains that were draped in dusty bay windows, and dreaded housework not half as much as they dreaded the shame of being known to be without servants. In certain pleasant, old-fashioned parts of the city practically every other house had a modest sign tucked away somewhere among the fuchsias and marigolds of the little area gardens. "Rooms." "Modes." "French Taught Here." "Piano Lessons," said the signs, and each sign told its own story of cramped and shabby elegance.

Those parlors, to which I made calls with my aunts when I was a little girl! The drawn shades with San Francisco's dusty summer wind rattling them, the trembling grass in a pink vase, the portrait of Pappa enlarged in crayon and standing on an easel, and the coal fire laid in an iron basket of a grate, with a paper fan opened over it. They were all alike.

Sometimes these down-at-heel ladies who murmured of sickness and failure above my head made cupcakes for the Woman's Exchange. Sometimes they pawned household treasures: gift books in full leather bindings, like Flaxman's *Bell,* or pictures like Burne-Jones's *Ophelia.* Sometimes it was silver forks. Their effect upon one's courage, one's hopes, one's daily drudgery was devastating.

The men of these households were proud, patronizing, usually idle. They worked elegantly at intervals, with an air of bestowing a favor; quite often they tossed off the idea of pay for any services, as gentlemen of leisure should.

"I told Hardisty I'd be glad to go up to Redding and

take a look at the horse," one of my uncles might say grandly. Or, "The Colonel told me I handled the desk so well he'd like me to take regular charge of it."

"But you didn't?" the women might ask, fluttered but quite without expectation.

"Oh no. No. May someday," the superior male would answer negligently. And after asking the ladies if they had any commissions downtown, he would stroll forth in the afternoon sunshine.

Yet these were clever men, entertaining, amiable, and physically fitted for any sort of effort. The trouble was, they simply didn't like effort; they didn't like work. When betrayed into employment, they could return from a casual three months' or six months' engagement laden with stories, able to embellish the simplest human situation with their certain brand of fascination. Years later I was to meet two other brothers, the fabulous Mizners, of the pioneer family of San Francisco, whose attitude toward hard work was similar. Like my uncles, they always had, almost within their grasp, the means of making great fortunes, and their conversations were maintained on the millionaire level.

When Wilson chose to expand upon his years in the Yukon, just his straight-faced recountal of the persons and situations he met there were enough to start the laughter, and eventually his listeners quite frankly raised their collapsed heads from the dining table and wiped their eyes. Very simply he recounted to us one night the untrammeled actions of his dinner guests on an occasion when he had placed hasheesh in their after-dinner coffee cups. It was Wilson also who commented, when a rejected woman friend had felt sufficiently frustrated to jump from the thirtieth floor of a Park Avenue hotel, that her bad luck had probably started as she passed the thirteenth floor.

Addison had magnificent upstairs art studios on Fifth Avenue. Here as a decorator he garnered treasures from South America, Europe, and the Orient. A pair of oxblood vases, bought in San Francisco's Chinatown for perhaps fifteen dollars, were separated, one to go on the mantel in the studio, one to travel all the way back to China, to be smirched with dust and ash, bundled in enormous wrappings of Chinese newspapers, packed in a much-stamped crate all red wax and impressive symbols, and custom-stamped in San Francisco.

A Washington lady of high degree had admired the single vase in the studio. But Addison wouldn't sell it; his agent in China, he said, was waiting to find the mate. The symbols on the vase stated that it was one of only two in the world, and, reunited, they would be museum pieces—priceless, of course. The lady waited, the crate arrived, she was present at its breathless opening, and there was the mate! They adorn her drawing room today.

In 1925 Addison Mizner became interested in the development of Boca Raton, one of the Florida beach developments. Cigi and I went down to stay with Arthur Somers Roche and Ethel, and went out to share the festivities of the opening. I've not seen Boca Raton since that extraordinary night of divine warm Florida darkness, with the Atlantic duly playing its part, the moon very much on the job, and the "Taverne Intime" looking like a bit of old Spain, with its low tiled roofs and creamy walls, its bell tower, and its dovecote under the eaves.

But everything else was missing. The "yacht basin" of real estate promise was not even outlined, the two golf courses had not been laid out, all about the intimate tavern, that was intended to be merely a promise of the titanic hotel to come, lay watery lots, outlined with the little street markers so familiar in Florida boom years: Park Lane; Fiftieth Avenue. Except for a workmen's cottage at the gate there was no other building in sight. And in the distinguished throng that attended the opening whispers were already afoot that the enterprise was bankrupt, worse than bankrupt, that a certain great Delaware family had sunk fifty millions in it, and yet it was not launched.

But in the enormous entrance salon, where workers were still busy with putty and glass at the exquisite tall windows, tables for several hundred guests were sparkling with crystal and silver and fountains of flowers bloomed on all sides. One detail of the meal, which had been flown almost ready to serve from New York, was caviar in prodigious quantities, served in frozen swans of ice.

My neighbor was Marie Dressler, one of the human beings given that last great gift of all, magnetism. She had me enthralled, and years later, when we chanced upon another dinner, in Hollywood, at the height of her eventide fame, we could pick it up with some of the features of our Walpurgis Night still remembered.

Another note that evening was supplied by Wilson Mizner, hurrying up now and then to his brother with apologies for interrupting the conversation, but explaining that he had a buyer for six of those lots in Section D-26-24. Going to put a twenty-room cabaña there . . . tennis . . . yacht . . . scads . . . Addie gravely confirmed the sale.

But Boca Raton, and the Mizners, too, had some deep water to cross before any yacht dropped anchor in the yacht basin.

To go back to my leisure-loving uncles, it is only fair to say that neither of them ever made a woman unhappy or left a child to face the precarious circumstances they knew. They were courteous in manner, clean in speech, noble in the plans they made for prosperity just ahead. Their womenfolk adored them, cooked and kept house for them, and "loaned" them money when there was any.

The older aunt had married, and she and her husband lived with my grandmother; the younger one had come on to New York earlier than any of us, and was somewhat precariously established as a music teacher and vocal coach. Her living, that is, was precarious, but her life was full of excitement, variety and, strangely enough, complacency. She preserved, in the midst of a bohemian circle, that infantile Celtic chastity that includes words, intonations, thoughts, reading matter. The briefest contact with her displayed it: she had the purity and ignorance of a child. She had met some of the country's greatest musicians in her earlier teaching days in San Francisco, among them Walter Damrosch and David Bispham; now she took on their more hopeless pupils, and the pupils rewarded her with rich gifts, seats in their opera boxes, visits to Newport and Oyster Bay, exquisite garments hardly worn, freedom of beautiful apartments when the owners were in Europe or Santa Barbara.

She was more than ordinarily pretty and she had a perfect figure. Her rich hair was dark and glittering mahogany, like my mother's, her hands were slim and exquisite, her voice lovely in singing, and her wit electric. She lived in one room in the old Grenoble Hotel on Seventh Avenue for many a year; sometimes, when money was short, lunching on a can of soup heated on an electric iron in her hotel bathroom, sometimes carried off for weeks to one of the most luxurious camps in Canada. She had influential women friends; she had new admirers every year; lovers she kept at a distance through some instinctive block of mind and soul. She didn't know the block was there, but it always betrayed itself and saved her from—or perhaps deprived her of— the natural results of the chances she took. I have heard her innocently repeat coquettish conversations she had had with some man whose reputation was that of a howling wolf in a Siberian forest. It is my profound con-

viction that any one of them could have taken possession of her person, given the accommodating hour and
place, without disturbing her spirit unduly. Nor did
mild abnormalities impress her unpleasantly. But even
while she told me of the crybaby antics of this pair
of tassel-gentles or that, until my blood ran cold, she
showed signs of active nausea if one of her infant great-
nieces or -nephews poured a stream of soured milk down
the maternal back or needed the eternal changing.

Her attitude toward life was that of a Victorian girls'
high. Not all girls' highs, but a church school situated
in some healthy factory town, where the teen-age females stream home in slanted autumn sunshine, arms
locked, loudly assuring each other—and any eavesdrop-
ping boys—that they wouldn't marry the finest man
alive and bring up a bunch of nasty little kids. To the
end of her life at eighty-six, Aunt Mary liked schoolgirl
mischief, she had a "crush" on some other woman, she
had a "trade-last" for me, she was "going to get even"
with some stately matron of her own age.

We saw very little of her in our early married years;
she was too popular, too busy. Her advice, if ever we
were mad enough to confide to her any domestic problem, was, "I'd walk out on him! No man is ever going to
tell me where to get off! Don't be anybody's unpaid
cook!" If she had children they'd better have tin ears
and copper bottoms!

But she liked Cigi and Bill, and even practiced her
arts upon them quite openly, to their quite open interest. When at fifty she married a quiet old friend who

had lived in the hotel longer than she had, she became the proudest of wives.

"Those three little letters, 'Mrs.,' on my card, I could kiss them!" she told me.

Jack Reed, later to be the John Reed of *Ten Days That Shook the World,* had joined the staff of the *American Magazine* for a while, and he happened to be at our table one night when she came to dinner. He had written a sort of rhymed account of the personnel of the *American* and he read it to us that night. He was immersed in a pretty engrossing love affair at this point, as I learned later, with a lady far above him in position and fortune, if not, it may be conceded, his equal in vigor of character, violence of political tendencies, and general challenge of manner.

In his rambling poem he had put all the personalities in the office, including, briefly, Cigi and me. He promised me a copy—incidentally, never sent. He came into my small kitchen to supervise the making of a favorite cheese dish and told of his hope of organizing a march through New York streets of the suffering wives and children in a great Philadelphia strike—miners, I think —which did come off a few Sundays later with great effect. Aunt Mary didn't like the casual, friendly easiness of all this but when he gave me a careless glance and said, "Baby, hey? Oh, God!" she formed for him an active dislike that caused her to follow his Mexican adventure, and the supreme achievement in Moscow a few years later, with a sinister satisfaction. In those days refined persons did not speak so to pregnant ladies.

Jack had a lesser adventure, about which he wrote Cigi a long letter, but whether it actually happened to him, or he heard it of someone else—the familiar doubt arises even as I recount it. I have never seen it in print before, and he did use the first person in relating it, so herewith he gets the benefit of the doubt.

He and a friend crossed the ocean on a cattle boat, a popular way for impecunious young males to get to Europe at that time. The boys' job was to care for lowing, restless, frightened stock, in the steerage, and had their food and lodging, and, one hopes, baths, as pay. The boat was so odorous, the prospect so uninviting, that they had scarcely got under way before Jack's companion hastily handed him his watch, pocketbook, and identification papers and leaped overboard. Authority on the boat took a rather dim view of Jack's explanation of the other's absence, and upon arriving at Liverpool he was detained and held under suspicion of foul play. A brief investigation proved that the swimmer had safely made some friendly shore, and Jack was freed to go on to meet his own strange destiny. More than twenty years later Mark and I stood beside his honored grave in Moscow.

A short life, and not too gay, but how packed his days were! I wish I had today the poem to which we paid so little attention the night Aunt Mary came to dinner.

After we bought the Port Washington house our chief interest was naturally there, with the typewriters and the little children. Teresa and Bill lived only the dip of a shallow canyon away, and Teresa's Jim was presently digging away on the sandy shores of the Sound, with Frank and any other small cousin the time provided. For Mark had married her Navy man, Charles Conway Hartigan, a lieutenant now, and Mark and Happy came to Port Washington for more than one long visit, and after a while brought the incomparable redheaded Bunga, explosive, original, definite even in a high chair.

Mark had been married to Happy very suddenly, after a dance at the old sail loft in Mare Island Navy Yard in California. Orders had come to the dancing crowd; men of the *Louisiana* were to report the following afternoon, to sail immediately. The eighteen-year-old Mark had looked into the eyes of the twenty-four-year-old Happy, and they had taken Bill Benét and Hap's fellow ensign Bill Spears into their counsels. So the dawn found all of them, including Laura and the ubiquitous young Stephen Vincent, driving in a surrey to San Rafael for the necessary papers, and Mark and Happy were married in the Catholic Church at Benicia that afternoon, with the Colonel to give her away, his warmhearted wife, Mother Bun, for witness, and Laura for bridesmaid. They all went back to Benicia Arsenal for a wedding breakfast, and then the Hartigans went to Vallejo and found a small flat. After the fleet sailed Mark followed it to Coronado, where other young Navy wives assembled—one of them, incidentally, being Wallis Warfield Spencer. Mark and she, then Mrs. Simpson, were to renew their early friendship years later, in Paris.

The Hartigans were stationed in Annapolis for a while, and we and the Benéts went up and down for visits. We found few city attractions as strong as the country pleasures of swimming and summer picnics, and our own absorbing family occupations were all that we could handle. For I was writing magazine serials— always two yearly—and articles, and usually a longer novel, not for serialization. And competition was keen, with Faith Baldwin, Juliet Wilbor Tompkins, Clarence Budington Kelland, Arthur Roche, Red Lewis, Edna Ferber, and a dozen more all in the field.

There is surely no pleasanter experience in human affairs than the emergence from good, stiff, realistic poverty to increasing easiness in financial matters, to still further expanding security, to comfort beyond any point of expectation, to actual luxury, and the last supreme height of achievement, the right to indulge one's fancies in books and trips and hospitalities—and even clothes, although this last subject covers some of my chief annoyances, embarrassments, and occasions of boredom in this life.

As for thousands of other Americans, this delightful destiny was ours. Having known sharp necessity without being too much aware of its inconveniences, we relished every inch of the change, even though our growing prosperity did not reach any very fantastic heights. But the pleasure of living just as we liked—able to buy fine writing paper and trips to California and first-night theater seats and to shop for old chairs on Third Avenue, new hats from Fifth, and lunch at the Ritz—never lost its charm. And these delights still have their newness, for me, although without the old companionship, the old conferences and plans, the old "Katy, will you kindly give me your undivided attention?" they are no longer what they were.

"Joe," I said not very long ago to my older brother, "when we were left absolutely without money, with four kids to raise, we didn't worry much, did we?" And Joe replied in honest surprise, "What was there to worry about?"

Which has given me one of the maxims I like to spread among the younger folk of the rising generations: "The only real security is insecurity." Or to put it more briefly, and in more modern form, "Do it yourself." They pay no attention.

To have had many years of unbroken companionship, so sure that it passed unnoticed as the air one breathed, is to have lived in a very real sense. Something of oneself dies when it is interrupted. Things are there, but not the same things. Looking backward, it seems to me that a great part of my good fortune was due to the fact that the two men with whom I was most closely associated were two men who were indifferent to money, as money, yet in their ways entirely unlike.

Joe, through our youth, was absorbed in the designing, construction, and improvement of circuit breakers and transformers; at about the time of our marriage, with less than a thousand dollars capital—the thousand borrowed from the always solvent Fred, then working in the steel mills of Germantown—Joe had opened a shop in a carpenter's abandoned shed in Napa, a hundred miles north of San Francisco. Over the door of this hut I had read the sign, "Pacific Electric Manufacturing Company," which looked as if it were worth more than the shed itself, and there Joe worked on blueprints, waiting for custom, and absorbing every word of George's *Progress and Poverty,* even to the elephants mad with pride. This became his second obsession, and with neither George nor Joe was money especially an object.

Cigi wore his rue with a difference. Money meant less to him than the thrilling game of making money. In our earliest days he had affirmed and reiterated his faith in those homely rules that rich men have always had on hand for the use of impecunious friends. Early hours, thrift, saving, if only a dollar a week, stern self-discipline in spending, and the proud right to retire at night owing no man a penny—this was his doctrine, and although I was more or less indifferent to the details I was perfectly willing to go along with him.

My own concerns, during the prewar years, were largely domestic, the novels I wrote being mere extensions of those interests. *Poor, Dear Margaret Kirby, Saturday's Child, The Story of Julia Page,* were among

the first, the second of them written while I was in-
valided with a sharp attack of arthritis following the
suppressed and hidden misery of the loss of my children. Weeks of rest, a diet of milk and only milk, lazy
hand-writing on my novel, delicious communion with
Teresa during the days, with little Frank and Teresa's
Jim to amuse us, and long sleepy evenings listening to
Cigi at the piano thundering away at the *Ring* operas
downstairs put me back on my feet, and in 1915 we
went home to California for a visit. Incidentally, a year
later, when Cigi and I went on four successive Thursday afternoons to hear the *Ring* cycle at the Metropolitan, the miraculous interweaving of the themes with
which pain and helplessness had made me familiar was
one of staggering joy and Wagner's music is my favorite
out of all the world of music to this day.

The home visit to San Francisco was all it could be.
All three brothers had tottering progeny in three nurseries now, Cigi forgot his mother's ominous predictions
that he would be swallowed up by my family, and
made of himself a fourth brother whose bond with them
was never broken; my little aunt Kitty promised to visit
us in New York in the spring; we stayed in the hotel
with Cigi's mother, who took me to meetings of the
Browning Club, of which she was San Francisco's
founder.

During this visit we stayed part of the time with Joe
and his small, bright-eyed little gypsy of a wife, Marjorie, who had first been my sister Mark's friend, and

then mine, in the old house in Mill Valley, under magnificent Tamalpais.

San Francisco was getting ready for the Panama-Pacific Exposition, and the war in Europe was never mentioned. The long strip of water front, stretching from the last of the godowns to the old fort that had been built in the Civil War at the Golden Gate, shone like a Maxfield Parrish painting in creamy walls and towers, and these fairylike structures were studded with jewels that flamed in the long rays of the setting sun, rivaling Bagdad itself at night.

Just nine years earlier San Francisco had lain stricken and destroyed, a smoldering level of ashes that sent a strong choking miasma into the salt air. Now she had risen in powerful beauty, and her people pinned badges on shirts and coats before the great gates opened, and in they streamed with no wretched inspection and recognizance, taking possession with a royal confidence.

We had reluctantly to turn eastward again after a few weeks of it, but I've always been glad that we missed the last night, when the people stood about dazedly, watching the glorious gold and red and apricot of the lights flame up and die, and the last sparkle of the jeweled walls vanish, and the silent dark stretch above them, pricked only by stars. For it was a beautiful fair, not too big, neighborly and intimate, and set against the waters of the Bay and the far slopes of Tamalpais and the Marin Hills. And it must have been a well-managed fair, for the city's merchants boasted that it played to capacity from the first hour to the last, and proved a good investment as well as a good time.

Life went on, that year of 1915, with almost too much felicity, in our two houses in Port Washington. Teresa and I basked in the new leisure and luxury of it. My typewriter worked steadily six mornings a week; it was under contract now, and had dates to keep. Novels followed each other at six-month intervals, and my mind was always busy with plots and counterplots.

But at noon Teresa came up for lunch, and perhaps afterward we prayerfully and cautiously backed out the Dodge, and with baby Jim in Teresa's lap and Frank wedged between us, we drove over the beautiful autumn country, to Roslyn, to Manhasset, to Oyster Bay. On the way home we sat in little ice cream parlors and had cocoa, and usually the Benéts dined with us or we dined with them. Teresa had a Polish Sophy in her kitchen now, and I "Ma's Kate." Our men talked magazines, we talked babies. Teresa was having a second, each of the three brothers had one or two, and Mark and her small redhead had come up to Port Washington for summer weeks, Bunga being a charter member in the "Cousins Club" that was to flourish in California some years later.

Sinclair Lewis and Grace, Addison Mizner, Herb Roth, Fontaine Fox of the "Toonerville Trolley," wonderful Harold Webster and his irrepressible Ethel were neighbors. These were not the days of two-hour pre-dinner intervals of cocktails, and Saturday nights at clubs that got themselves into the papers; everything was on a simpler level, and the months spun by in silent happiness and tremendous activity, like a top.

But gradually we all began to talk war, utterly ignorant of what the word meant, only vaguely aware that every country had soldiers—we caught occasional glimpses of ours now and then—and navies, of course. But somehow to think of actually using them was strangely upsetting. We had our ocean walls; people talked a lot about the absurdity of thinking that any nation would be mad enough to attack across our oceans.

War seemed dim and far away; politics did too. But it was at about that time that a spirited campaigner from Sands Point, one Harriet Laidlaw, later a good friend to us both, reproached Teresa and me pityingly and sadly on our harem attitude and gave us pamphlets to read. And within a few days Teresa was keeping from me the secret that she was a boiling suffragette, and I was concealing the same horrid secret from her. It was our gracious grandmother who had warned us years ago not to take an interest in any of the downtown, smoking, saloon-frequenting, political preoccupations of men, and we were afraid to confess our defection. Once admitted, we entered into the cause with vigor, and Teresa, about three days before her second baby was born, made a speech that literally converted the town.

Two miles away, in Plandome, lived another vehement feminist, the author of *Little Lord Fauntleroy*, Frances Hodgson Burnett. Her garden stretched to the shores of the bay, and in the comfortable rambling house tea was of course served daily, and we and the small children could come in for tea when we would.

All her books had been worn threadbare in our hands, in the early nineties when we got hold of them, and Teresa used to sit literally at her feet when she told of the "one she knew best of all." In old age she was heavily built, generously spreading in figure, and willing, even then, to talk of the idolized boy she had lost, not Lord Fauntleroy—who was Vivian, a man now, married and with a daughter—but the other child, who had made quite a sensation in Washington when the wife of Dr. Burnett walked abroad with her handsome little sons, dressed, I could only gather from what she told us, very much as the *St. Nicholas* artist, Reginald Birch, dressed Fauntleroy, in knee-length velvet, with a silk sash and a *point de Venise* collar. Just what Dr. Burnett's sons thought we could only surmise.

One day, when I was on an afternoon train from Port Washington, Mrs. Burnett got on the same train at Plandome and we made the trip together. She told me then she so admired one of Teresa's babies that she would make a serious offer of adoption, even at her age, if she thought there was the slightest chance of its being accepted. I told her that there was none; that my sister was in danger of breaking the First Commandment every time she looked at either of her children.

"Ah," said Mrs. Burnett resignedly, "that's the delight of adorable puppies. One may always adopt a puppy!"

She was worried about a lawsuit that had to do with something indiscreet she had written in a personal letter and some friend's betrayal. I had had my own worries on this point; one never learns a healthy fear of the written word in time. But as we got out of the train in New York she had a fresh worry.

"Oh, my luggage! I left it! It's in my room. My boat to Bermuda leaves in two hours. Oh, get a taxi boy—tell him to hurry—oh, what can we do! My nightgown —my toothbrush—my bag—my boat——"

I shouted, as we raced toward the taxi stand, that it might be easier to step over to Macy's or Gimbel's and get a nightgown and a toothbrush. She halted, gazing at me with a glazed eye. There was a pause; then her breast fell on a great sigh.

"Of course I might," she said gently and sweetly. "And slippers and soap. Soap on boats, you know, is— and I can carry them in my hand?"

"You could buy a small suitcase."

Another stare. Another deep breath of relief. "Oh, my dear! What would one do without friends in such a fix!" All was peace again. As impulsive, as volatile, and as warmly human as she had been when, a trembling newcomer, she had dared the literary heights with *That Lass o' Lowrie's* nearly forty years earlier she was to the very end. She told us that on her first submission of a manuscript she had written, after agonies of indecision and debate with her sister, "My object is remuneration." It usually is.

Writing is hard work; nobody works just for hard

work. Fame, as Christina Rossetti puts it, is but a "gathering jeer." But remuneration is something else again. One name out of every hundred lives: Chaucer, Milton, Clemens, Dickens. Who reads George Moore, Thackeray, the Kingsleys, today? How often nowadays does the librarian stamp dates in the novels of Frank Stockton, Richard Harding Davis, Robert W. Chambers, Jeffery Farnol, S. Weir Mitchell, William Dean Howells, and Mrs. Humphry Ward? We seized upon them hungrily as fast as they appeared.

Cigi and I, elated with the power that money gives, had been planning a trip abroad; Germany first, just because Mrs. Burnett loved Rothenburg, had had rooms over a city gate in Rothenburg, and had been able to watch the soldiers drilling from her drawing-room window.

But war stopped that. Ah, if that had been all! We gave up the plan, kept closer to home than usual, for the first deadly threat of polio was abroad, went out to Sands Point to a quiet cove and nearby rocks all but submerged in clear water, where even small children could be floated on the hot, soft summer mornings. This choice spot may have impinged upon the estate of Burke Cochran, but we cared no whit; they were fine people, they wouldn't eject us. One day an Englishman passed by near enough to fish three-year-old Jim Benét out of rather frightening water. We knew instantly that he was English by his words: "I say, this man's gone in a bit deep!" He was afterward known to Jim as "the man who called me a man," but his real name was Shane Leslie.

The dreamy lovely days, with the luncheon baskets, the wet little footsteps in sand, the afternoon drives, went on, under red and gold and yellow leaves that turned brown so soon, but Teresa and I were knitting on olive-drab wool now, and Mark wouldn't come up from Washington at all. Happy was on duty on a destroyer; there weren't going to be any unnecessary partings.

Early in 1917, it was war. Incredibly, war! Cigi went up to an officers' training camp in Watertown, and while a dark cloud of we knew not what hung over us, we were all nevertheless thrilled by the slogans, the uniforms, the service flags with their stars. That war was dressed up, romantic, exciting. We loathed the Kaiser with all our hearts; it was our mighty destiny, as a nation, to go out and kill all the bad people, so that the good people could live in peace. It was as simple as that. I even wrote bold analyses of the international situation, and published a small book, *What Price Peace?* It is long out of print, but if ever I come upon a copy in some old bookstore, chagrin at my own arrogant assurance will keep me from reading it.

American women, simply because it didn't seem possible that we were or ever could be at war, dramatized the events of 1917 with some real satisfaction. We were safe on our side of the ocean, much lesser seas had kept

England safe for all her stormy past, and knitting, and raising service flags, and seeing one's favorite restaurant filled with uniforms and sounding with martial music were emotionally satisfying. Nobody was worried; we couldn't lose, the minute we got in, things changed. Patriotism was everywhere. When magnificent Geraldine Farrar came out on the stage of the Metropolitan Opera House and the orchestra touched the first bars of the great anthem the packed house rose to its feet with the roar of a tidal wave.

Cigi came home from Watertown R.O.T.C. a captain, a sight that called for a burst of dinners and weekend parties and even tears from unknown ladies in the streets, who caught at his arm and said, "God bless you!"

That winter there was an immense bazaar for the Allies; and practically every enthusiastic socialite who volunteered to help was accepted, with strange results financially. Once open, this affair got rapidly out of hand; when streams of persons surged through the great decorated hall and autographed the wrong books and walked off importantly with treasures which someone else had just bought, gay debutantes refused to make change with laughing abandon and distracted society dames, as saleswomen, rushed to and fro asking what was the price of this and that, and eventually unable to find the buyer who wanted to know about it. Bedlam seethed back and forth, and four distracted directors asked me please to sit near an exit and identify a gray-haired woman in a seal coat who had bought in good faith a book for three dollars and seventy cents.

The book was a volume of the memoirs of Kaiser Wilhelm II, had been inscribed affectionately to Theodore Roosevelt, and had been priced, after due discussion, at three hundred and seventy dollars. The purchaser never was identified.

With some others, I autographed books too, and got very tired and presently found a quiet chair in a quiet corner, where I was joined by a quiet man whose face was entirely familiar but whose name escaped me. I knew I liked him, but that was as far as identification went. He called me by name, and seemed tired too, and we sat for a while, resting, out of the current of madness that still seethed in the bazaar. Presently he asked me if he might confide in me a personal problem that was distressing him. Sympathetic, but mad with puzzlement as to his identity, I listened to a story that involved the supernatural, other persons I knew only by name, and his own sense of having failed those he loved most dearly. Aghast as my mystification deepened moment by moment, I could only pray that, having perhaps felt some relief in airing the matter, he would go his way.

But it was at this moment that Fannie Hurst bore down upon us. This was before the most heroic dieting in the entire story of reducing human poundage had brought Fannie down to about half her normal weight. When we met her in Florence a few years later she had the figure of a high school sophomore and tucked under her arm was a yellow cocker puppy to complete the effect of a cover for *Seventeen*.

But on the day of the bazaar she was the original Fannie, of striking opulent beauty, clothes that slightly suggested the Orient, a turban, and earrings the size of amber ash trays. For years Cigi had been one of her devoted admirers; he considered her literary judgment of infinite value to his awakening prowess in letters, and consulted her whenever she had the graciousness to let him carry his manuscripts to her for tea and talk. Fannie, simple, gracious, unaffected as to her own great art, really helped him.

Still floundering in the sea of my complete ignorance of the identity of the man to whom I was talking, the first words of her greeting smote me with the ultimate horror.

"Kathleen, introduce me. I've wanted to meet this man for a long time. I think I've read every word Basil King ever wrote."

The earth steadied, the mist cleared away. If I called my companion Basil once in the next five minutes, I called him that fifty times.

There was a coal shortage that winter, and when a ton of coal was being sent down the sidewalk chute of some lucky house it was not uncommon to see strangers standing about wistfully watching, perhaps making tentative suggestions about half a ton.

There were northern lights over New York one night, and when Cigi came home with captain's bars on his shoulders I managed a dinner party for him, and sacrificed an old icebox, a straw perambulator, and two kitchen chairs to make sure of a good roaring fire. That week, introduced by the charming little Mrs. Martinez, whose husband had been music critic on a San Francisco paper before they moved to New York, we went to supper with the fascinating Geraldine Farrar, and carried our trays down to the furnace room.

Cigi was stationed at Camp Dix, in New Jersey, and for the summer of 1918 we rented a fine old Quaker homestead in nearby Mount Holly with its own big pond, its own great trees, a corn patch, a barn whose roof was eighty feet above our heads and swooping with bats. Teresa answered our telegram of invitation with a simple "Oh, bliss, yes," and Mark to the question, "Could you and the children get away for the summer months?" responded almost as briefly: "Like a fire horse."

So we gathered in the dim, vast, cool, old-fashioned homestead, three sisters, seven children, three oddly assorted maids, who turned out to be entirely congenial: brown-skinnned Cynthia, German-born Johanna, Irish "Ma's Kate."

Our officers—Bill Benét was in an air force camp in Florida—came to us when they could; and often we went over to Camp Dix for concerts and for suppers at the officers' mess. Cigi was promoted to major in August. Daily we drove to a beach of the swift, cool-running Rancocas and swam about the big hulk of a river boat that had been wrecked there long before, obviously for our express convenience.

This summer Bill, a small boy who had recently lost his mother, joined the family. The following year, to make postwar passports and travel a little simpler, there was a formal adoption and Bill became one of an increasing crowd of cousins.

These were halcyon days, and we knew it. Never was summer to be so golden again; there was a crystal quality about it that made me compare it to the beauty of the bubbles we used to blow from clay pipes when we were children. They grew greater, those bubbles, more frail, more pulsing with delicate color, and then they burst, and only a cool little smudge of soapy water was left to brush one's cheek. We took our first moving pictures that summer, but I have never had the courage to face them. The laughing, the radiant Teresa, knee-deep in the river, with a bewildered baby on her shoulder; the reading Teresa, looking up from her book on the lawn out under the great elms and maples, the busy little sister, raking paths, filling her arms with flowers, threading the high cornstalks or lifting the heavy dark tomatoes from their vines! It would have been too much, once the dark came and the dream ended, to see her living and joyous in pictures, again, as she was that summer.

We extended our stay to three full months, and before they ended she knew that a fourth child was coming; she was always shaky and cold in the first stages of pregnancy, easily tired and more serious even than her usually serious self. In telling me what she suspected— but I had suspected it already from her changed mood —her lips trembled. We were sitting outside the hot little post office in Mount Holly, which the children were storming for the mail.

"The very first thing I want to say is that he's welcome," she said.

"Women in wartime; it is our thooty!" I reminded her, my own heart sick with jealousy. And we both laughed shakily.

In late September we all went into Philadelphia and put Teresa, Cynthia, and the three small children on the Washington train. Mark's house in Washington was cool and empty, they would be met by Bill, who was temporarily in Washington, and be joined by all the rest of us two days later. The day was hot, and Teresa looked so pale that at eleven I suggested a second breakfast, and as she and Mark and I shared it in a tearoom we saw her color come back and her courage with it. The war was going to be over, we'd all be done with anxieties and separations, and she was fortunate, she said. She was fortunate to be going to Colonel Benét and Mother Bun, to Laura and Stephen, in the cool big arsenal at Augusta; Cynthia would go right on with the children and Teresa could be spoiled, and read, and rest, as I had been indulged a year or two earlier, in my own sick days.

She went through the gate to the train, came running back; she was in my arms, her face wet. Once again we were playing the parts we had chosen so long ago from Mrs. Craven's *Récit d'une soeur;* I was Pauline and she Eugénie. Mark and I had last kisses, we were all laughing as she ran back to the train.

Last kisses, for when we got to Washington two days later, by some change in wartime schedules Bill had been able to get reservations for his party that first night, and as he could accompany them, the only sensible thing to do was to bundle them aboard and make one long jump of the two trips, straight through to Georgia.

"I gave her my good-by kiss," writes Pauline of parting with Eugénie. "Oh, it was a very tender one! It could not have been more tender if I had known it was our last!"

M y sister Teresa Thompson Benét was thirty-seven when she died, in January 1919. The deadly flu of that time, that piled soldiers' coffins like cordwood at Camp Dix, and covered all our mouths with antiseptic gauze, was mortal to pregnant womanhood.

She was never very ill. Usually in those last months she was glorious in health and beauty; Laura wrote me that she was at her loveliest, coming downstairs in a new velvet gown at Christmastime, with her children about her. The big army house was warm, there were devoted people, dark-skinned and white, about her, eager to save her any trouble, to keep her rested. She interested herself so deeply in Augusta's wartime activities that she won an extraordinary tribute from her associate workers and the press when she died; Mark and I, nursing flu cases in Washington, could think of her as safe and loved and happy.

There had been all the more reason for that feeling of security when November eleventh brought Armistice Day, and cooks poured out of the Washington hotels in their tall white caps and paraded in Connecticut Avenue in the dark night, and flags blew, and our children and a thousand others went out with whistles and dishpans and anything else that would afford a noisy background for their wild shrieking. "Peace!" roared the newspapers, in letters eight inches high, and "Peace!" said all our hearts as the dawn whitened Georgetown's brick houses and our night of rejoicing was over. Washington didn't go to bed that night: we had won, we had ended wars forever. Cigi would come home now, and Bill and Happy. Everything would be as it had been.

Cigi wanted to show himself to his mother in all the glory of maple leaves, and I had serious surgery to face. We left our boys—real and adopted, for Bill was a member of the family now—with Mark, and warned the very few persons who knew anything of my condition to keep it from Teresa until I was completely recovered. In California Cigi and I danced at the big Del Monte Hotel, down near Monterey, on New Year's Eve, and on January fourth I had emerged sufficiently from more or less crucial interruptions to write Teresa. I had arranged four letters, carefully predated, to be sent her for this interval, but only two were necessary. No air mail existed to speed letters, and mine reached her on the fifteenth, and she wrote me instantly. I have the final sentence of her letter.

"But even knowing that you're on your way out scares me, Katy. My darling—my darling, if your eyes are really reading this, you'll know I'm in heaven. And if they are not I'll know that you are."

We had left for Washington when that letter reached California, and it was sent after me. When I read it she was indeed in heaven. We joined Mark and the children in Washington on February seventh and somehow they told me; they had not intended to say anything that first night but I felt uneasiness and constraint in the air; the children were solemn, obedient, quickly banished. I asked outright, "Teresa?" and the answer came in all their faces. She had had but a five days' illness, had never been alarmingly ill, had left them while lying in a lawn chair in the Augusta sunshine, with her beautiful eyes following a bird's flight into the skies, and her last look for Bill. Her eyes, when they fell upon him, during their brief six-year idyll, had always held a sort of radiance that was better than any smile. Bill was her world.

She was born in San Francisco on New Year's Eve, and grew into an extremely pretty little girl. It was immediately evident that she was a small intellectual, too, for she taught herself to read before she was four, watching Joe's struggles perhaps, and my six-year-old contempt of learning. Her memory was prodigious, and she easily got by heart any sonnet or quotation that caught her fancy.

Years later a grieving mother stopped at my library desk with a copybook into which a loved and lost daughter had copied her favorite poems. She wanted this collection published but had first to give credit for the more than two hundred selections, and she had tried in vain to find anyone who could help identify them. Teresa, coming in at that moment to join me for lunch, had leaned an elbow on the desk, seized a pencil, bit her lip, looked to the ceiling, and begun scribbling. "That's Fiona Macleod—Hood—Sir Walter—Aldrich—that's your *Battle of Bunker Hill*, Katy, here's Holmes, Noyes, Newman——" And so on, like flashes of lightning, and even with an occasional "That's anonymous."

Teresa was the spiritual force that carried our orphaned ranks through the first years of the century. Nothing ugly or quarrelsome ever had been in her nature, she maintained our home scene on a serene level, by her very presence quelling anything like strife or dis-

157

sension in our ranks. I never heard anyone speak angrily or coldly to her: I never knew a moment when her time was not at everyone's disposal. The fatal monosyllable of the psychiatrist's couch and the neurasthenic ward was no pitfall to her; she never started a sentence with an "I," she never had nerves or moods. And despite the fact that her normal expression was grave, and her mind often off on some poetic tangent, she could be merriment itself and see a lot more than the surface fun in any predicament. She had a ringing laugh, with just a note of reluctance and reproach in it, as my mother's laugh had.

She organized us; she rolled butter balls every Sunday night so that one of my mother's housekeeping touches was preserved, and she set as dainty a table, for our Friday meal of hot crusts and milk, as my mother had for guests at home. Aunt Kitty backed her up, championed her dislike of slang, careless gossip, and crossed legs and yelling in halls, and we kept to their standards. Teresa adopted a uniform dress for her years in Paul Elder's bookstore: an inexpensive dress of corduroy velvet made Russian fashion, with a fastening of two big buttons on her left shoulder. When young William Benét came to the shop he was not long in finding her out, and in the ensuing years many of his most beautiful poems were written of her and to her. They were very much in love and were happily planning for days of peace and companionship, joy in their restored relationship, and delight in their children. These were ended now. There are many faces I want to see, beyond the vcil that is life. There are many hands I want to touch again. But I know whose eyes will first meet mine, whose square small hand will be holding mine as I go.

In May 1919, Mark and Happy came up to New York from Annapolis, with the small babies. Happy had an opportunity to go to Rio de Janeiro on a special mission, but Mark was reluctant to go away for three years unless we promised to come down there for part of the time. We all went to dinner and talked madly over the table. The Hartigans, who were deep in books of Portuguese grammar, were to go immediately, but shortage of shipping delayed us, and they had been four months in Rio before we got passage for ourselves and the two boys. We sailed on the *Vauban,* and plunged into the glow and the beauty of the Brazilian capital with enthusiasm that had begun with the departure from the dock in New York, and my lazy pleasure in a deck chair, watching them load the hold, cranes screaming over the hatches, ropes swaying overhead, and New York noisily minding its own business as if nobody was going on a fairyland cruise and feeling salt water rocking under her for the first time. I had been laid low again with arthritis; I was back on a milk diet, but an English ship's postwar table was not such as to make me feel myself much abused, and when after a golden cruise we finally reached the most beautiful harbor in the world, and took possession of an enchanting little house in the

Rua San Salvador, I was halfway cured. Milk in any
state at all appetizing would have been difficult to get
at that time, for there was no ice in Rio, and all milk
was boiled to rags before being delivered, hot in the bottle. The only cream procurable, as my sister observed,
was the ever popular *crime passionel.* But on boiled milk
I grew steadily better.

Our house was sunk deep in a narrow, packed garden,
with a high fence of arabesque iron, and a gate from
which a bell dang-dangled if anyone desired entrance.
All about were larger houses, all also deep in bushy gardens, whose open shutters—for there were no glass windows—gave passers-by the full benefit of magnificent
piano scales and chords pouring out to meet and mingle
in the hot streets with the musical cry of *"Galinhas!"*
from the venders of cooped and muttering chickens. No
ice meant no meat refrigeration in 1919, and I have seen
Maria, our cook, fondly kissing against her brown cheek
a little dove that she served twenty minutes later crisp
and broiled for my luncheon.

Happy Hartigan was on a special mission whose object was to assist the Brazilian Navy to get into stronger
and more usable shape. Of the practical details of this
undertaking we heard little, for Rio was perhaps the
gayest capital in the world, after the war, the members
of the mission were young, and in the exotic setting of
the beautiful city, the bay with its chain of islands, the
music and moonlight that kept the nights swimming
with romance, there was much to occupy them along
lines not strictly nautical.

One event will perhaps illustrate with what simple trust the two navies regarded each other. A spectacular review was planned, with appropriate speeches and music, with open house on the ships, and thousands of visitors streaming into town for the occasion.

It was only when it was successfully over, and the wearied crowds had dispersed, and carloads of flowers had floated wilting away from the scene upon the languid tide, that Happy discovered that a command to unload the artillery had not been issued, or had been disregarded. Any one of the thousands of visitors might playfully have pulled a cord or pushed a lever with a result that the navies, the dignitaries, and the international relationship would have been blown sky high.

But no such catastrophe disturbed the serene reign of Edwin Morgan, then our ambassador to Brazil, a dignified, cultured and gracious New Yorker, wealthy and a bachelor to boot. Mr. Morgan's dinners were special occasions for which I abandoned my invalidism and joined the others. The house itself was one of Rio's old and beautiful mansions, and everything in it was an item of individual treasure, rare, precious, and somehow exactly in the right place and put to the right use.

One night our host happened to be talking of his own boyhood, and mentioned the fact that with his brother and sister he was taken up for the summer months to the high mountains, New Hampshire perhaps, or Maine. The little Morgans were very specially guarded children, and it had been customary to make this move in the family carriages, with the inevitable stops and changes, unpackings and overnights that that form of travel demanded.

But on one occasion their mother daringly suggested the train. Dinner on board, only one night's delay, and a morning arrival at their destination.

So with hampers and bags and nurses and parents they all got on the train, and when night came the small excited faces were washed, slippers and dressing gowns unpacked, while the children watched in fascination the making up of berths and stowing of gear generally.

Then suddenly the trio disappeared. The children were nowhere to be found. Nothing to be alarmed about, of course, they were exploring, playing a game. They couldn't get off the train. It was all right, but still . . .

And back they came, just as their absence began to cause some faint beginning of uneasiness. To questions it was the five-year-old Edwin who explained.

"We had to go through all the cars, Mother, didn't we, and kiss all the people good night?"

In the dreamy late mornings I was quite well enough to go swimming at Copacabana, picnicking at Santa Teresa, or wandering down the narrow shopping street called the Paysando, climbing the steps of Gloria Hill, where the swarming babies, goats, dogs, chickens, and mules were guarded by handsome, gypsy-type mothers who looked as if they might at any minute break into choruses from *Carmen* or *Il Trovatore*.

My orders were to be in bed when the sun went down, so the more sophisticated excitements of night life in the most dramatically picturesque city in the world had to be retailed to me by the others. But my typewriter clicked faithfully after breakfast and every day found me feeling freer and freer of the frightening arthritis, so all my memories of Brazil are happy ones, even including the horrible taste of boiled milk. When we left for home on the *Alban* I was well again. The captain and I played cribbage acidulously, accosting each other as "Mr. Swiveller" and "Marchioness." What once would have been called a mutiny, but in our more enlightened time is known as a strike, delayed us on this trip for a week in Vitória Harbor, Brazil, and we had a chance to climb to the old monastery up on the mountain, accompanied all the way by the singing of water in a mossy flume.

It was the death of Cigi's mother that brought us to California, in a world that was so sadly disorganized and changed for me that our discovery of a ranch in the Santa Cruz Mountains, and the decision to spend our summers there, was just a vague event in a new life that was all a dream from which I dared not try to awake. As we inspected the formal six-room bungalow, the various sheds and lesser buildings, the great redwood grove that was soon to shelter our outdoor kitchen, and the slope where Cigi said we could someday put a pool, there was no hint that La Estancia would come to mean what it did mean to all of us.

With my brothers and their wives we walked out the wood road, looked down over the tops of mighty trees into the canyon, and just before we left for New York and another winter's work we secured the whole place, two hundred acres, partly planted to prunes, mostly wild and untouched hillside, oaks, redwoods, chaparral.

T hat winter, four years after the Rothenburg plan had been disrupted by the war, and with no special affection for Germany that tempted us to fulfill it, we made our first visit to Europe, enthusiastically guided by Effendi, who insisted that we fully flavor London by going to Brown's Hotel in Dover Street and occupying the identical suite that he always reserved for himself. First days in London are like nothing else in the world, to Americans, anyway. There is so much that English letters have made deliciously familiar, and yet that one feels can't be going on quite seriously with no play-acting about! To have one's staid currency changed into the big white fluttering pages that are pounds, to hear the fine speech, the fine voices all about one, to walk past immemorial landmarks under immemorial elms, and to eat hearty, unpoetical fare in such a place as, say, Simpson's, is to be sharing buns and milk with Rumpty in Rumpty's perch. France, whose poorest ragout is browned and bubbling with a hundred subtle savors and sauces, is scarcely a stone's throw away, but that has never affected John Bull's unspiced apple tart, cold slabs of unsalted bread, large boiled potatoes, and sharp-cut wedges of that pale cabbagelike vegetable that is generically described as "greens." But how delicious they are, the "silverside" and the great turbot wheeled to one's table, and the cold toast separated from its fellow toast by a colder wall of china!

Thanks to Effendi, half of whose introductory letters we never had time to deliver, we had a royal time from the moment we stepped off the boat at Southampton. A car was awaiting us, and we lunched at Virginia Waters', and toasted the King. At Brown's, where we had a string of rooms and a canopied great bed, we found a letter from Hugh Walpole and another from Mrs. Belloc Lowndes, both asking us to dine, and a note from Heinemann's publishing house, signed "Paulding," suggesting arrangements for a tea for a "few writing people." When, all aglow, that first night, and twisting about like weathercocks as every few feet of the way streets and shops waylaid us for raptures, we dined at the gloomy old mansion of the Ritz, Philip Merivale, who was to win the heart of New York with his performance in Miss Eva Le Gallienne's production of *The Swan,* came across the big dining room to sit with us.

Delirious with this social success, we staggered out into Piccadilly, and passed "circuses" and Trafalgar Square and Nelson and the lions, and amazingly were in the Strand. It was all there, and awaiting us!

The next morning, sobered by cold toast and jam and tea, we came down to earth and decided that our first call of obligation must be on my publisher. Cigi showed the house porter downstairs the address of 50 Albemarle

Street, and he advised us in the low, conspiratorial, fatherly tones that all porters and policemen use in England to go back through the hotel and use the other door.

At this door stood a round-bellied great taxicab, which would have made some of ours at home look like mosquitoes dancing about armadillos. To the apple-cheeked driver Cigi repeated the address sharply—all gents speak smartly to social inferiors in English fiction, and although he did not add "my man," the feeling was there. The driver hung toward us from his right-hand seat and asked hoarsely, "Did you wish to drive there, sir?"

"Did we wish to drive there?" I murmured, climbing in. "We are in England, Cigi. When we engage a car and get in, giving an address, we are asked if we really wish to go there."

The driver imperturbably drove us some two hundred feet and stopped at the publishing house of John Murray. We disembarked in a slightly chastened frame of mind, and afterward Cigi explained that the outrageous size of the tip was because he, Cigi, was unfamiliar with English money.

John Murray, publishers, the men of whose house had been friends of half of London's writers for a hundred years, made us warmly welcome in an office perhaps twenty feet square, warmed by busily chewing little flames upon coke, in a grate with round iron bars. All about the grate little pots of daisies and primroses were ranged to the number, perhaps, of a hundred, for Easter was approaching, and the grimy downstairs windows of business houses would wear fringes of spring flowers

Missy and Jojo, 1884

Maria Teresa Thompson

Frederick Rand Thompson

"Mother"

The Moroneys. Seated: Paul and Margaret Moroney, with Lee, Frank, Mary, Charles. Standing: Margaret, Josephine, Paul, Jr.

Teresa

James Alden Thompson with Teresa, Jim, Kathleen, Margaret
in Mill Valley, 1898

"Aunt Kitty"

Laura Benét

Joseph, Margaret, Kathleen, Jim, Teresa, Fred in Mill Valley, 1901

Kathleen and Charles Norris, San Francisco Fair, 1915

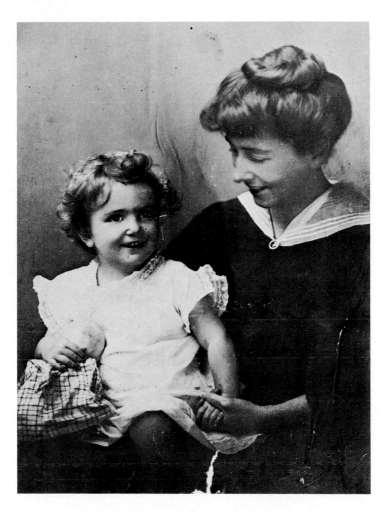
Laura Benét with Rosemary, Augusta, 1917

Ben Hampton, Harry Wilson, Kathleen Norris, C. G. Norris, Frank

Behind the scenes at *Mrs. Partridge Presents*, Blanche Bates, Guthrie McClintic, Cigi, Charles Waldron. Standing: K. N. and George Creel

At "Pickfair" with Douglas Fairbanks and Mary Pickford

Jim, Rosemary, and Kit Benét

Hawaii, 1933

Cigi with Beatrice Lillie on the *Europa*

At the California Ranch, 1925. Jim, K. N., Joe, Mark, Fred

Ethel Barrymore, Noel Coward, Alice Duer Miller, K. N., Julia Sanderson, Alexander Woollcott

Frank Lawton, Vincent Youmans, Noel Coward, K. N., Cigi

Bohemian Grove. James A. B. Barton, Theodore Roosevelt, Nelson Double-day, Cigi, Dan Longwell, Walter McLellan

K. N.–1925

MINA TURNER

William Rose Benét

With Kate, 1935

Frank and Alice

Kate with "Poopah," 1935

"Treehaven," Mill Valley

"Green Blinds," Port Washington

"La Casa Abierta," Palo Alto

Theatricals at the ranch, 1928

The Spanish Kitchen, Palo Alto

along their sills. Sir John asked us to lunch—upstairs, as it happened, for his home quarters were in the same building.

At a more formal luncheon a few days later we were perhaps a dozen, and when Lady Helen asked me if we were comfortable at Brown's, I said that we were more than comfortable, that the fine old porter had secretly pleased my hypocritical American soul by calling me "my lady."

"Oh, that," said Lady Helen, "is because M'ma lived there for a long time, and she is Lady Brassey."

This electrified me. It took me back to Mill Valley, and my father's fashion of wandering through San Francisco's old bookstores at noon, and bringing me, perhaps in my fifteenth year, a large book that bore in gold scrolls upon its green cloth cover the words: "*A Voyage in the Sunbeam,* by Lady Brassey."

"Not," I said to Lady Murray, "not the *Voyage in the Sunbeam,* the first steam-powered yacht to sail from England! Not the lifeboats named the *Gleam* and the *Ray;* not the boys put off at Italy for school, and Mabel and Nannie and Baby?"

"I," said Lady Helen simply, "am Baby."

A t the Heinemann tea was the very winning actress, Clemence Dane. For she was an actress at that point, and explained that she had had time for the writing of her play, *A Bill of Divorcement,* because of the enforced idleness following an accident in which her leg was broken. The success of the book and the play and the movie must have turned her in a different direction, for later I found a book of hers that seems to me a little classic, *Legend*. This slim volume really describes just one scene, the reminiscences of a group of artists and writers in a studio, as they discuss the illness of one of them, and presently the arrival of the news of her death, and what it does to them all. My copy was lost long ago; I wish that particular story might be reprinted.

Hugh Walpole asked me what two special desires London meant to me at the moment, and I told him I wanted to see Robert Scott's diary of the South Pole journey and had an overweening curiosity that my sister and I had shared from childhood about bread sauce. A few days later he and I found the shabby, half-legible last penciled words of Scott in the museum, and I told Hugh of Apsley Cherry-Garrard's book, *The Worst Journey in the World,* which I knew by heart. Later I was lucky enough to find the one-volume edition for Hugh and we marveled together that what forlorn, scared little Lashley could do in the face of an antarctic blizzard, Scott could not. Lashley was sent back with the second four of the twelve men who set out for the pole; Cherry-Garrard, to his deep disappointment, was sent back with the first four. Some years later Cherry-Garrard came to have tea with us at the Savoy; Hearst's top editor, Ray Long, was there and the lovely "Miss Lucy." Cherry-Garrard was painting pictures then, and we did not talk much of the Scott expedition. Like the pictures of Teresa in the summer of 1918, it was, as Lady Dead-lock puts it, a case of "If I were not dumb, you must be deaf."

As for the bread sauce, we followed the Scott museum visit with dinner at some club where grouse with bramble jelly and bread sauce was the main course—the first grouse that Cigi and I ever had tasted. These days were full of "firsts," and no subsequent visit to England matched that one for a quality of discovery and delight.

We went afterward to Paris, reaching there on a warm Thursday afternoon in Holy Week; the floor of the Madeleine was covered that afternoon by an immense cross made of spring flowers, and while we watched black-clad forms came in to kneel and rose to go away again, as women with tear-swollen eyes contributed their little handfuls of violets and primroses to the great emblem of our salvation. There were some Hollywood friends in Paris—one earnest soul from Culver City told us just where we could get ham and eggs American style, and gum and doughnuts as well. Also there were the New York artists May Wilson Preston and Jimmy Preston, and May told of her street dispute with a bus driver who would not stop for her. She said she called him a cheat and he returned with a flood of vituperation of which she did not understand one word. But May was more than equal to the occasion; she knew he was calling her names, and as he stopped for breath she floored him with a scornful "Oh, *je suis, suis-je?*" and swept upon her way.

On the boat going over and on the boat coming back was Samuel Goldwyn; we had had some communication in New York before sailing but had postponed any meeting or any definite plans for the use of my stories in pictures, as Sam's secretary informed us that he was leaving immediately for Florida, and we told him we were heading for the Coast. Having made these deceptive statements as mutual protection against getting involved, it was surprising to meet in the first hour on board the *Berengaria* and find that we liked each other very much and were not afraid, on either side, of being untimely trapped. Mr. Goldwyn told me on this trip of his admiration for the lovely woman who later became his wife; and although our paths separated not long afterward it was good to realize that that marriage had taken place, that a fine boy had been born who was one day to marry the daughter of an old friend of mine, Sidney Howard, whose first play, *They Knew What They Wanted*, made him famous in New York overnight. Sam and Cigi and I talked plays, and of the new film success of Douglas Fairbanks, in whose company years before Cigi had had a small part, at about the age of eighteen.

When we went down to Culver City some months later and I had a studio to myself in the Metro-Goldwyn-Mayer plant, there were some old friends to find again: Arthur Somers Roche, working there with his gypsy-pretty Ethel and two small boys; Clayton Hamilton with his wife and two more small boys; and Rupert Hughes, whom we had often seen at Irvin Cobb's house. These hospitable persons were more than enough to launch us, and for one season we shared the breathless thrill of saying "how do you do" to practically every celebrity in the entire colony. The very air one breathed, of course, was thick with talk of pictures—pictures—pictures.

It was Charlie Chaplin who once reassured me, when the personal lives of some friends—himself included—were being poisoned by the whirl and heat and hurry of it all, "Hollywood has no trouble that a good picture doesn't cure!" I hope it was true in his case.

Most actors have a secret desire to write, and most of the writers I have known hunger for the footlights. Twenty years ago I played the part of Ma Cagel in Lula Vollmer's *Sun-Up*, and enjoyed every moment from the first rehearsal to the tenth and last performance. Afterward I played the boys' mother in *The Swan* and still later Ethel Barrymore's part as the century-old grandmother in *Whiteoaks* at the Community Playhouse in Palo Alto. These experiences are great fun and give one a full realization of the importance with which players rightfully regard themselves. There is no food for vanity quite so potent as that last flurry of make-up and comb in one's dressing room while the house fills to the last possible inch, and while there glows in one's heart the expectation of an enthusiastic reception.

The director gathers his trembling group about him, at the last minute.

"Now listen, you're all good. I've never had a show of which I felt more confident. You're wonderful! Everybody just take it easy—all right. Get in your places, you two . . ."

Some of my contemporaries, Fannie Hurst and Edna Ferber, for two, got immense fun and satisfaction out of the stage and movie plays they saw produced; Edna's talk went heavily theatrical when Ethel Barrymore was playing her "Emma McChesney" stories, and perhaps she was as disappointed as many of us were when John and Ethel Barrymore didn't play the parts so obviously fitted for them in *The Royal Family,* on which Edna and George Kaufman collaborated.

But I never had a play produced, except for a few wartime sketches picked up here and there where programs for enlisted men were being given. And in Hollywood, although as many as twenty of my stories were bought by various companies there, and some of them played by top stars, while socially all was gas and gaiters, as a writer I never felt happy or at home. I did stay one pleasant week with Mary and Douglas at Pickfair, but these two were never the rioters who gave Hollywood the reputation it had then, and our evenings were decorously spent over jigsaw puzzles, peanut brittle, of which a fresh tin was opened and placed in readiness for us every night, and a picture. Not T.V., of course, but a real picture selected at the studio where Fairbanks and Pickford reigned supreme for many years, and sent up to the house for our delectation.

Mary was at the height of a popularity that no other single woman has ever reached or ever will. We knew in America that her name on any theater bill meant magic, but I had to travel over the Orient and Europe to realize that long after we had lost sight of *Tess of the Storm Country* and *Rebecca of Sunnybrook Farm* and a score of others the films went on circling the globe and winning fresh millions of friends for the first blazing cinema star.

One evening she told me that she was jealous, and I naturally asked of what. Oh, she confessed, laughing, of anyone who looked at Doug, of any star over whom the critics raved, of everything! I studied her, a small form exquisitely dressed, in a big chair, a beautiful home and incomparable gardens about her, a great studio that hung on her slightest smile or nod, a great fortune, a husband almost—but never quite—as famous as herself, and the backing of a fortune that enabled her to do everything that she so loyally wanted to do for her own people. Mary Pickford jealous! It amused me then, as a random admission, but later I came to feel that professional persons, writers and painters, actors and movie folk included, are all spurred by that very intensity of ambition that we call jealousy. They must be, to preserve identity at all.

The golden light of success and youth and love and laughter shone over Pickfair in those days, and knowing

Mary as I came to know her, I know that, however the thirty intervening years have treated her, she is still the wonder child I called her, at heart.

One night at dinner at Rupert Hughes's home a weedy young man got up to sing, and produced a baritone so pure and perfect that we all sat rapt under "Mandalay" and the toreador song from *Carmen* and, yes, I think "Trees." Lawrence Tibbett was singing in a movie house then; old-timers will remember the days when every movie show started with the Pathé news, went on to a comedy, presumably with a chase or a real lion in it, and then changed the mood with a singer and a few good songs as prelude to the big film. Tibbett was that singer in such a Los Angeles movie house.

Cigi, always a transformed personality when good music was in question, warmly invited the young singer to come to New York, promised him that he would send him a letter to Gatti-Casazza, at the Metropolitan, and assured him that fortune and fame were ahead.

This was not an unusual procedure; if I were to count the promising young men suddenly fired by Cigi's enthusiasm to ambition, I would need all my fingers and all his. Many of them duly came to New York and most of them made their mark. It was only a short time later that Tibbett came on to create a sensation as Ford in *Falstaff,* and brought his family rushing up to our New

174

York apartment to report it. After that we felt it a point of honor and pride as well to hear him whenever we could; and there are some of us who more than once heard the voices of Caruso, Pol Plançon, and the De Reszkes and who yet feel that the soaring full easy flow of Tibbett's big baritone outgloried them all.

There was one evening at the house of the popular George Barr and Laura Baker when Tibbett was—to put it mildly—in voice. We must have had three hours of it, tottering out into starlighted Park Avenue at midnight speechless with magic. Exactly what the distinctions and achievements of Mr. Baker were I never ascertained, but I know he had something to do with the Relief Administration after the war, when he went to practically all the capitals of the world and was decorated by them all. Anyway he had a remote dresser drawer packed full of medals and ribbons, never seen by anyone except when his wife Laura gave a secret preview. But we all loved George and his peppery little wife, who gave us all unstinted hospitality, and on one occasion gave us, herself included, a delightful laugh when George rose to toast the guests of honor and Laura firmly interrupted to say that he had named the wrong guests. This, in a manner of speaking, opened the whole thing for nominations from the floor, and the question was settled to the satisfaction of all, even Laura.

It was George Baker, at the head of his own table, who warned me once of the fatal error of asking too many celebrities to the same dinner.

"When they get to comparing long runs and new contracts and royalties, whoosh!" said George.

L ooking back at those New York years, it is impossible to omit Franklin Pierce Adams, who was known as "F.P.A." and who had a newspaper column that everyone read and in which every one of our aspiring group was anxious to appear. He had built up an astonishing number of contributors and had reached the point, when we first knew him, where he could firmly discard any offering that did not meet his extremely critical standards. Frank could turn you down wearily, absently, almost as if bored. He introduced types of verses and plays on words that were greedily copied and circulated by other columnists. "Tobacco is a loathsome weed, I like it," upon which there were infinite variations, was one, and such little twists as "Should a nincompoop have an income?" and "Who put the low necks in the loan exhibition?" were typical. When he accepted half a column of parody on May Sinclair under the caption "Bats in the Belfry" I was set up for days.

F.P.A. himself was a small, gentle, tired-looking little man with strong Hebrew features. One factor in his success was his incredible booklore—the poems and the history at his command, his familiarity with Greek and Latin. When his contributors decided to give him a dinner, with the then little-known Robert Benchley as toastmaster, the hundred and fifty who attended indeed represented the young literary, dramatic, artistic elite. Frank himself did not attend. At this dinner Alice Duer Miller read a sonnet that, she claimed, Frank had discarded as worthless. It began: "Let me not to the marriage of true minds admit impediment. . . ." Benchley arose with a manuscript six inches thick, observing that, as we were giving Frank a watch, he thought the history of watchmaking might interest us. He then fumbled with the mass of papers and began, "Some three centuries ago, in a remote Bavarian village . . ."

Married to a brilliant, hard, critical woman who never would yield him first place, F.P.A. yet managed to attain a height of quiet popularity and influence that opened all doors. Irving Berlin, Alec Woollcott, Neysa McMein, Edna Ferber, Alice Duer Miller, Jack Reed, Madge Kennedy, Ruth Gordon, Dorothy Parker—it would be hard to name any one of the rising crowd of beginners who did not find in him a confidant, friend, and cap and bells.

Some few of us took it upon ourselves, privately and timorously, to warn the confident Minna, who had been an actress and was a personality in her own right, that his was a unique character and needed gingerly handling. But we had to watch the wreckage of a marriage that perhaps never had been right for either.

There was a happier time coming for both, when they decided to part. Minna went on to her own independent career in Washington, and for Frank there was a second marriage with the gentle, aristocratic Esther Root, who built for him a real home that was presently filled with handsome, vital children. But this time was far ahead of the days when we were all beginners, and acceptances in Frank's newspaper column were a sort of recognition of merit that was casually mentioned in the course of a conversation but gloated over in secret. Frank had an uncanny way of sensing which newcomers were destined for success, and even before the magazines knew them the names of Inez Milholland, Charlie Towne, Clement Wood, and Edna Ferber were familiar to the faithful.

After a while the name of Neysa McMein occupied a prominent place in the column. Neysa's name had been chosen by numerical selection. There seemed to be no special reason why a young artist, coming unknown from some Western state, should quite suddenly be discussed and quite inexplicably important—that is, until one met Neysa. In a careless, carefree, slipshod sort of way she seemed at first glance to be just one more beads-and-sandals bohemian, with a big untidy studio near Fifty-seventh Street. There was nothing left-banky about the neighborhood, anyway, and nothing of the Trilby atmosphere cultivated or suggested. What happened in Neysa's studio happened naturally, but it was the sort of thing a good many other newcomers to the city, strugglers like herself for recognition, sought in vain.

She was an artist; she drew girls' heads in crayons and pastels, and they were exquisite, absolutely of the moment, no two alike. She was exquisite herself, with fine eyes, a big mouth, a lovely face, though it was not always free of smudges of chalk or crayon dust. Her soft knot of heavy hair was gold, untidily bunched on her neck. Her voice was low and her speech unhurried; nothing ruffled her. She listened more than she talked.

And she might well listen, for everyone went in and out of the big cluttered room—everyone who was any-one, that is. I don't know how she managed to dispose of bores; she was quite ruthless in a quiet way, and she may have had her own system. But the others came, the artists, the singers, the players and writers, the poets, the famous folk who came over from France or England to be with us just a few weeks; they were all there. Neysa went on drawing girls' heads; she told me once she never could put two together, and as far as I know she never sketched a man. One summer, when her work was fa-mous on the covers of many magazines, she stayed in the city to take drawing lessons at Columbia; it must have been a startled class of undergrads who beheld the great McMein in their midst, faithfully following in-structions.

Noel Coward was her slave; he read us scenes from *Cavalcade* one afternoon, fresh from the oven. Alec Woollcott immortalized her in one of the best of his sketches. George Gershwin hammered away at his "Rhapsody in Blue" on her old piano. Beatrice Lillie, in the dim-witted way that made one feel that she couldn't possibly realize how funny she was, gave us an impersonation of her own small son that eclipsed any-thing she ever did before the footlights. Edna Ferber, William Bolitho, Frank Sullivan, Ruth Gordon enthu-

siastically autographed her copies of Dickens and Scott,
with appropriate Victorian sentiments; Dorothy Parker,
Harold Ross, enchanting Madge Kennedy with her
sentimental tribute to Strephon and its ribald finish—
everybody was at home there. Neysa's negligent "Come
up tomorrow" was equivalent to a command. Quiet, untidy, dusty, her small figure worked steadily in the very
center of the scene; she made no effort to entertain anyone; she was amused rather than amusing.

Neysa, after setting some fifty rumors afloat, married
a quiet young engineer, one John Baragwanath. But the
"second-year high" element that was never quite absent
from her doings was evinced in her plan for her honeymoon. She left, alone, for Europe, on her wedding day.
It sounds rather like something a teen-ager would
threaten, while eating lunch from a paper bag among
her school peers, but Neysa carried it out. It was her
first look at Europe.

When she returned she told me of a barbarous act of
penance she had seen inflicted in a Roman church—my
church, of course. According to her story, Neysa, having
loitered too long over some obscure wall painting, had
found herself locked in the church overnight. Aroused
by the sound of chanting at midnight, she had hidden
behind an arch and seen a slow procession of monks and
nuns enter by torchlight. They were escorting a frightened girl novice to one of the great pillars near the altar,
where an opening was speedily made in plaster still wet.
Into this orifice the bound girl was placed, the plaster

opening was closed, and the solemn train departed chanting, as it had come.

Neysa had, of course, rushed to the ambassador. But she had been warned to keep the peace; international relationships must not be jarred. Whether the poor postulant had room to turn in her vault I don't know; certainly Sir Edward Bulwer-Lytton turned in his.

Neysa was unstirred by my brisk accusation. "Well, somebody told me that," she mused. "I didn't know you'd heard it."

One evening that was memorable to me in its excitement was at Irving Berlin's house, when Ruth Draper was one of the guests. This extraordinarily gifted woman, slender, quiet, able to fill a whole stage with personalities without a change of position or costume, was alone in her field, and the generation that is too late to have known her knows nothing like her, and never will know anything like her. People used to stream out from her one-woman shows loudly contending that there actually were soldiers or peasants or children on the stage. "In that Italian church, George," one might hear some voice saying, "I suppose you'll say that those American tourists didn't come in?"

She had one sketch in which she differentiated one Irish brogue from another—Mayo as it were from Clare, or Cork from Roscommon. On the night I met her I had the audacity to try my own brand upon her, but she did not rise to this bait. She answered with extreme politeness, "Ah, that's southern," and the conversation ended abruptly, leaving me somewhat red in the face.

But it wasn't Miss Draper who made the night what it was, nor Jimmy Gleason with his rustic soliloquy, nor even Harpo Marx with his goggle-eyed brand of magic. It was when our host took his place at the piano and played and sang his newest song, "Always," not published yet, not even copyrighted, but instantly placing itself, to those of us who listened, in that select category that holds "Sweet Adeline," and "In the Evening by the Moonlight" and "Drink to Me" and "Maxwelton's Braes." It seemed a miracle to me that night, as it does today, that this quiet, unassuming man, impressive to the casual observer, at least, in no way, should contribute joy and harmony to groups of youngsters loafing under summer trees, to the very heart of the singing circle around the home piano, to earnest white-tie-and-tail quartets walking out upon a hundred stages in the hundred years to come.

Miss Draper's extraordinary art could permit her to offer two numbers on her program, "The German Lesson" and "The Italian Lesson," and have no hint of similarity between them. The aristocratic lady, continually interrupting her Italian lesson with messages to the cook, to the children's teacher, to the new puppy, and finally in telephoned undertones full of love and longing to a new conquest, was pure comedy. The German lesson, with a passionate lover of Heine or Goethe or whoever it was struggling with a large class of uninterested children, was pathos. She read a passage, relishing each word, like a drink of fresh, cold water, and must interrupt herself more than once to say "Schtop dat!" to some small offender who was either climbing over the back of his chair or stretching his gum into a long loop. I saw him with my own eyes.

There were giants on Broadway in those days. Did anyone ever see Ruth Draper without tears as she stood, one small forlorn French wife among so many thousand, holding the baby up to get his first glimpse of his father, coming back up the small-town street with his regiment, home from the war? The bewildered look turning to fright, the loving low murmur of promise to the baby ending, the agonized appeal to Jacques—to Hilaire—where is Jean? Jean. My man! Where is he? It was all war in epitome.

For a few winters we were madly social. One day after shopping far downtown I drifted into the Thirty-sixth and Madison home of a very fine old lady who had been my mother's friend in a California girlhood. She had said so often that I must lunch with her, any day without warning, that I really did it.

"This is nice," she said when we two were settled at the sort of meal that rich old ladies have formally served when they have come down from more serious cares and pleasures to a real, fussy concern about sauces and salads, "because tonight there'll be twelve of us here——"

It was no time for me to be criticizing old ladies! I was not yet an old lady, but I had been so swept into the dame-of-fashion attitude that I never looked at the dinner-engagement list until it was time to dress. We were dining with her that night.

But I had valid excuses. Two novels every year for more than twenty-five years, many short stories, fifty-two newspaper articles, and the heavy mail all these involved might well have kept me busy, too busy to worry about dates. Cigi presently began steady work on his own heavier type of fiction; two years or more, and much research, went into each book. Also he carried the responsibility for every practical detail of our lives: interviews, photographs, talks in newspaper offices or editors' sanctums, personal and business relationships with all the experts who handle royalties, insurance, investments, taxes, sales. To say nothing of the domestic staff and the children whose teeth, wardrobes, schooling, general progress were of far more absorbing interest to him than to them.

When croquet fanatics set up their wickets in long stretches of Central Park he sometimes joined the gallery but he never played. I played whenever dire emergency demanded a fourth player, not otherwise. Harpo Marx was ringleader in organizing these games; wherever he went, in the luggage box of his car a croquet set went with him. Other enthusiasts were Alec, Neysa, George Kaufman, Dick Leonard, Bill Hanley, a newcomer from the California theatrical world, and presently to marry Madge Kennedy, and others whose names are lost. One day Ruth Gordon, small, homely, packed to the brim with magnetic fire, stood dreamily watching us. Someone, at a crisis, missed a wicket at six inches, and the ensuing universal gasp and paralyzed silence held the players while Ruth said in her young, wonder-filled voice, "He wanted it to go through, didn't he?"

This reminds me of the comment of a maid in the lonely house of Commander Spears when his wife and two small sons were awaiting news of their sailor, away in the war.

"My God," murmured the mistress, "the Germans have entered Holland!"

"An' din you want 'em to?" Sarah, bringing in the breakfast, asked sympathetically.

Ruth Gordon, to my thinking, has not always been given her rightful place among our great actresses. She brought something original, inspired, and different to every role she played. I especially recall her impersonation of Nora in Ibsen's *Doll's House*. Nora, a bewildered, well-intentioned little girl, finding herself quietly following other people's directions into obedient wifehood and motherhood, secretly buys some forbidden candy when she takes the children for a walk, and of course hides it from Torvald's keen eye. The hurried childish gesture with the meek little striped paper bag of caramels is almost her last before the dam breaks, the quiet power is released, and Nora, without raising her voice, thunders the pronouncement that eighty years ago awakened half the women of the world.

W hat the friendship of two New York women meant to me after Teresa died has to have its own place in the story.

Friendship is a rare luxury. Liking people is one thing: being glad to see them, going to their house twice a year for dinner and always asking them to the big football lunches, sending Christmas cards. But friendship means more than that. It demands propinquity, constant meeting in off hours, exchange of problems, exchange of books, ideas, likes and dislikes. With nine tenths of one's friends this is impossible. After rare meetings one parts on a troubled "Why don't we do this often? This has been so nice. Well, do. Please remember to. We'd love it." We say, year after year, "Why don't we try to see more of the Lawrences? We love them and they've always been lovely to us." And years go by, and birthdays go by, and on their silver wedding we were in Europe, and on ours they were in Mexico. And presently it's the Golden Wedding . . .

It was my fortune to go to New York armed with but two introductions and knowing not one soul in the city except Aunt Mary. The introductions were to two sisters, Cora Cook Rowan and Jane Cook Tobin. These two played so remarkable a part in all the New York years that no story relating to me could leave out their names. I had been married some weeks before I could command courage to make the trip far downtown to Eleventh

Street and ring the bell on a three-story brownstone bearing a neat brass sign: "Stephen M. Cook, M.D." This was their father, distinguished among the physicians of New York two generations ago. All three of us had husbands, all three were not long married, and all three were within the next year to become complacent mothers. Their husbands, Joseph Rowan and Joshua M. Tobin respectively, come into this narrative but slightly, although they did their full duty by us, taking us to dinners and shows, and using those many and sometimes strange ways that old New Yorkers know, to get us privileges: special tickets for this and that, special places to park at big games, special tables in pack-jammed special restaurants. Everything we did, as a party of six, was done with a sense of being highly favored. On one occasion we finished a Sunday lunch at one of the grandest hotels, only to have the headwaiter bow deeply while waving aside the bill and say that we were Mr. McDonald's guests: George McDonald, himself a highly privileged person, had observed us from a nearby table. On another occasion Joshua Tobin, member of an old Albany family, could drive along several miles of sidewalks to get us somewhere on time.

This particular breed is distinctly New York. The manifold ways in which true natives of the city, with a heritage of some hundred years behind them, can find and press advantages and obtain favors, and get Judge Somebody to say it is all right about that ticket, and Attorney Somebody Else to say that the boy will go scot-free, must inevitably impress outsiders like ourselves, who have never known such favors, as black magic. Mysterious folk classed as "clients, customers, or a fellow Bill knows" could open up sales lofts in the thirties, and sell $300 coats for $139.50. Amiable "Miss Annie" or "Miss Lou," fifty years old, with dyed hair and smart figures, in the smartest shops would waylay us. "Jane, that English coat is down to eighty-five—was three-forty, you know. Better come in." Or "Cora, don't you wear that hat another minute. Come in this afternoon. I've got a beaver, with cock feathers . . ."

We lunched together on that very first day of my shy call, and thereafter, for thirty-five years, lunched together whenever we could—that is, every day unless some other plan had right of way. I should estimate that this meant some two hundred times a year for the twenty years that we lived in New York City or on Long Island, and perhaps a hundred times a year for the remaining fifteen. We made three European trips together, and three times the "Cookies," as Cigi called them, came out for visits to the ranch.

Both were handsome; Cora dark and slender with magnificent dark eyes; Jane a striking gold-blonde, with black eyes, brows, and lashes. Both were sophisticated, witty, and fundamentally and refreshingly decent and good. They danced and played golf, they managed luxurious households, they loved their men, they had children and adored every phase of the children's growth, but they would no more have missed Mass daily, or constant recourse to the Sacraments, than they would have cut their throats, or their children's. Their company was infinitely exhilarating, and for years it was my very special luxury. We lunched at each other's houses, at hotels, at a favorite little French restaurant off Ninth Avenue in Fifty-seventh Street, at charity affairs, at counters; and when we were all at the ranch we drove down to lunch at Pebble Beach or Cypress Point or came into San Francisco to eat sand dabs at the Fairmont or abalone out at the Cliff House, or shop among the crab kettles at Fisherman's Wharf.

And there were letters, hundreds of them, letters full of laughter, and for a while of sorrow and tragedy, all shared, all woven into the tough fabric that was our friendship.

Our name for Cigi, when we traveled, was "the Protestant Gentleman." This awesome character is a familiar bogey to little girls in Catholic boarding schools. He observes the misconduct of the aforementioned little girls and reports it to Sister Superior, or to their teacher. "A Protestant gentleman who saw you girls in chapel yesterday was very much dis-edified," Sister Philip Liguori tells the class severely. The girls never see the Protestant gentleman, but his influence is immense, and in giving Cigi the title of this nebulous character we felt we were doing him honor.

After Teresa died Port Washington seemed a completely strange place to me, and before we went to Rio de Janeiro we sold Green Blinds and began to spend some of the winters in California. But it was Cora and Jane, inspired in words and more than inspired in silences, who made me feel that I myself had come back from the shades and was living again.

For two or three years Teresa's children lived with their grandparents and Laura and Stephen, first in Troy, at the arsenal, then, when the Colonel retired, in Scarsdale. Separation from them, who had been as close to me as my own, was a steady heartache to me, eased somewhat during the second summer at the ranch, when Jim was loaned to us. It was small comfort to visit them, for their presence naturally made my grief for Teresa's loss more acute, and parting from them, after a visit, was hard on both sides. They were loved, sheltered, amused, educated, trained as are only the fortunate children of the world, but they were never for one hour mine in the old way. It was only natural to suppose that Billy would marry again, and perhaps choose a wife as devoted to the children as their grandmother and aunt were.

A very close friend of Teresa's and Billy's, Henry Hoyt, a man of real gifts and great charm, coming home after the armistice, found something of the infamous "dear John" situation at home and joined Billy in his return to bachelor existence. Not long afterward Billy met Henry Hoyt's sister; they had all been friends as children in Washington, when the senior Hoyt had held some political appointment under the first Roosevelt and the Benéts were stationed there. Henry's sister, twice divorced, was writing poetry, and Billy was the first to pronounce it exceptionally beautiful poetry, which opinion, through his eager handling, shortly began to be shared by the world of letters. This was Elinor Wylie, born Hoyt, and first married to one Philip Hichborn, of Washington.

Tragically, Henry Hoyt, heartbroken over his domestic picture, took his own life; Billy found him dying in their apartment. Heartsick at the loss of his friend, and ill himself, Bill had the added misery of having to tell the sister the hard news. That winter, Elinor nursed him and presently they were married. And now the picture changed completely, and from feeling that Teresa's children were safe and loved and intelligently handled, my agonies arose in full force, for whatever else the gifted Elinor was, she was of all women in the world the last one fitted for stepmotherhood.

She might have been quite beautiful, with her colorless clear-cut face, superb dark eyes that were framed by a great mop of curled dark hair, except for an expression of faint discontent about her mouth and a restless use of the eyes that were always looking for something else. We all make curious mistakes in self-analysis, but hers were tragic; trying to reconcile her actual character and her destiny with what she wanted and hoped them to be, and yet knew they were not, kept her spirit in a state of continual unrest.

She had had a brilliant Washington wedding and had taken possession of a house that was a show place in Washington; she had borne a son. When the baby was less than two years old she fell deeply in love with Horace Wylie, a friend of the family, who had several children of his own. They went away to England together, leaving both nurseries behind; they rented a country place north of London and lived there for some years. It was in this comparative isolation that Elinor battened on old English novels and achieved her passion for Shelley's poems. She made this a personal affair, stating frequently, when I knew her, that she herself actually was Shelley redivivus. She also gained at this time the charming, slow-stepping style that shows in her prose work, *The Venetian Glass Nephew, The Orphan Angel*, based on Shelley's life, and *Mr. Hodge and Mr. Hazard*, this last, to my thinking, her best novel. One of these won distinction as the Book of the Month.

Having left her own child motherless and having at least contributed to the fatherless situation of Horace Wylie's children, it still pleased her to claim a deep devotion to Billy's trio, a position that she could in no way maintain. She told these bewildered youngsters of her loss of several babies while in England, their names, the grief she had felt in their deaths. She wrote of herself, in a *New Yorker* profile, "She's always longing to turn back the page, and live with children in a golden age."

But with the actual children about her she was capricious and willful, sometimes going to some pains to amuse them—especially the youngest girl, Kit—in whimsical ways, but more often ignoring them as far as possible. Her greatest preoccupation, with me, was self-defense. It grew wearisome, the constant explanation of her own erratic career. In some moods she would disparage my own incurably domestic interests, stammering eagerly that it was no virtue in me to like kitchens and picnics, I was just made that way. At other times she would challenge me to say that anything she had done I might not have done in her place. Then she would assert that after Horace Wylie's wife had agreed to a divorce she, Elinor, had asked to have his children sent to them in England, so that I need not think my taking Billy's children to California was anything unusual. (The Wylie children did not go to England.) In canonical ways, too, she was endlessly argumentative; her three marriages were all legal, even in Catholic eyes, as she defended them. Nobody was worrying about these points or discussing them, but she could not leave them alone.

While all literary New York was reading her poems and admiring the sudden rise of the new poet—for, if she had only appreciated it, she was taken seriously from the first, as few new writers are—Elinor was fretting over imaginary slights and disparagements that never existed. For example, she rushed from our dinner table one night and flung herself upon a bed, raging because some innocent dinner guest had observed that G. B. Stern was the most important woman writer of the day; at another time she was reduced to suicidal fury because a newspaper commented upon innocent matching of couplets at the home of poet Clement Wood. "It sounded as if we were hayseeds!" she raged, telling me of it. "Nobody makes fun of me like that!" At a dinner to which we were all invited she sent late regrets because Edna St. Vincent Millay was also to be among the guests, and when Billy, with his inexhaustible good nature and indulgence for the whims of the other sex, observed soothingly that she needn't be afraid of playing second fiddle to anyone, the fireworks really began.

In fact, despite beauty, brains, youth, wit, a talent close to genius and fame, she was troublesome. Three men—one might say men of distinction—had married her, and many others had indicated their admiration in unmistakable terms, but "dissatisfied" was the word that inevitably was fitted to her, and everyone who knew her wondered what on earth she wanted. Billy never wrote to her the poems he wrote to Teresa. But after his marriage to Elinor the Teresa poems were not included in his first collected works.

With her other gifts Elinor had a subtle wit. It evinces itself sharply in such poems as the one beginning "I was, being human, born alone. I am, being woman, hard beset." And no one ever could capture the fascinating Stephen Vincent Benét, with his round, little-boy face, his Spanish eyes, his big glasses, as she did in the lines "A canvas of Rembrandt's might be your proper field, but oh, that resemblance to Master Copperfield!" And she ends this poem with the signature, "your sister-in-law, and in outlawry."

Elinor died suddenly, and Billy was destined to marry twice again. Edna St. Vincent Millay's eight-line tribute to Elinor is one of the most exquisite things she ever wrote.

Bill's third wife was an extremely handsome young actress, Lora Baxter, from whom he parted with much amiability on both sides a few years later.

The last wife of William Rose Benét was indeed the woman of my early fears: motherly, clever, herself a successful writer of children's books. Marjorie Flack showed from the beginning the home quality that embraces not only Thanksgiving and Christmas parties but schooling and rubbers and understanding and love. Had that been the second marriage, we might have lost the delight that Jim, Rosemary, and Kit were to me and all the Western branch of the family. The thought would keep me awake at night even now if I did not feel that Marjorie and Billy and I would have come to a treaty by which the California summers would have been mine. Teresa's grandchildren loved this stepgrandmother, and holidays at her retreat at Pigeon Cove, on the Massachusetts coast, were a part of their story. Marjorie Flack Benét died in 1958.

The saga of the ranch went on from 1920 to 1945, and broke, the last of the great soap bubbles, just before the end of the Second World War. Our first year began simply enough in 1920 with Cigi and me and the two boys taking possession, and luring brothers and their wives, Frank Norris' shy, exquisite small daughter, and the small cousins, increasing in number steadily, down for rather rough weekends. The small main house always suggested to me the architectural books my father had picked up for us as children —the *Shoppels Modern Homes* with their cupolas and gingerbread work. We had not quite reached the time of Spanish tiles and patios when all northern California set up grills, cloisters, terraces, pools; we climbed, when sated with outdoor joys, into sleeping bags.

We dug for the pool, we picked a grove of redwoods as a cathedral roof for the outdoor dining room, and year by year we expanded, adding a tennis court, a girls' house, a guesthouse, and a tent platform for the boys. The great lawn that dipped below the porch was clipped, and a baby set of little color-belted wooden mallets and matching wooden balls was handed to the children as a sweet Victorian game for them to learn.

This beginning of croquet naturally led to violence, mayhem, bloodshed, and tears, and an adult apiece began to appear on the green, championing this child or that, asserting that it was Rosy's turn and you were dead on that ball anyway. Shortly the children were banished, balls of a special composition were ordered from Germany, the mallets grew heads hard as cannon balls and longer handles, and the real purpose of our buying the ranch was at last made clear to us.

"I've seen hard times and good times in my day," said Harpo Marx, "but the things I remember are the croquet shots I've made and the ones I've missed."

"He's gone down to his room to commit suicide," Alec Woollcott said dispassionately as an especially engrossed player lost a game at the penultimate wicket.

"Can these people possibly be reconstructing a game of croquet?" demanded Jim Stanley, who was breakfast guest at the hotel in New York one bitter winter morning, as some enthusiasts began to dispute a decision made in the hot beauty of a summer day in California six months earlier. For army talk and navy talk, stamp-collecting and mountain-climbing talk, doctor talk and clergy talk pale into mere casual chatter when the croquet players get together. And here must be mentioned the name of Richard Anthony Leonard, long associated now with the National Broadcasting Company in New York, but a mere boy when he first came to the ranch and asked amusedly if that wasn't a sort of kids' game. Only a few years later, scantily clad in shirt and slacks, freely perspiring and dead serious in a ring of breathless spectators, it was Richard who won the first and only "Rover Emeritus" medal ever struck, by finishing the fourteen wickets and both poles on his first turn. True, he played the third ball. True, two played balls were lying in somewhat approachable positions, but also true, nobody else did it for a long, long time.

Gradually the ranch came into being, the loveliest mountain retreat ever known to man, as far as we knew. We built other cabins, on the crest of the ridge looking down upon the great canyon that lay in a picket line of mammoth redwoods a mile below. We built little Rosemary a place for her puppet theater in Drury Lane. There was "the Jims'" house and "the Joes'" house, and when Fred and Nell and small David, and the prettiest child of all, the oldest of the cousins, Fred's Babs, were anywhere in the neighborhood they had their quarters too. The cousins surged over the place and built up a thousand customs and traditions that made every summer increasingly memorable. They climbed the easy ladders of the great redwoods up to a hundred feet, and hung like sloths in the green layers of the branches, they built houses of the light madroña and bay logs from the woodpiles, they swam and dived in the emerald pool, and walked on the linked roofs of the ranch buildings. They cooked at the grove, climbed the hill for breakfasts high up on the summit, and they wrote dramas and performed them.

It was a scene from an Indian harem that the grown-ups especially remember, when the children worked up an entertainment in the barn. The Sultan, who was luxuriously prone in a nest of cushions, shouted without preamble that he wished to kill all his wives, and dragged in to him were all the delicious little girl cousins in saris and yashmaks; all duly fell under his scimitar except the last, redheaded one, who slew the Sultan himself.

While this was going on two lanky twelve-year-old boy cousins fanned the murderous Sultan. "You two were his servants," I said later to one of them. "We were the enoughs," he answered simply. I was foolish enough to try to draw forth this word again, on the porch after dinner, but something in my expression must have put the boys on guard, and they agreed that, yes, that was it, they were the Sultan's butlers.

In another show Mark's Conway, at seven, clad only

in a loincloth, ranged growling in a box stall. The sign above him read, "Pung-pung, He eats only grass."

California's hot summer days and cool summer nights, her fruits piled high in the center of the board, the scented piny shadows of the mighty sequoias, the starry glory of moonless nights have been sufficiently recorded, but we could add to these the voices of children, ringing up and down the hilly slopes, the music that presently poured from the very heart of the forest, the long table and charcoal pit in the grove, with half a dozen cooks elbowing each other out of strategic positions, and the pool that was the very center of every hot day's adventures. The wide strips of lawns about the pool saw domino and bridge games going, and there were movie cameras and midnight swims, and the rescue of at least one too daring child every weekend. In the kitchen were white-clad Orientals whose one object in life was to destroy any ideas of dieting.

In the house on Saturday nights we had every game that a ring of persons who like each other can play, and often that special amusement called by the New York crowd "the game," with the accent heavy on the first of the two words.

Mark came up from Rio with her children, who spoke in their smallest years with a faint Portuguese accent, the oldest once accosting me uncertainly, "Tia Caterina, are these the gloves of my brother?" Jam, to these infants, was *geléia,* and fresh garments *roupa limpa.* In moments of stress they addressed each other in belowstairs Portuguese, the three-year-old Connie sometimes withering his sister with a proverb or two. *Amor sem dinheiro no tenha valor* was one to remember.

For two summers we borrowed the Benét trio, but this had to stop, for from the first of August on they began to anticipate the end of vacation and the agony of parting, and to me every moment of the last weeks was equally hard. Autumn and schools and return to the cities were naturally not appealing to any of the children, but our separation from Teresa's three was necessarily complete, for Billy and Elinor lived in Connecticut now, and such visits as I could make were few and uncomfortable. One winter, unhappy away from them, we went to England, dawdled down to Sicily in search of the sun, found we would have been warmer and more comfortable in London, but still stayed on in dramatic Palermo, where the Mafia supplied the Adriatic beneath our lawn with a few of its enemies now and then, floating face up, and our boys swam daily in the same waters with no suspicion of ill. It was here that our apple-cheeked Syracusan maid reminded me one Sunday morning that the signor would be late for Mass. The signor, I said, was not a Catholic.

"The gracious signora married a Turk!" gasped Costanza, aghast. I found a murmured reference to this question useful in later mild domestic crises.

When we came back from this Italian visit, both with manuscripts, we found matters not too serene in the Benét household. Elinor really was not well, and between struggles with the children's winter coughs and colds, her shifting kitchen help, and her own mad desire to get at her *Orphan Angel* she was battered flat. Within ten days Billy had agreed that the three children should be delegated permanently to our care. It was a time of ecstasy for me, fitting the small travelers out for the Panama trip home, removing the boys from their Connecticut school, with no protest from them, in mid-April. All four were with us at the rail when the *President Harrison* sailed on a languid balmy spring afternoon, and after that, until each in turn went off to a home of his own, they were ours.

The trip through the Zone took three weeks then, or almost that, and they were heavenly weeks, and it was sheer felicity to get the ranch machinery in motion somewhat early in the season, and in the meanwhile drift about San Francisco, the rocks and beaches, Chinatown and Fisherman's Wharf.

The long bright pageant of twenty-odd summers followed, good for even the littlest ones to remember to the last detail, as they indeed have to adult years, and their own turn at parenthood.

It was not so long ago that Kit, over at Santa Cruz beach, finished some cautionary directions to her own quartet by turning to me with a stricken face.

"I sound like a grownup. Oh, heavens, I *am* a grownup!"

Every year Cigi and my brothers went up to the redwood grove where the Bohemian Club held its yearly encampment, for Jinks Week. And every year they brought back various visitors to the ranch, some of whom came many times. Nelson Doubleday and Colonel Theodore Roosevelt were among the early ones, George Creel had a working table in Cigi's cabin and did many of his *Collier's* articles there; Tom Beer came and went with no special formality; and Dan Totheroh wrote on the ranch the play, *Distant Drums,* that opened later on Broadway, and a child's book that he dedicated to Rosemary, ten years old.

Herbert Hoover, in the summer of his nomination to the presidency, came to lunch once or twice with his lovely wife, whom I not only loved but deeply admired. Blanche Bates came to play bridge under the redwoods on the lawn, shriek alike at bad luck and good, and, grabbing a trio of carefully chosen companions, rush from the dinner table for the remotest cabin on the ranch for more bridge. Sometimes the men of letters sat with an eclectic half dozen of us all night on the porch, busy with the simplest of games, "Who Wrote It?" The music of Cigi's carefully selected program would die out of the redwoods, the croquet players turn out the big locomotive lamps that lighted the field and come in with soaked boots green with torn grass, but the book game went on until five o'clock sunlight filtered through the layers of redwood foliage and another day was begun.

During a San Francisco campaign for America First we had the Lindberghs down, Charles the Silent climbing the almost perpendicular mountain with us, hewing his way with an ax through the choked chaparral, rejoicing in the heat and sweat and silence and protection of it, while the incomparable Anne won every heart on the place, hands down. Elsie Janis sparkled through one weekend, and Edna Ferber, on the Coast to attend a political convention, placed her approval on La Estancia. From England came Tennyson Jesse and the delightful Totty Harwood, who stayed with us for a fortnight, and one Lawrence Irving, grandson of the great Henry, and son of the H. B. Irwin who wrote almost the best and first of the factual murder books. In a stay of perhaps less than two weeks this Englishman wrought great havoc in the harem that was left there during Jinks Week, and is still remembered with romantic sighs. Alec came and stayed longer than the fortnight originally planned, he and Harpo electing to make complete preparations for departure, and at the last moment, with the car at the door, enthusiastically announcing that they were staying after all, and so making our chorused goodbys sound overly sentimental and rather flat.

Frances Parkinson Keyes came, and we found ourselves very much in harmony after a three-day friendship, even though circumstances did not give us a chance to pick it up again for some twenty-five years, in Venezuela. At the time she came to the ranch her first best seller, *Letters from a Senator's Wife*, had launched her on a long series of best sellers, but I think at that time she had not tried fiction, and I could cheerfully assure her, to her amusement, in a long late night talk on the porch, that fiction was much less in danger of libel suits.

In my entire career I was never subjected even to one, although I occasionally received haughty letters from ladies of high degree asking for an explanation of my use of apparently sacred names. "Frankly, I don't like it," one offended reader wrote me, because I had quite accidentally used her family name for my fictional family. As a matter of fact I took it whole from a nice old fellow who used to work around the ranch during the summers, quietly entering the county farm when the weather grew cold, and often asking me questions about the attractions of San Francisco, which he had never chanced, during his seventy years in Santa Clara County, to visit. Another lady wrote me that she proposed to bring suit for my use of the name of a poem she had written some twelve years earlier, and which had appeared in the church weekly. Inasmuch as the weekly was copyrighted she felt that she had me in an awkward fix. But names cannot be protected by copyright. Sinclair Lewis was quite safe in using *Main Street*, though Joyce Kilmer's book of poems had been published under that name three years earlier.

It is strange to look back upon the complete preoccupation we all had in our own work in those first postwar years. Every writer wanted to talk about writing —but exclusively his own.

Sinclair Lewis took Cigi and me to lunch in Washington one day and asked us to come up to his apartment and hear the first chapters of *Main Street*, which was to set the world ablaze the following year and lead best sellers for several years. But we begged off; we had something else to do. It was probably the all-important business of finding attractive tin cups for ranch luncheons. Red told us that day that it was the great American novel and perhaps it is; there are some others, not so sensationally received, that I would name first.

Of course we had honeymooners at the ranch as the young cousins grew up and spread wings. Caswell Adams of *Herald Tribune* ringside and newspaper fame, and his irresistible Mary were among the first, Madge Kennedy and Bill Hanley, both of whom had spent holidays there before, the cartoonist Herb Roth and Mildred, Maude Fay and Commander Powers Symington, the one fresh from triumphs in opera roles in Europe, the other recently retired with Navy honors.

But the occasions that brought distinguished folk to the ranch were not more popular than the weeks that went by with no special distinction, when the dreamy everyday routine went on day after redwood-scented day. Perhaps it was the man with the ponies this week, breakfast up on Deer Hill whenever a sufficiently energetic group would essay it, a three-day picnic in the bare little cottages of Santa Cruz when the men were at the Bohemian Grove and the household staff on vacation. Always the murmuration of starlings went on, under the oaks, about the lunch table, through the blazing flower beds. Bridge games at the pool were interrupted by the diamond splashing of small sunburned bodies and the shouts of "Looky! Look what I can do! Count while I'm under water!" that distracted parents from that special concentration that is needed to play a doubled slam.

For several years two diminutive Sicilian donkeys played a large part in summer amusements, their furry offspring, limp, comfortable, about the size of a well-grown cat, being carried casually about on the hip of an eight-year-old Kit, Kathy, or Peggy. A cart, covered completely with carvings of Romeo and Juliet, Julius Caesar and Cleopatra, came with the donkeys, and frequently made its appearance upside down, having hurled hysterical children in every direction, in flight. My dream of orderly children driving an orderly "Neddy," a dream probably borrowed from some old bound volume of *Chatterbox*, never came true. But there was always excitement where the donkeys were, and that was all the children wanted.

It was on real rides on real-sized horses that Peggy added a dramatic contribution to one occasion. We were all up at Tahoe then, during a Jinks Week, and there had been some question of ten-year-old Jane's riding at all, because of a recent appendectomy. Doctor and mother had agreed it was safe, but seven-year-old Peggy was so apprehensive and so vocal at the start that the riders turned back and presented themselves before a group of mothers with the suggestion that Peggy be removed from their company. Last of all of them, fat little weeping Peggy and her pony came bumping in, to address the maternal jury with a frantic plea: "Oh, please, all of you, be merciful to one who is in your power!"

Mercy was duly extended, with Peggy's big sister Jo, maternal at eleven, delegated to keep the conscientious objector quiet.

At the ranch these mothers were assisted at mealtime or bedtime by high school girls who came up as sitters and had as much fun as anyone. My sister's caustic comment upon the term given them was that it encouraged them to do nothing but sit, but they were a lot better than that. My criticism might have been that every one of them had a long important message to telephone to Ma every night, with supplementary messages for Stan, Buck, and Chub.

But to the sitters, I have no doubt, their vacation jobs meant only incessant changing of small clothes, keeping little rebels quiet at dinner, cutting up countless chops.

The ranch remains a golden memory of golden days, a picture of the time when almost all the women wore comfortable blue cotton coolie coats, frogged high at the neck, and extending halfway down wide oriental trousers; when the children lived in bathing suits and rubber-soled sneakers that give off frightful odors when taken from hot little feet. The hot walk, in and out of oak shadows, to the spring, the clicking cameras, the blackened old six-quart picnic coffeepot, the lines of wet bathing suits, the empty Coke bottles left in conspicuous spots, the annual rattlesnake and the heated bargaining for his skin, the tennis balls so disappointingly lifeless, the wriggling and scratching of poison-oak victims, the smell of citronella and cocoa butter, the flowers, flowers, flowers that filled the houses and crowded the walks, and the click of croquet balls and shouts of "Fresh on the world!" from the croquet field.

The croquet field. I wonder if any hour in the world holds the peculiar bliss of a holiday morning, with the breakfast triumph of griddle cakes, monogrammed with all the children's initials, well out of the way, and the scent of coffee dying on the warm air; the young mothers down in the latticed laundry, and the children roaring at their first swim, Cigi's music drifting out over everything, the croquet-free grownups already setting up a bridge table in the shade, and oneself with a select three worthy opponents, calmly, confidently, taking the first two wickets and obtaining a desirable place for the black ball at the third . . .

No, there is nothing like it. Not in this world. It was one of our players who chose "No rest for the wicket" as a slogan for the game, and George Kaufman who added, in his own sad and absent-minded manner, "with mallets toward none!"

When we were at the ranch, Cigi's was the supreme authority. It was always an unpretentious place, but with a staff of perhaps seven or eight expert assistants to keep the kitchen humming, the porches swept, the lawns in emerald perfection and attend to the last tiny detail that could, in simple mountain-house fashion, keep his guests comfortable, he gave everyone within the reach of his affection a very wealth of memories for more than twenty summers.

Rules were rules, on the ranch, and the swarms of children who spent long holidays there—sometimes as many as thirty at the six o'clock first dinner in the grove —learned to respect them. On hot mornings they could swim before breakfast, but anyone who did not appear, shining and hungry, at eight o'clock was asked in a roar that echoed through our glorious mountains if he supposed the place to be a boardinghouse. Many were the morning amusements, with the pool for their center, but no child could appear after luncheon before half past three, and the quieter they kept to their lairs, with pillows, books, and whispers, the better for one and all.

Among themselves there may have been feuds and vendettas, but in earlier years a trip to the five-and-ten and Disney movies in San José assuaged the worst of them, and as the nursery ages began to give way to the teens there was no quarreling at all.

The fact that we were all scattered about among a dozen cottages, and the added fact that nobody came to the ranch who didn't want to come, may have contributed to the general harmony, but it was Cigi's genius for management that made the whole beautiful experience possible at all. It was only when Cigi's long trial of illness ended, in the summer of 1945, that we could fully grasp just what he had given to the cloudless ranch summers that were never to be the same.

Every September our paradise was closed and abandoned. When schools opened everyone settled down to work, either in hotel experiments, broken by travel, for him and for me, or in the Casa Abierta in Palo Alto, where we lived for more than twenty winters. Here, in the big garden, I had my outdoor kitchen, and croquet games proceeded with unabated ardor, and here Cigi's limitless interests in the affairs of the constantly enlarging family group and the circle of our closest friends found endless outlets. The concern he felt for the new households extended to every detail, and the newlyweds who had been children on the ranch a few years earlier were expected to spend at least some of the summer weeks there, and come to many of the garden lunches in Palo Alto. The day of rest was crowded, for him, with activities. We all came home from Mass to a long, vociferous breakfast table embellished with great platters of fruit—some of it from the ranch—and Kayo's famous popovers. Then came croquet challenges, the long lunch break with broiled steak and bowls of salad in the garden, and a lingering afternoon on the croquet field until winter dusk drove us in. Sunday nights were open-house nights for the children of the family, and after a buffet supper there were games until midnight.

After the New Year Cigi and I always went to New York for a few weeks and perhaps extended those weeks for brief trips to Florida, Cuba, Washington, Bermuda. Then back to California, to sandwich in the necessary three months for novel writing—my writing, that is, for Cigi kept a much slower pace, wrestling with every one of his seven novels as if it had been a labor of Hercules. His was not a natural gift; he fought his way from page to page, and sometimes made my blood run cold by tearing up the patient work of weeks, or even months. But he loved it; his adoration of his brother had given him a reverence for the profession, as indeed his mother had, and he could not take it lightly.

His reward was that reviewers took him seriously from the first and analyzed his work with a kindred respect; he really enjoyed the flagellations through which he put himself, his typewriter, and the hours he spent in the libraries of the Stanford University. He went down to Bakersfield to capture a background there, and spent an absorbed and thrilled three weeks in a lumber camp in northern California. And discouraged, despairing, exhausted, he enjoyed every moment of it, as he enjoyed life. His club, his home, the ranch summers, the sea trips and land trips were all part of a pattern that deeply satisfied him; he had, like Sidney Howard's Sonoma ranchers, what he wanted.

Love for him, his impulses, his generosities, his eagerness to share any responsibility or predicament of those he loved, lives on. The children of early ranch days have families of their own now, and the tradition of "Uncle Cigi" is handed down as fresh as it was when he left us in the last year of the second war.

On whatever trade or profession he attempted, the peculiar force of his personality would have made its mark. He was not only tireless in energy, he was imaginative, enthusiastic, and he had that genius for taking pains that never stops. Repeatedly various firms, especially those of publishers, tried to get him to join them, but after his four years of war he had begun to write, keeping heroic hours and agonizing over the turn of a phrase or the motivation of a character until he was exhausted. It was never easy for him. But he was never deflected.

So violent were his emotional phases that even the youngest members of our enlarged family regarded them with amused affection. As, for example, the time when I was called to the telephone from a long dinner table filled by young cousins. In passing Cigi at the top of the table I paused to put a casual kiss on his forehead, saying surprisedly, "Why, you feel as if you had a fever!"

"I've thought all afternoon that I had a high fever," he answered in a subdued tone. I went on to the telephone, returning in a few minutes to find an unnatural hush holding the diners and Cigi sitting with a solemn face staring at nothing with a thermometer in his mouth. In a moment he removed it, studied it seriously, observed in a cheerful voice, "Absolutely normal," and the resumption of the usual dinnertime clatter went on. My sister, congratulating him on his honesty, observed that she would have announced, "One hundred and six," and broken the thermometer.

He had always expressed a horror of small cats, and when a diminutive silver Persian staggered out of our spare bedroom at the New York hotel he was angered. It seemed a small enough thing, he observed, to keep cats out of his way. I explained in confusion that I was merely holding the cat and would hand it over to a new owner as soon as I could find one, and before I went out I shut little Rajah up firmly for the afternoon. When I came back at five Cigi was asleep, as he often was at that time, and Rajah was curled close to the collar of his pajamas.

I hastily removed the cat, but later Cigi told me seriously that by chance I had got hold of an exceptionally fine little animal, that I appeared not to be able to discriminate between cats, and for Rajah's long and honored reign he was Cigi's cat. A detail of this sudden change of front was the appearance of two stout books on the care of cats, and not less than fifty pounds of sand, brought to our hotel room and deposited there for Rajah's complete comfort in the hotel and on the train trip.

After a childhood starved for affection and family serenity it was Cigi's fortune to marry, hesitantly and with foreboding, into a large clan, every member of which he subsequently came to love, and by every member of which he was loved in return. This was evinced by his nicknames; no relative-in-law ever had so many. He was "Chas" to his brother Frank, "Doc" to Jeannette Norris, "Chuck" to Irvin Cobb and to James Montgomery Flagg, who did his portrait in crayons, "Poobah" to his grandchildren, "Maje" to Walter McLellan, his friend and secretary for twenty years, "Don Carlos" to Aunt Kitty, "Nunc" to the undergraduate body, and "Siege" or "Cigi" to all and sundry.

He was essentially lovable, partly for the laughable inconsistencies and absurdities of his character, but mainly for the tremendous strength that made itself felt through every current of the life we lived together for thirty-six years. No one who knew him at all could escape his vital interest in anyone's and everyone's affairs; if he could help, he was in high spirits for days. The vigor with which he arose every morning, fresh, groomed, ready for the day, gave me the background I needed for undisturbed work.

The summers were a cloudless stream of reunions and house parties at the ranch; effortless as far as I, or any other person but himself, was concerned. He gloried in details, lists, checking, and rechecking. When with a party of eight undergraduates, twenty horses, a guide, and a cook we rode up into the High Sierra for five glorious weeks it was to discover that nothing had been forgotten. At everybody's belt hung a light canvas bag containing some fifty-two items, ranging from pencils and aspirin to fishhooks, compasses, corn plasters, and lump sugar for the horses. The laying out of all this regalia beside the sleeping bag on the lawn, on the night before our departure, was part of the fun. He always liked to start any expedition at unearthly hours. "Four o'clock right here tomorrow for orange juice!" was the parting warning on this occasion, and on many a morning we saw the sun rise on our breakfast fire at the top of Deer Hill.

In the thirty-six years we had together I never bought a dress for myself or by myself. I may add to this statement that I never saw a dress or a hat that I wanted to buy. It was his custom, twice a year, to go to the shops of his choice, look over the field, and then come tell me about it. A few days later I spent an afternoon trying on clothes, avoiding any glance into a mirror if possible, but revolving before Cigi obediently, to get his reaction. Sometimes a new saleswoman would assume, naturally enough, that I was leading my husband into extravagance, and address him coaxingly as to what this dress or that "did" for Madam; but usually they were old friends and tried rather to please the gentleman sitting watching them so closely, with his foot-long cigarette holder in his hand. The handsomest coat that I ever wore was a surprise presentation in his study one morning, and I turned about, wearing it, to catch Rosemary's eye.

"Marten?" I said noiselessly. Rosemary kept her face straight and answered, also without sound, that it was another type of fur. I never wanted mink: never noticed it on other women.

If ever I did, in the earlier years, bring home some simple garment that had caught my eye, he was unhappy about it. It wasn't my sort of thing. He hated me in it. How about the rummage sale?

All through the ranch years my midsummer birthday was made gay with gifts of the blue cotton Chinese coolie suits, high-throated and frogged, and by their counterparts in stiff tribute silks and brocades, lavender, gold, moss green. And when perhaps twenty giddy contestants gathered in the game room on Saturday nights it was charming, to my eyes at least, to see that almost all the female players were similarly dressed.

The impossibility of capturing Charles Gilman Norris, and putting him down on paper, impresses me more and more as I write. He was busy, loved, successful throughout his sixty-four years, and those who remember him get a certain amused and admiring light in their eyes when his name comes into any conversation. We shall not look upon his like again.

My work fell into a pattern that it followed for many years, and would have followed for more had not the increasing payment for the stories, from magazines that used them as serials, counterbalanced the increasing taxation upon family incomes, so that to write three serials a year was absolutely to lose money. We cut them down somewhat, but not until Cigi's management of our affairs had put us beyond the reach of financial anxieties.

And this, even as I and mine profited by the situation, has always seemed to me unfair—I mean that a product such as mine should pleasantly, and without suspense or strain, roll up such substantial rewards, and the greater gift of certain other writers find so uncertain a market.

There were poets in our group during those years whose work earns the term "genius" today, there was one American woman poet who adopted England for her home and once told me that at her most productive moment she had never enjoyed even temporary financial security, and I knew an American writer whose exquisite essays often adorned the pages of the exclusive *Atlantic* but who held an onerous and underpaid position as a sorority matron all the days of her life, for the satisfaction of going to bed at night with the rent paid and tomorrow's meals secure. And this was too common a story, as so many biographies testify.

For my own work I can honestly say that it was the very best I could do. In every one of the more than seventy-five novels that I wrote between 1912 and 1945 I strove to improve upon the last one. Until a plot appealed strongly to me I would not begin to work upon it, moving about with other activities restlessly as it wrought upon heart and brain, and finally settling down to that irresistible combination of new typewriter ribbon and new box of perforated golden paper with a low inaudible growl, like a dog with a bone.

Croquet, solitaire, cooking, the raising of basketfuls of cocker puppies and Persian kittens, endless walks and talks, picnics and plans with the undergraduates, plans for their marriages, trips to Europe, Mexico, South America, gathering bookshelves full of prim old New England female biographies, or books on polar exploration—these were some of the interests that filled the pauses between novels, but when I fell upon the blessedness of a plot at last, the work went rapidly.

Most of the critics did not take my work seriously, but then neither did I take the critics too seriously. My writing I took with deadly seriousness. My contemporaries won prizes. I never won a prize, never was given an honorary degree or had a book selected for one of the clubs. But I rejoiced in writing, in the fact that magazines, if they had one serial, wanted another, and in the heavy mail which began to pour in from small towns reached by the big magazines and by the syndicated articles which were scattered all over the Union. Many a time some unknown woman's agitated letter, perhaps penciled on a lined tablet of dime-store paper, gave me a plot for the novel that was simmering somewhere unformed in my mind. And over and over again the fearful power of money upon human lives was impressed upon me—the wills, the lawsuits, the ulcers John gets under the long office strain, the nervous breakdown Mary has as the bills come in, the constant gnawing thought of it that rides us all.

Sometimes in a bus or a restaurant or a symphony concert I have looked at the faces about me and wondered, "Are you thinking of money now, and what are you thinking about it?"

"With men, it's the way the women waste money," said one of California's greatest psychologists when he was asked what were the most frequent causes that brought patients to his consulting rooms. "With women, it's because their husbands don't make enough."

It would seem that marital wreckage and divorces, even though they have many names, can almost always be brought down to that one word.

As for plots, most writers of fiction early grasp the fact that anything is a plot, and no plot—from the Venerable Bede down to Ellery Queen—can be stolen. *Jane Eyre,* that most plagiarized of plots, could be quite safely rewritten by a dozen of today's writers without any danger of sameness or similarity in the result. For years I had in a biography library in Palo Alto a faded old volume decorously called *The English Governess at the Siamese Court,* and never realized that in it a twentieth-century gold mine lay hidden. The successful play, *The Children's Hour,* and Miss Tey's magnificent *Franchise Affair,* to say nothing of Theodore Dreiser's *American Tragedy,* are true stories, and, if one wishes to go a trifle further back, so is Browning's *Ring and the Book.*

It was while we were still reading manuscripts for the *American Magazine* that a stout, battered, novel-length story of childhood was submitted; it was read with small attention and refused. It came back a year or two later and was declined again. When it showed up, even more battered and hopeless-looking, for the third time, it got more serious consideration. For by this time Cigi was what he himself called the "sporting editor" of a religious weekly, the *Christian Herald,* which had a fine circulation in church groups and into which, we thought, this much-vended tale might fit. It did fit.

It ran serially for some weeks; the sum paid for it was absurdly small, and yet it was Mrs. Porter's *Pollyanna*, which was destined to take America by storm, run over its hundred thousand, its million, and appear as the vehicle for more than one movie star. The plot? No plot at all, really. But there is no one in the English-speaking world who does not know what you mean when you describe someone as a Pollyanna.

On my desk for half a century has lain a double pack of miniature playing cards; complicated games of solitaire are my escape hatch when the story goes, as all stories do at some midway moment of panic, into mere words, words, words, and the players become lifeless puppets. I've tried darning and shelling peas, but the cards seemed to hold the only magic; at any difficult moment a few games cleared the way and showed me which way the plot should jump.

Thus my writing, if it lacked some of the suspense and doubt of the general run of fiction, was strangely serene. Short stories were sandwiched in here and there; quite often, for his birthday, Cigi might find two or three at his breakfast plate. And two or three times in the more than thirty-five years of activity I kept a long story going, a story not intended for serialization. When anyone asks me what one, of all the books, is my own favorite, I am apt to pick one of these: *Certain People of Importance, Little Ships, The Venables,* or *The American Flaggs.*

Cigi handled all contacts with editors, and told me only good news. Arthur liked it. Ray liked it. Miss Lane liked it. I swam blissfully in this friendly current. As far as I know no editor ever made any suggestion of changes in any manuscript, and Ray Long, of the *Cosmopolitan,* and Gertrude Battles Lane, of the *Woman's Home Companion,* kept me busy. Arthur Vance of the *Pictorial Review* liked an occasional serial, and we had pleasant relationships with Otis Wiese of *McCall's.* Once or twice when Miss Lane was supplied, *Collier's* took a story.

Miss Lane was my especially indulgent editor and my close friend. There was a real affinity between us, as women, that transcended any business relationship; not that I ever talked stories to anyone—any reference to what I wrote made me feel then, as it does now, uncomfortable and awkward. The gift, if it can be called that, was a natural one, and it was too richly repaid for me ever to consider haggling about terms or resenting the literary honors that came to other writers. Of one of my stories William Dean Howells wrote that it had a quality that had not been shown since Dickens dared; Theodore Roosevelt approved of *Mother,* and a cardinal from Rome wrote me some years ago that an Irish-American tale of mine had been read to a certain ailing old saint on one occasion and had made him smile. So that my kindlier critics, if few, were of the choicest sort.

My stories were not of the Irish-born but of the second-generation Irish in America, whose standards, ideals, attack on the English language, and curious use of gross overstatement, or of mild understatement as forceful as any exaggeration, delights anyone with even a trace of Irish in his blood. Having more than a trace of it myself, I studied these transplanted Celts with affectionate attention and tried to transcribe some of their ways in simple stories of the hard work they did, the poverty under which they struggled, and the joy, beauty, home love, purity of spirit, and romance they managed to put into it. Pride, dignity, and chastity are their birthright, and in the easier conditions of the New World they kept them all, and could spread out into undreamed luxuries and freedoms as they increased and prospered. When a fine strong girl who worked in my kitchen for a while gave up a long-awaited visit to the homeland so that she could send the hoarded hundreds to an aunt who was widowed in Ballyclare with a houseful of children, and later put off her own marriage so that she might send for a younger cousin and get her well established in domestic service in New York, she did only what was expected of her. Later she did visit Ireland with her husband and small sons; "there was Yanks on the boat very kind to James and me," she wrote on a postal, "as us to thim." And there one sensed pride and dignity. "Yanks" were Irish girls like herself, but ones who had worked in New England.

"Ma's hair would have you kilt!" was characteristic of the overstatements that went on in my kitchen. "Jo laughed till it kilt him" was another current phrase.

The understatements were even more effective. My favorite example of the latter was given me by a magnificent woman of something less than sixty, who had raised a houseful of ten children by her own efforts, the husband and father having died just after "our Jule" was born, some ten years earlier.

"But Jule's not the youngest, what about Jimmy?" I asked, eying the stalwart seven-year-old who was the darling of them all. It then appeared that Jimmy was an adopted son, and while I sat in simple wonderment —or perhaps it was reverence—she told me the story.

Jimmy was "posthumious." His young father and mother had come to board with Ma Callahan before the birth of their child, their plan being to get the expectant mother to the hospital in good season. But as indications of labor commenced so did a blizzard, and at daybreak the only car that could be moved was the family truck. The young wife duly got into the truck, her husband at the wheel, and with every good wish from the family seeing them off, they started up "Bur'rke Cochran's hill."

"But, d'ye see, the hill was slippery as glass," the story ran, "an' they couldn't make it. The car slipped, an' him flung off one side, killed dead, and her the other side, and the child borrn into me own hands of a dead mother lyin' out in the snow. 'Be good to him, Ma,' she says to me, shutting her eyes." There was a silence. Then, "You'd have felt sorry for thim," Ma Callahan said simply.

Much of what is called Irish wit is not funny at all, to the speaker. A group of American-Irish women, all long past middle age, was once discussing the sudden death of a friend.

"She was with the family at dinner, then she went to lie down and simply went to sleep," someone said.

"Doesn't it make your mouth water?" our hostess asked seriously, and she seemed a little shocked when in spite of ourselves we could not but laugh.

My Irish grandmother's approach to mirth was majestic and suspicious. My father told us that her grim, unamused face, at the minstrel shows of the sixties that San Francisco found side-splitting, was enough to finish off Mr. Bones forever. He said that Aunt Kitty and he had a second show when at breakfast she painstakingly took the evening's performance apart, dissecting it and asking patiently if this or that was supposed to be funny.

It was when a pretty, affected English girl congratulated her in the boardinghouse days upon the "delicious English plum pudding" at her table on Christmas night that my grandmother made the withering retort, "And since when did the pudden' cross the Channel?" But I don't think she thought it was funny.

Aunt Mary, appearing heretofore in these pages as a music coach in New York, very much at home with the fashionable clients of the big singers and producers, was once in a delicacy shop in Sixth Avenue, making purchases for her frugal supper, said supper to be heated on a reversed electric iron in a hotel room, when the handsome woman waiting upon her paid her a compliment.

"You've certainly got beautiful hair, dear," she said.

"Thank you," said my aunt, freezing at the familiarity.

"Well, I had lots of hair," said the proprietor, making three slices of tongue, some macaroni salad, and two doughnuts into a package. "Lovely hair," she went on ruefully, "but my girls made me cut it. You wouldn't know me."

"I don't know you," said my aunt, stressing the second word, laying down seventy-four cents, and sweeping from the shop.

Memories of gala nights punctuate the years. Once a year the Lunts gave a party, and once only, and that was an occasion not to be missed. My love and admiration for these two has never flagged. They remain as fresh, unspoiled, and honest in their art as they were when they began. In some verses I wrote for Cigi for our thirtieth anniversary I speak of prizes we have brought back from the long journey: friendship with the Lunts stands high on the list.

Almost once a year Madge Kennedy starred in a Broadway play, an event that brought the faithful out in droves. There was a thick-starred evening when Condé Nast had a preview of a Pickford movie at his house, and Mary and Douglas were there to add the last touch of excitement. There was a production of *Iolanthe* that drew us all to the theater again and again, and a strange Russian musical play called *Carmencita and the Soldier* that had as a backdrop a score of dark, looming Seville balconies where señoras sat all through

the play, fanning and studying the disgraceful go-
ings-on of the cigarette girl and her low associates.
There was a fabulous dinner before a fabulous concert,
after which a few of us climbed up the dark stairways
behind the stage at Carnegie Hall, because we were going on to Sasha's or Jasha's or Toscha's to make a night
of it. But here on these dark stairs, waiting for the musician to freshen up after the concert, in high heels and
with a heavy Spanish shawl dragging off my shoulders,
it suddenly came to me that I did not want to be here
at all, and I went quietly down the dark stairs and
through passages and out into Fifty-sixth Street, beautiful in light falling snow, and took off my best slippers
to wrap them under my shawl, and walked home in
blessed peace and quiet to a waiting bed, a lamp, a
book. It was a milestone.

And there were duds, too, in the picture. There
was a proposal from fascinating little Marie
Meloney, who was for years editor of *Delinea-
tor*, that I consent to a plan to send me to Brussels, to
abide for some weeks in the royal dwelling and write a
study of the royal personalities. Queen Elizabeth had
mentioned only two American women as suitably
equipped for the task; the other was, I believe, a friend
in whose house in Kennebunkport we had been guests
the previous summer: Margaret Wade Deland, who
wrote the "Dr. Lavendar" stories.

She either did not accept or perhaps, as a close friend of Mrs. Meloney's, I had been asked first. Anyway, we considered the idea, at first thought so thrillingly flattering, but on second and third thoughts not so glamorous to a woman with the blood of one Warren, M.D., of Bunker Hill fame, in her veins.

The journalist guest of Belgian royalty must rent and insure the use of some quarter million dollars' worth of jewels from Paris, and must wear gowns commensurate with great state functions. This was rather too suggestive of the plays that John and Neysa Baragwanath used to put on for evening entertainments, followed by staggering questionnaires as to what city we were in, what century, why we knew the wife was rich, why we knew the clock on the wall was five minutes fast.

But more than that. The writer selected to accept this easy, intimate friendship with the Queen must agree to remain in the aforesaid palace lodgings until eleven o'clock each morning. At that time, or earlier, she would be apprised of the royal plans for the day and informed whether or not she was to lunch, drive, enjoy afternoon coffee, or dine in state at the palace. And every word she might write about this exalted experience at any time must be submitted to palace censorship. Natural enough conditions for the Queen to exact, of course, but far from natural concessions for an American lady to make, especially as said American lady could not take husband or sister along to share stifled laughter behind doors, or lie awake half the night dissecting the elements of monarchy. So that came to nothing.

And some years before that event had come the commission from splendid Gertrude Lane of the *Woman's Home Companion* to visit the still glamorous widow of Grover Cleveland, the beautiful Frances Folsom whose marriage at nineteen to her former guardian, who also happened to be President of the United States, had shaken all girlhood, in the eighties, with wild dreams of similar conquests. And this might have been—would have been—an assignment of pure delight.

But just as the magazine's plans and mine became definite Mrs. Cleveland announced her engagement to be married to a Princeton professor and warmth faded out of the enterprise.

Cigi and I decided long ago that every fourth dinner party, whether at home or abroad, was a dud, and every alternate plan or offer that made our breakfast table wildly animated came to nothing, and so philosophy carried us through.

We joined the more exciting group only occasionally, loving some of them—Alice Duer Miller, Madge Kennedy, Harold Ross—unreservedly, and admiring the others tremendously, but still—not quite belonging. There was sometimes an unacknowledged element there that aroused uneasiness. Was everyone quite sincere? Weren't our bones among the myriad whitened bones that were heaped upon the glittering sands of that surging sea of production and achievement and failure and success? If not, why not?

Some of these folk came down, in later years, to the Doubledays' country place at Oyster Bay, and here there was unmitigated fun, with perhaps Gertrude Lawrence adding her own brand of irresistible fascination to the scene, imposing Somerset Maugham very much at home, croquet at its peak, and the normal life of a family moving cheerfully in the background: children on ponies, children on the tennis court or in the pool, Nelson and the radiant Ellen keeping half a dozen weekend enterprises going at once.

It was here that Edna Ferber, watching a croquet game, felt impelled to reproach Harold Ross during the course of a hard-fought game.

"Harold, you pushed that ball with your foot," Edna said sternly, adding, "Anyone who would do that would cheat at bridge!"

And Harold, coming up blandly, with his own half-submerged air of a manatee leaving the deep, asked innocently, "Don't people cheat at bridge?"

I t is natural for Edna Ferber's name to come into any story of those years. She showed from the very beginning a certain firm hold on the American scene, and the fact that many of her novels have become screen successes as well as library classics proves that we, her contemporaries, were right in feeling hers a unique approach. She had already had a novel published when she came from Chicago to New York; it was a tale of a newspaper woman, *Dawn O'Hara*. But I had never heard her name when the first story she submitted to the *American* came to my hand (Cigi often brought home manuscripts for consideration), and instantly it stood out among the others. I think it was called "The Frog and the Puddle," and in spite of the almost fifty years that have passed since I read it, one detail remains in my mind. It was the story of a small-town girl, an office worker, new to the city, somewhat discouraged and homesick, at night, easing her hot and tired feet against the coolness of the iron legs of her bed.

Until sometime shortly before the second war we two writers were warm friends. It was a real sorrow to me when she changed, for I never changed. We were never neighbors, never intimate, but we shared many, many good times and friends and kept in touch as Cigi and I came and went between our two cities. Her wit, her keen intelligence and passion for analysis, and her enthusiasms made her always prominent in any group, and wherever she was there was laughter, and quite possibly the challenge and the high scorn that were characteristic of her.

On one occasion I was preoccupied with some family matter during the first days after a return to New York, and learned from Cigi that Edna had heard we were back and was in high dudgeon. The old-fashioned word was surely written for her. I happened to be broadcasting for books for sailors that night, from a newspaper office, and seized this chance to put a personal in the agony column. My plan was to cut this personal out, the following day, and mail it to Edna, but that was needless, for Frank Case, manager of the Algonquin

Hotel, saw it and put it at her breakfast plate. Frank had not the faintest idea that it concerned anyone he knew, but he chose to assume that it was meant for her. Edna read:

> Edna, your folks from Cal. are here. Charley is drinking again and Katy is fit to be tied. Come round right away.

Edna instantly got it; she came round right away. This personal was immediately picked up by one of our own weeklies and later, in the London daily to which, as a crossword puzzle fan, I then subscribed, I found it quoted again, with an acid hint about American culture.

Edna's own message when she first took her mother to Europe was passed from hand to hand. Julia was loved by everyone, because Edna so loved this splendid, courageous Jewish woman who had taken care of a blind husband and two little girls for many years. Edna spoiled her, and everyone who went to Edna's hospitable magnificent apartment paid tribute to Julia. From the steamer Edna cabled:

"Julia calls the deck the front porch. What shall I do?"

She also used to tell of treating Julia to the special duck dinner at the Tour d'Argent. As all traveling Americans know, the preparation of this dish is not a mere culinary feat but a ritual. The naked, deceased duck is first displayed, and then as it is borne away to be cooked a sauce is made right at your table by crushing another whole duck and pouring the rich dark blood into a mixture of sweet butter, chervil, scallions, and a score of seasonings, rushed out from the kitchen by Antoine, tasted rapturously by Jean, served with a flourish by François. Julia, herself a notable cook, is reported to have tasted the dish, pronounced it excellent, and asked for catsup.

My pacifism, as the Nazis came to power, my charter membership in the newborn America First, and possibly the fact that in 1935 I had a meeting with Hitler, in those days when we were all ignorant of the bloody purges and horrors ahead, and made a routine report upon him, cost me more than one friend. Germany, mercilessly crushed by conditions after the first war, was still shockingly poor, but when we went there she was eating again, she was organizing again, and much of the credit for her recovery was given to this dapper, strange little man.

But I would never have asked to meet Der Fuehrer. He asked to meet me. I was as indifferent to his existence as I had been to a chance for a friendly talk with Mussolini a few weeks earlier. The condition in the latter case was that every word of my article should be approved by Il Duce himself, which made the whole prospect lifeless.

But Hitler had a reason for wanting to meet me, and he confided it to his pal, "Putzi" Hanfstaengl. Cigi and I had known Putzi when he managed a Madison Avenue shop that sold fine European art reproductions. Hitler knew that decently hidden behind our Massachusetts battery of D.A.R.s is the secret of my father's great-uncle Benjamin Thompson, Count Rumford, the gallant beautiful soldier of Revolutionary days, who deserted his friend George Washington, left for England, and threw in his lot with King George. Fighting wasn't his forte, anyway; he was a physicist, a humanitarian, a soldier of fortune, if a soldier at all. He was eventually to invent the cooking stove, get himself a niche in the London Society's museum, and a statue in the park of a Belgian city for his services in cleaning up the panhandlers and beggars with which the city was infested. Also he got a title, Count Rumford. His wife had been born in Rumford, New Hampshire. They had one child, a spinster daughter who endowed a home for orphan girls in Rumford, now renamed Concord. His second wife was the widow of Lavoisier, the chemist.

He was Hitler's idol. And Hitler had heard that I was his several-generations-removed niece. How, I don't know. It seems the Fuehrer winced when Putzi told him that my maiden name was Thompson; he had had some rather trying experiences with the sharpened and brilliant pen of Dorothy, of the same name. Perhaps Dorothy, experienced European reporter that she was, had suspected the bloody brutalities that lurked under his ceremonious manners and dapper little frame, but I had no such suspicions, and we went with Putzi to the Reichskanzlei to be presented. Goebbels and Goering were introduced, and left, and Hitler asked me if my name was Benjamina, praised my remote relative, and observed that all Germany asked of the world was peace and a right to hold her own country. Germany, he said, had been very sick and needed strong medicine. That was all.

Whatever it was, my first inkling of how they felt about it was the cut direct from some of our friends in New York. Alec Woollcott and I were alienated at the time, because he had published in a magazine the story of our adopted son. Billy had always known that his father had deserted both him and his mother and was long dead, and had pleased me very much, as an eager little boy of perhaps fourteen, by hunting through New York streets until he found "the French laundry where Mother worked." Like Trilby, she was a *blanchisseuse de fin*. She died the day I met Billy, and he became one of the children of the family. I thought Alec had dressed up the story too much and that it might hurt Billy, then in his teens. But Billy was not disturbed, and I was perfectly willing to make the peace. This was when I learned for the first time that there was a general resentment against me that had nothing to do with Alec's story about Billy. The idea was that because I was opposed to war, any wars and all wars, I must be in sympathy with Hitler.

Alec found a pair of my gloves in the reporter's seat we used alternately at a famous trial, and made immediate peace when he returned them with the note John Brooke wrote to Meg March under similar circumstances. But Edna and one or two others never forgave me.

Smarter pens than mine have tried to define Alec, but this glove episode illustrates one of his qualities that

I found most endearing; he had read every book my sister and I had read in the nineties and he remembered them all. Miss Alcott, Elizabeth Phelps, Sophie Swett, Mrs. Molesworth, Charlotte M. Yonge, Laura E. Richards, Trollope, Rosa Nouchette Carey of *Queenie* and *Uncle Max*, Kate Douglas Wiggin, Mrs. A. D. T. Whitney, even Miss Warner's *Wide, Wide World*—he must have read them as we did in Mill Valley days, over and over, packing them along wherever we went all over the garden and the woods. As for Dickens, for whom I name no compeer even today, Alec and I together could have reconstructed any of the top half dozen novels word for word, had the originals been mislaid.

Alec was also a passionate player of those imcomparable games, cribbage and croquet. When he came to the ranch in later years a before-breakfast croquet game was always in demand, and we had locomotive lights to illuminate the lawn for a last game at night. And even when the players came in, soaked and cold from the heavy mountain dews, he was ready to shuffle and deal the fifteen-twos and fifteen-fours.

He could be a strong friend, intuitive, even tender sometimes, and he had an insatiable appetite for talk. I remember his wit, his inexhaustible tales, his accurate, reverential use of words. He could be petty and his interests could be surprisingly trivial—as, for example, his careful citing of ghost stories and dreams. When I introduced him to a Town Hall meeting in San Francisco, to talk on "Dreams," I slightly altered Kit's wording when she was about six. Kit had said, "This is

Charlotte, my dear little friend that I hate," and I repeated it for Alec, and he was delighted, as I knew he would be. But his talk was later described by my brother Joe as whipped white of egg and water.

Whatever was weak, whatever was strong in him, no one has ever quite filled his place for a good score or more of us, and that, I think, is as he would like to have it.

A brilliant bird of passage was the English novelist Pamela Frankau, daughter of a distinguished writer father, Maurice Frankau, who rested her wings for a while in the quiet backwater of Woodside, a small settlement tucked away in the coast range to which neither bus nor railway had yet penetrated. Woodside's residents traveled by motorcar, preferably chauffeur-driven.

Pamela had done some writing at this time and had some work published but was suffering from one of those lulls all creative artists experience, and was homesick for curling, choking yellow fog, four o'clock tea, and the delicious sound of Bow bells shaking the sunless air of London. But she approved of the ranch enough to put it into her novel, *Willow Cabin,* and this book established a new and wider fame for her, and has been followed by three or four more fine stories, all preeminently successful, so that the great G. B. Stern in her book *And Did He Stop and Speak to You?* gives Pamela's work and Pamela herself an important position in modern letters.

Apricots, sand dabs, eucalyptus, and wild lilac, to say nothing of the three hundred sunny days a year that we boast in the Santa Clara Valley, failed to hold her, and Pamela is back in London, very much, I imagine, in the mood of the pale young Frenchman, burdened with a wife and two colorless children, to whom Cigi and I made offers during dreary war-shaken 1921, in Paris. The hotel elevator, we told him, was no place for him, he had been a gardener's son, he loved gardens. His forty-dollar-a-month salary was only a quarter of what his salary would be as gardener on a California estate that was tenanted for but a few months every year.

"But it would not be Paris," he said, coughing. This was his only argument. It sufficed.

The summers flew by; teen-age agonies of acne, unpopularity, and inhuman parental disciplines gave way to hoarser voices, prettier complexions, and sorority and fraternity crises that entirely eclipsed any dim ambitions for higher education. As Jean Ingelow puts it, our hearts had scarcely time to beat before a "shallow seething wave sobbed in the grasses at our feet."

The seething wave was young love. It was when Frank entered Stanford University that we built the large Spanish-California house in Palo Alto, and he and his cousins kept us in touch with the undergraduate body for the ensuing years. We had Sunday night open-house suppers, followed by charades, games, and theatricals that pretty well demoralized the house, and that were followed in due course by affairs of the heart. Frank led off with his Alice, for whom my descriptive adjectives here would sound somewhat unusual, to put it simply. Surely, surely it is not the common run of good fortune to have an Alice step as naturally into her place in a big family and into the family's heart as Alice did. I could go a good deal further on this subject; for obvious considerations I refrain. But I will say——

No, I won't. Another of the marriages among the cousins took place in Shanghai, for Happy Hartigan had been out there for some years as Naval Attaché, and when he returned to Washington it appeared that the redheaded Bunga had left her heart there, and with her mother she went back the following year to be married to James Alexander Barton, oldest son of Sir Sidney Barton, who had been Consul-general at Shanghai and later made a name for himself at Addis Ababa.

Mark and Bunga were escorted by Cigi and me, and also by the two Benét cousins, Kit and Rosemary, the bridesmaids-elect, the adored teen-agers of our household. The bridal gown and the bridesmaids' costumes went along with us, and there were on board the *Empress of Japan* enough Shanghai folk who knew all the Bartons, and enough Navy folk who knew the Hartigans, to make the trip one long festivity. Jimmy Barton came out on the packet boat to meet us as our ship came slowly up the Whangpoo, and the days that followed were a glorious mingling of oriental thrills and wedding plans, and a look at the new China blending with the old. Jimmy's tall brother Hugh was there to stand up with him, and Jimmy and lovely Bunga were thoroughly married—once in the Old Cathedral in the French settlement, once by mere legal recognition of the marriage in the American Embassy, and also in the English one to hold the double citizenship that was to stand her in good stead a few years later, when the world-shaking troubles began.

It was during these weeks in China that what I have regarded as the great Sino-American episode took place, leading to nothing more serious, however, than a whitened band on my hair, not unbecoming, and a little bewilderment on the part of a Manchurian giant named Foo Long. Foo was our hotelman, room boy, waiter, steward—he was everything, and in a long white cotton robe he roamed the halls with his fellow servants at all hours of the day and night.

So one midnight, when I had just laid down Churchill's *Crisis* and turned out my light, it was not too surprising to hear a tap at the door and see Foo open it and stand at polite attention. I snapped up the light.

"Missy ring, want telephone?" he asked politely. I was alone, and separated from Mark and the girls by our sitting room. Cigi had gone off with pals to take a look at Shanghai night life, and we were high above the city on the top floor of the Cathay. I said briefly that I had not heard the telephone, that I wanted nothing, and good night. Foo disappeared, and I settled down again.

But he reappeared five minutes later, himself turning up the light, and this time I got frightened. He asked if I wanted a cup of tea, and advanced slowly toward me with a smile. He closed the door behind him and moved up between our beds steadily, his eyes on mine. In that minute I went through all the agonies of violent death. Even if there was no rhyme and no reason in my terror, I thought I was going to be strangled, I thought, without daring to move my eyes toward them, of the open windows and the bathroom that had a lock on the inside door, I thought that no scream would make itself heard over the night racket on the Bund far below.

Foo came closer, stretched out a hand, and removed from the bell plate the heavy copy of Churchill's *Crisis* that I had been reading. All switches on the small metal bell plate that is marked "Amah, Waiter, Valet, Cleaner, Errands, Office," thanks to *The Crisis*, had been ringing violently, in the boys' waiting room, where these over-worked attendants had pallets on which they sometimes snatched some sleep.

Foo apologized. I laughed heartily—it must have been a ghastly sound—and apologized, too, and the episode closed. But even a return to *The Crisis* didn't put me to sleep until Cigi came back.

When we left China it was to come leisurely through the Suez Canal, ride on camels, enter the Sphinx busily into our journals, and wind up with a look at Paris and a week or two in London.

When the *Bremen* stopped at Le Havre, to pick up

passengers on her homeward way, among those we were interestedly watching, as they filed on board, was the ubiquitous Noel Coward, without mention of whom no contemporaneous diary, biography, or memoirs can be written at all, apparently.

As he came across the gangway at the French port Mr. Coward caught sight of our welcoming group and called cheerfully and with ringing clarity:

"Just a moment, good people. I'll sign your books directly!"

This outrageous greeting might have caused some coolness between the parties, but nothing was further from the truth. Our teen-agers took this traveling companion instantly to their hearts, did actually secure photographs autographed with passionate devotion, and carried these mementos triumphantly to the walls of their college rooms some years later.

They became especially unmanageable when the British playwright gave us a dinner whose menu, duly printed and tasseled, was composed entirely of such dishes as "Potage à la Famille Norris," "Hors d'oeuvre Hartigan," "Crêpes à la Rosemary" and "Café Diable Kit."

My own complete breakdown came at another dinner when I was trying to explain to Noel my evil effect upon waiters, all waiters, everywhere, and their grim destruction of my wits and self-possession. Our waiter, perhaps conscious that this was our last night afloat, meanwhile demonstrated my meaning with such thoroughness that only an act of will kept my helpless head from the middle of the plate.

By the time the *Überkellner* had moved each of our water glasses a few inches sideways, poured eleven drops apiece into each of our full wineglasses, asked Noel, Cigi, Mark, and me, at moments when our respective mouths were full, if everything was all right, dismissed an assistant who was really doing very well, and given us two sugars from an adjoining table while removing the salts and peppers in the middle of the main course, Noel was openly destroyed, Mark was gasping, "Behave yourself, Katy!" and Cigi was deep in silent and dignified yet uncontrollable convulsions.

Irvin Cobb himself could not have supplied a sturdier top hat and stick to that one.

Two summers later Bunga came back to the ranch for the arrival of her baby, and in September Mark and I took him and his mother back to Shanghai. General MacArthur, with his mother, was on that trip, going to the Philippines to fulfill his strange destiny. It sounded a peaceful, uneventful sort of assignment then, but when it came time for Mark and me to return the Ethiopian trouble was shaking Europe, and making impossible the use of the canal route. Yet we had promised to meet Cigi in Vienna early in December. We might have sailed back to California with our trunks. Instead we decided to make the trans-

Siberian trip, by train. Exactly why we did this seems obscure at this time. But we shipped trunks to California, packed our necessities into "corries," and set forth from Peiping by rail. Kind friends saw us off at the station in Peiping and I suppose one of them must have said, "Remember, all baggage must be checked again at the Japanese frontier," but if he did we paid no heed. We stopped at Shanhaikwan for breakfast as guests of a cordial Scotsman who introduced himself, and on parting scrupulously gave Mark his card because we mispronounced his name. It was only upon reaching Mukden, tired, bewildered, and assaulted by a towering downpour, that it was revealed to us that all our bags, nine in number, were still at Shanhaikwan. There was no train until the next day. We went to a dark Japanese hotel with gloomy leather chairs in the lobby, and worried. And what a special type of worry travel worry is, so hopeless, so blind! We had no word of Japanese or Chinese and no friends, and they disliked our small Persian kitten, and had the best of us with two English words at least: "Kot. Dont."

It was my sister who remembered the friendly Scot of the breakfast hour, dug out his card, recalled that he had said he always went to his club on Tuesday nights, and called Shanhaikwan, the Scot, and the club. We got him by a miracle: he was apologetic but could do nothing. The Japanese demanded that baggage be opened before being forwarded. Mark, frantic at the dim and wavering telephone, shouted that it was unlocked. This shocked the Scot. "Oh, I say, no!" he cried.

But as with trembling hands I held the baggage checks and with frenzied eyes Mark read the numbers, this friend in need gave us a shred of hope. The station was a mile from the club, the night train went in seven minutes, but he would do what he could.

Racked by suspense but heroically reminding each other that it wasn't as if one of the children were ill, we tried for some hours of sleep.

"We must think what Lady Brassey would do," said Mark helpfully.

"And at any moment Mr. Moto may arrive," I reminded her.

Whatever cosmetic comfort we had in the long, hot night was derived from two small powder boxes and two lipsticks; there were no towels or soap, no bath, no nightgowns, and the double windows were hermetically sealed. But sleepless, disheveled, and carrying our cat, we were at the station when the train came in at seven the next morning, to experience that most blessed of human emotions, relief. There were our bags, and fifteen minutes later, in a sun-flooded hotel window, we were enjoying the most delicious meal we had had for a long time.

That day was a long one. My stateroom on a tinny sort of train measured some five feet by eight. When a metal shelf with a flat straw mattress was lowered from the wall, half the width of the room was filled. Above this shelf was a narrower shelf on a chain. Mark presently came in with a too graphic description of the sanitary conveniences available, and a suggestion that she occupy the upper shelf that night. Two Japanese officers had arranged to share her stateroom, and she preferred mine. "We must sit rather matey," said a delightful Englishman, a friend from Rio days, who joined our train for a few hours. Ours was a troop train, with a hasty "First Class" chalked above some oriental designation outside. There were no sheets, pillows, blankets. We sat up all night, listening to scuffles and chatter in the passages.

The frowsy, sleepy morning brought trouble again, for the hotel porters considered our straw suitcases too lowly to be handled, and it was only by luck and financial persuasion that we waylaid a boy with a sort of pushcart and got them to the hotel, only two blocks away.

Our train did not leave for some hours and we could walk out over the wooden sidewalks and between the high wooden fences so characteristic of a Russian town, and across wide dusty streets that looked either half destroyed or half finished, and thoroughly dismal in either case. Almost immediately we went forth to seek a trunk store and roused its owner, asleep in a back room, to sell us four substantial leather bags. Our train that day passed troops, and we saw a Chinese prisoner with his face running blood, also a small Japanese woman who screamed with such horror at some news one of the trainmen gave her that we congratulated ourselves upon not understanding the language.

Solemnly shaking hands, we exchanged real congratulations when we at last had reached Manchouli, hours

245

late, had stood on the platform in a bitter wind while our luggage was inspected, had convinced the porter that we actually had engaged two rooms in the shabby old wagon-lit that was part of a miscellaneous assembly of cars that made up the train, induced him after some consultation with the authorities to open the extra room, and seen our bags stowed in a spacious overhead storage space that in these trains is intelligently placed over the passage. We were under suspicion of capitalistic snobbery.

Between our rooms was a generous washbasin set in marble, about us were our rugs, our two Sterno stoves, our typewriters, our well-packed hamper, our cat. An immense samovar at the end of the car was always ready with boiling tea. We were alone, warm, comfortable, successful so far. Over delicious dark Russian bread and sweet butter, strawberry preserves and hot tea, we had a congratulatory meal.

"The leather bags were your idea, Katy."

"You were the one, Mark, who thought of telephoning Shanhaikwan."

Our thirteen days in this warm, dirty, slow-moving train were bewildering but not alarming. We did not know the country through which we were moving, we did not speak the language, we did not know the time; all clocks in Russia keep Moscow time. We saw Stalin's face at every little station, a photograph blown up to some twelve feet square and covering the front of the building. We saw hundreds of log cabins, lightless and dark in the dark winter weather, with smoke trickling from chimneyless roofs; chimneys were once heavily taxed in Russia. We saw shawled and bundled women coming down with pots and pitchers to get hot water from the engine of our train. We saw rough corduroy roads leading into dense forests, and we saw feathery snow falling, falling, falling.

But in all the incredible nine thousand miles between Vladivostok and Moscow we never saw a power vehicle —not a car, truck, or bus. Not one.

At intervals a loudspeaker shouted a message in explosive Russian, and Mark and I waited with bated breath for the outbreak of a revolution. But the announcement was followed by some pleasant familiar American voice, on an old cracked record—Libby Holman singing "Give Me Something to Remember You By," or Helen Morgan with "My Bill."

We attempted the dining car only once. We were the only Americans in the wagon-lit; there was only one other woman in the passenger cars, a well-known Vienna-born tavern singer from Shanghai who could for sheer delicate beauty have been Marlene Dietrich's daughter. She was hopefully brewing wheat germ under the impression that it was instant American coffee; we had coffee to spare and won her undying gratitude.

In the dining car food was coarse, plentiful, and calculated to sustain human life in a cold climate. Fat is heating; the borsch was an inch deep in it. We skipped the soup. The same soup plate accommodated as a second course a goulash so formidable that I knew the meal would be my last if I essayed it. I went through an elaborate pantomime indicating that my lungs, throat, stomach were in deplorable state. Then I clucked alluringly, framed the shape of an egg with one hand, and scrambled with fork in the other. The waiter got it—an omelet! He presently brought me an omelet, fringed with dark reminders of other meals, odd bits of onions, a splash of some green substance, and a burned wax match. A person who must eat as carefully as I must should not travel.

Again I was in an ugly predicament. We were sufficiently impressed by the somber strangeness of Russia not to wish to make enemies. When the waiter turned his back I wrapped my omelet in a handkerchief and unobtrusively slipped it into the capacious bag where money, papers, make-up, credentials were carried. When he passed us again my plate was clean, and he smiled approval. Our meal finished with large, firm, yellow cakes with currants in them, which we carried with us to our rooms. After that, we preferred very appetizing meals of our own preparing.

Moscow was dark, disorderly, and crowded with action when we stepped out of the train early in the morning. Jitneys were running as they did after the San Francisco earthquake, over rough widespread street corners that seemed to have no boundaries. The imposing old mansion of a Grand Duke where we presented our credentials was filled with loudly talking men and women shabbily clad. It was hard to imagine the glittering social life of the Tsars' day in this place with mud on the marble floors and groups of jabbering people gathered about the handsome French and Italian tables and chairs that were formally arranged in the four corners of the room. There was no comparing the great, forlorn city, where dust blew and crowds ranged to and fro, with any other familiar or even imaginable city; everything was in a state of flux and change, and such advantages and improvements as were brought insistently to our attention were as drops of clear water in a muddy river rushing in spate.

The great churches were used as government bureaus; no candles, no lights, no kneeling forms; we were told that one great church was the center of an abortion clinic, and also explained the extremely simple process of divorce under the new regulations. These have since been changed.

We were also shown the beautiful new subway, all sparkling glass, chromium, marble, but unused that day. The fare was high then, about half the daily pay of most workers. We also saw excellent new apartments, in which the tenants were oddly matched; one that we saw housed an old lady, a boy of twelve, and an office worker, not related, but apparently content. And we saw exhibits of papier-mâché foods, regulated to the ages of children from infancy up; and impressive photographs instructive to pregnant women, and other educational displays. We filed by Lenin's famous and beautiful tomb, in a line of spectators three blocks long, but saw only that part of the Kremlin. The Kremlin, scented by the incense of a thousand religious ceremonies through hundreds of years, is all business now.

"Our leader died for his people," said the guide. "Ours too," my sister said gravely.

What was pleasantly impressive was the quiet stream of work people filling the streets at half past four and listening to the suggestions of loudspeakers, audible through all the city. Entertainments were cited—two of the statistics that I jotted down from our guide's talk were that there were sixty-five theaters in Moscow, and that there had been eighteen hundred churches. The loudspeaker informed the home-going crowd of good buys for dinner in the markets, a fresh haul of fish in, cheeses available, and announced, on Gorky Prospekt, a windowful of Russian-made shoes, available for the first time. Another thing I liked was that the commuter trains left the station in darkness; when I was a worker and a commuter I used to long for that hour of darkness at the end of the office day.

One innovation provided treatment for office workers who lived alone, without family ties: these were hospitalized except during business hours. Boys who would neglect a cold, a wound, a case of injured eyes, were kept in wards between the hours of half past four in the afternoon and eight in the morning, fed carefully, and of course they got well.

And as our visit was some twenty-five years ago, unquestionably much that was disorganized and unfinished then has been brought to completion.

Our last half hour in Russia had its own agitation. When we were at the border, with the peaceful green fields, the goose girls, the chiming church bells of Poland actually within sight and hearing, a hitch occurred. Just why the authorities wanted to detain the cat has never been explained, but it was the Russians who refused to pass little Piper through. My sister, who had not particularly enjoyed the long strange trip, here broke down. She would not desert the cat. "They would make her into a coat collar," she said to me darkly. There was a deadlock.

Then, on an inspiration, realizing that the inspector had command of only a few English phrases, I groped in the aforesaid handbag among passport and letters of credit, lipstick, rosary, compact, identification papers, pencils, aspirin tablets, and other trivia, and fished out my vaccination card. Freely using the phrase "United States of America," I displayed it and pointed to the cat. The customs clerk called in another clerk, and even a third, and to Piper all three referred as "United States kot." After some study they nodded reluctantly, and Mark, Piper, and I went on to meet Cigi in Vienna. The cat was four months old, the certificate more than a year; but it served our turn, and it is only fair to observe that few of our own customs officials are fluent in Russian.

On one of the holidays between stretches of writing a party of five of us went to London for the coronation of George VI. This, with the stupefying shock of the abdication of the beloved young man who might have reigned as Edward VIII, was a sad and nervous time for England. To the shops alone it brought unthinkable confusion; all the mugs, flags, plates, pictures, coins, vases, ash trays, teaspoons, and key rings bearing the pictured head of the monarch had hastily to be scrapped and similar representations of the hesitant, mild, unhappy successor hustled into their places.

And this detail, of course, was nothing to the uncertainty, the fears, the shaken confidence in the line that had never known any man to do less than fight with his very life for that long-disputed throne. There were tears in the eyes of Queen Mother Mary when the great moment of coronation came, when the second son returned from formal robing behind the great altar and stepped into view in the cathedral, when all the city bells and the trumpets went mad, and hundreds of boys' silver voices rang up to the sturdy, high old rafters with "God Save the King." And God, as we know, did save the King, and England.

Margaret Rose, delicious as an attendant with train and baby crown, wiped away her grandmother's tears with a small, anxious finger, and was restored quietly to her place with perhaps a grandmotherly admonition that one did not make a scene at a coronation in Westminster Abbey.

Having written my first sentence and my last in the expected article, late on the evening before, I went back to the hotel in a driving rain and fitted the story in between. The rain upset all plans for traffic but the dripping crowds surged gaily enough in the streets. Weary peeresses with their jewels safe in handbags and their long trains bundled in their laps sat for long hours on the stone steps of the Abbey. We all went to the B.B.C. headquarters from which I was to send a world-wide broadcast. And here a pleasant gentleman, having greeted and chatted with the family for a few inconsequential moments, glanced at me and observed, "When that light directly above me turns green, Mrs. Norris, you might begin," at which instant the light turned green. Gulping, confident this could be only a rehearsal, unfurling my manuscript, reaching for a prayer, I trembled into the message that was duly received in Peiping and California and other places, ending with a gasp quite audible to all listeners and a harsh whisper, "Is this final—is this *it?*"

Our American masters of ceremonies handled broadcasts a little differently. Rehearsals, voice tests, timing tests, position tests—one American station actually used a metronome to balance the rhythm perfectly.

O ur casual cousins! One wonders and wonders how they do it. When a packet boat brings mountainous heaps of luggage into the customs at a British port there is no fuss about checks or identifications. There it lies in a heap, and they pick out their own: "The two there, and that one, and the little one. And there should be one more!" And up to London they go, still in a conglomerate heap, and there one finds the luggage, safe and sound.

This sublime trust and superterrestrial honesty worked well for us on that same coronation holiday. Months earlier Cigi had secured four seats on the hospital porch, right opposite the Abbey, for his party: Cora, Jane, Mark, and himself; I had received the enormously important cards that would admit me to a balcony seat in the Abbey with the press. I had also received a sticker for the car that would bear me through the august gates that had been raised across strategic streets. Besides these, Cigi placed in a small brown pigskin bag a large sum of good American dollars, in cash, for after the English event we were going to some other countries where that little face of bewigged.George Washington is dearly prized. Then there were passports, identifications, hotel reservations, and any other articles that Cigi's foresight had provided for the rush and pressure of London in those days. And Jane had hastily added, on some undiscoverable impulse, her famous emerald, observing that she wanted it to be safe. This handbag was never to leave Cigi's hand. He was in charge of four irresponsible and elated females and he wanted to take no chances. But leave his hand it did.

A packet took us from the big ship in Southampton water, and it was crowded. The object of our immediate attention was Fanny Ward, the extraordinary grandmother with the face of a sixteen-year-old, against whom we happened to be wedged bodily in the crush, when Cigi said to me in a low tone, "Where's my bag?"

Horror, perforce subdued, paralyzed our stricken hearts. Everyone disclaimed even the slightest responsibility. Had Cigi handed it to you, or you, or you? No, he had not. We women separated quietly, like conspirators, hunting in couples, and Cigi went to consult the captain, charter a packet, return to the big ship, search staterooms, summon Clanconnell generally.

Mark and Jane worked their way through the milling throng, looking with stealthy suspicion right and left, and were back in five minutes with the bag intact, and as beautiful in our eyes as the Kohinoor. Among thousands of trunks, bags, sacks, crates, bundles, piled mountain-high on the rear deck, our bag had been riding conspicuously. A boat hand had just placed it on the top of the heap. "A lady dropped it to the lower deck as you was going up the gangplank," he explained, "and Joe Rich here brought it up."

Joe, even richer, was thanked, and we went to find Cigi, release the harassed captain from further concern, and honestly admit that it was a lady who had released hold on the bag. The matter of responsibility was then also thankfully dropped, and the coronation proceeded as scheduled.

In those years we were always meeting people who were supposed to have introduced Wallis Warfield Simpson to the Prince of Wales. It need hardly be said that Alec was first in the field, although the leaning toward Noel Coward was strong. When I was introduced to Lady Colfax that interesting note was whispered behind someone's hand, and was repeated when I met Lady Mendl, who had been a San Francisco girl and whose mother was my friend in newspaper days. Beverley Nichols was pointed out to us at a theater opening as having this same distinction. "Get him to tell you about introducing . . ." But now these perhaps possible introducers have been joined by so large a party that credulity staggers. One American woman of some position is so accustomed to relating that she was the responsible party, at a Riviera resort, when everybody was swimming and having informal fun, that she honestly believes it to be the truth. I forget whether either the Duke or the Duchess ever mentioned the real catalyst in their articles and books.

This passion for annexing any good story and retailing it in the first person often created confusion in the fast-moving, fast-talking, overexcited, and furiously jealous group that is formed by the creators of books and newspapers and plays and amusement generally in a great city. A good story, especially if it involves or, even better, embarrasses one of the elect, is seized hungrily, and whoever gets it first takes the lead as he retells it.

Irvin Cobb was a master storyteller. He framed his anecdotes with care, as one does a short story: plot, characters, climax, last twist. One lunchtime at the ranch he gave a simple report of a colored congregation in a small church in some Southern town, his own beloved Paducah perhaps. My three brothers were present and their enthusiasm and their questions developed the story right before our eyes; Joe, Fred, and Jim gurgled over the details of the return of a negro hero from the wars, his mother, in starched calico, in the front pew, his family and neighbors repeating in gradual, hot-Sunday, restless crescendo, "Yes, Parson, but who's that man?" as their love, their pride, their eagerness to hear the name they already knew so well swelled beyond all bounds.

The next time I heard that story, months later, it had indeed been given the stick and the top hat of our family proverb: it was a classic, the recital of which made one's throat thicken, even while tears of laughter were in one's eyes.

Irvin, enormous, laughter-shaken, deep-chested of voice, and "Mawey," his small and sparrowlike mate, were our dearly loved friends for many years. Mawey's name was not based upon her rightful cognomen of Laura but was rather an extension of "ma." Awkward as it looks in print, it was a genuine love name, and always sounded like one, given her by the irrepressible daughter of the house, "Buff," and the friends who swarmed in Buff's wake. Among these friends, incidentally, was an exquisite blonde child named Clare Boothe, with the maddening combination of blue eyes, darker lashes, and pure gold hair that were to work some havoc in preconceived standards of beauty a few years later.

One story Irvin told me was of his serious illness while on a lecture tour, in Boston. He and I agreed that we might have seriously considered signing up for these tours, always so lucrative, if it were not for the fearful price the visiting speaker must pay in social events before and after the lecture. A wealthy resident puts her big car and her driver at the command of the entertainment committee. The new Y.M.C.A., the site for the new library, the house Louisa M. Alcott's cousins lived in—these the visitor must see. The visitor is a little train- or plane-jaded and on the drive may be just a trifle disconcerted to learn that her luggage has been merrily, hospitably moved from the hotel, where blessed peace, and a book, and a bowl of cream of tomato soup and brown toast beckon her, and she is to stay in the Macknockbottoms' magnificent place, and yes, be let alone, and rest, and not be allowed to talk too much at dinner . . .

But the visitor—speaking for myself, or Irvin for that matter—loves talk, and so does the hostess, and they get into confidences, gales of laughter, until both are all but hoarse, and the little daughters of the house come in, and are introduced, and the newcomer finds herself bathing, brushing, powdering, getting zipped, under the eyes of the women of the family, and escorted down to dinner without having touched her back to a bed or head to a pillow.

"They stay until three o'clock because you talk all the time, they can't walk out and go home with you holding forth," Cigi said darkly more than once. This led to our resolution that we would observe silence on the drive home from any festivity, friendly, restful, pleasant silence.

"Going home from parties is horrible," I said once to the always-delightful-person-to-find-next-to-you-at-dinner, Marc Connelly. "You've eaten, drunk, laughed too much. The air has been too hot. It's too late, considering tomorrow. And I," I went on, "am always so dumb that I ask Cigi if I talked too much."

"And he hesitates?" said Marc, with exquisite understanding. "Yes, I know. But I'm worse off," he added. "I go home alone. And I hold arguments with myself. 'You were wound up tonight! Well, what of it? They don't ask you just to eat. I know, but holding the floor that way, having the maid stand at your elbow ten minutes with the soufflé. Oh, for heaven's sake, who cares? They laughed, didn't they? So you talked too much, and it's nothing but a dinner party, and if some of them were bored, a lot weren't, and you never need dine there again. . . . Oh, God, I wish I was dead!'"

But to return to Irvin Cobb's illness. This time he was in a hotel when some frightful sudden thing came upon him, and without anyone having dared even to remove his evening clothes he found himself dazedly in the charge of nurses, with Laura's frightened face rushed to his side, and the lowered lights and voices suggesting to his dimmed senses that this was it. He swooned in and out of consciousness without much concern, in his coma continually finding himself slowly descending a dark shaft, like Alice, almost reaching the bottom, and turning with some dim premonition of danger, slowly to remount the shaft again. This went on through some days of shaded lights, hushed voices, hushed steps, sound of a little girl trying not to cry.

"You were dying."

"I surely was, ma'am."

"And that's the way it felt?"

"Honey, it felt like you do when you're driving, and you come to a sign that says, 'You Are Now Leaving Boston.'"

A propos of story-robbers, we had one experience that seriously embarrassed a visiting English playwright, novelist, reader, and raconteur. This amusing man was at our table the night before he was to lecture at Town Hall, when Cigi told of the narrow escape from death that an uncle of mine had had, when holding a job in a mine in Mexico some fifty years earlier.

There was a stream and a ten-foot waterfall a few miles distant and Lee used to walk there in the early cool of the day, or after sunset, to have a plunge in the cold, cold water, and after a while, as he became more daring, to dive under the apron of the waterfall and come up on the opposite bank.

He tried this on a day when he had for audience some officials of the mine and some Eastern visitors and their children. They had all been swimming and were lined up on the bank when Lee proposed that he take the dive. But by some slip the violent overturn of the water caught him in its grip, and he was whirled about, chin to knees, doubled up in a helpless ball, realizing that death could be only a few minutes away. A desperate look through the veil of water showed him that his audience was enthusiastically applauding, and he said that a wild laugh burst from him as he visualized their consternation if the whirl of waters held him on and on in this mad revolution until it occurred to some one of them that something might possibly have gone wrong.

With a last drive for life he thrust himself out of the circle and lay gasping on the bank in a shower of congratulations. He never tried it again.

Whether our dinner guest that evening had a strangely brief memory, or whether he didn't know we were following on to the same evening party I don't know, but upon being besieged to tell a few stories he began with this one, saying it had recently happened to him in Mexico, and his look, in the middle of it, as he caught my attentive eye, was accompanied by incoherence and a sick consternation. The story fell flat.

Cigi and I, from the days of our engagement, had an escape hatch ready for any such situation. We called it "the earthquake break."

This earthquake break was instituted when we were first engaged, after the great earthquake of 1906. He belonged to San Francisco's nicest social group; I belonged to San Francisco's nicest Irish and bohemian group. So our general conversations when his friends or mine were about were apt to be full of pitfalls. I might launch forth, "As for the Ashers, everyone knows——" and Cigi, realizing what I was about to say from the tone of my voice, would cock his head, raise a silencing hand, and say, "Earthquake!"

Instantly, everyone had felt it. Distinctly. And while they compared notes I could change my whole attitude toward the Ashers and observe mildly that they were lovely people, I hoped to know them better.

Or it might be Cigi, violently pursuing something we had discussed when alone, who raged on, "The whole thing was a cheat, and if you ask me, Dick Wittington——"

"Listen! Did you feel it? Earthquake! Didn't anyone?" That was myself speaking.

But it didn't matter whether anyone did or didn't. Cigi by now would be altering his attack to "Dick was one of the finest fellows at Cal——"

Piracy went on in every direction. I remember a brief colloquy between Noel Coward and Vincent Youmans. Vincent rebuked Noel for having stolen a certain melody from him.

"I know," said Noel thoughtfully, with that characteristic wrinkling of his face that may mean amusement but looks as if he were about to burst into tears. "Where'd you get it?"

"I forget," Vincent said, musing in his turn. After which we all went on strolling about the deck of the *Bremen* in undisturbed amity.

An Englishwoman wrote me a distressed letter some

thirty-five years ago. She enclosed a letter in which she confessed to my English publisher a bold act of plagiarism and asked me to forward it to him. She had taken a serial story of mine whole, changing only a name or two, and had sold it to one of the minor English monthlies. She could only plead her poverty, the wartime death of her husband, and the needs of her two small daughters. Not seeing exactly who was injured by the transaction, I answered that I was sorry for her troubles and thought no other recognition of the situation necessary.

It has been my fortune to discover other cases of plagiarism. Two of our highly rated literary magazines have innocently used stories by Frank Norris from time to time, and in Italian I read some years ago an exact transcription, under another woman's name, of a tragic little story of two inexperienced country sisters caught in a white slavery trap, which had had great success in our country.

One sad case was that of a mother who brought me the writings of a recently dead son of fifteen. She showed me the poems she proudly thought to be his, clipped from different periodicals, and for which he had been duly paid. One was taken whole from Browning's *Ring and the Book;* one was an old one of Lucy Larcom's about weeds, and a third one, by Mary Mapes Dodge, I knew as a child.

"Everyone says they are extraordinary, coming from a boy that age!" the heartbroken mother said to me pathetically.

She was arranging to have them published, paying half the printing costs, and I couldn't be sure the publisher would recognize the poems. She had to be told, and I told her.

"David must have been full of mischief," I began. "He was always up to tricks, wasn't he? Of course he was. D'you know what he's done here? He's picked the quieter little magazines and sent them his favorite poems—he may never have known, or realized, that it wasn't quite a legal thing to do. You know boys! It was fun. Like sewing knives and forks to the tablecloth on April first, or dressing up as a ghost for Hallowe'en!"

Heartsick, I rambled on. But seeing her bewildered look turn to one of consternation, shame, and crushed pride was something I never can forget. Eventually, with her friendly printer, I talked her into publishing a neat little cardboard-bound volume entitled *Poems David Liked*. If any friend exclaimed, "Oh, I thought David wrote them!" she could answer, "Just loved them." And nobody is apt to hunt up old magazines and compare notes. Writers, actors, poets, newspaper people are all too busy to pry beneath the surface. We don't know much of each other, or want to. One of my closest woman friends expressed admiration for the "courage" Cigi and I had in spending winters occasionally in San Francisco. Those earthquakes . . . !

"But it must be interesting," she conceded. "Old Indian scouts riding down Market Street, and—oh, I don't know, driving flocks of sheep across the Embarcadero—

and all the Spanish names, and Spanish ladies smoking cigars."

And in answer to my look of mild inquiry, she adds: "No. You know I've never been there. But Mother's uncle went out, sometime in the sixties, and he thought it was simply fascinating!" She couldn't care less, or know less, or bother less to check details.

Some years ago, while speaking in behalf of peace in a certain small Arizona town, I was a little bothered by the steady attention given me by a woman in the front row. Her look was unfriendly, and little twitches of a scornful smile showed whenever her eye met mine. When she came up to speak to me, after the talk, she commented coldly upon my good luck in marrying the brother of an established novelist.

"I have here a story that would have been accepted instantly if you had written it," she said, "but because I am unknown as a writer no editor will even read it. I want to know if you think it is not just as good as thousands of stories that are being printed every day." She thrust a long envelope into my hand. "Read it," she said, "and then ask yourself why you should have all the luck and I should go on teaching school all my life."

Rather unwillingly I propped myself up in bed and took a look at the story that night. It surprised me. It was launched with some old-fashioned touches: " 'Tell us a story, Uncle Ben,' cried a dozen eager voices. Uncle Ben tossed a log on the fire, filled his pipe, and dropping into his favorite chair . . .' " That sort of thing. And it wound up with a statement that the love affair it described was true, because "it happened to a cousin of Mrs. Calvin Coolidge." But it was well done.

When I returned the manuscript I praised the story, said that I would like to send it to my special editor, and merely asked that the first and last sentences be deleted. I asked her to keep a copy, in case of loss in the mail, and of course congratulated her upon submitting to me one of the first really salable stories that had ever come into my hands in that fashion.

And that was the end. She never wrote again. Or no, not quite the end. Because some time later, when I was recounting this odd experience to an after-dinner group and had outlined the story, it was Frank Crowninshield who spoke up from fireside shadows. "One of Dick Davis' best, word for word," he said. My schoolteacher challenger had been testing my ability to know a story when I saw one, and had lost.

Jimmy Barton and Bunga and their small Hugh came from China for summer holidays in 1934, and again in 1936, and this new member of the cousins' group was a real acquisition. Jimmy played bridge and a dozen more card games, fished off the Santa Cruz coast for salmon, went down to Pasa Robles for the pigeon shooting, taught the small children to swim, went with Cigi to the Bohemian Grove for Jinks Week, entered upon the theatricals and charades with experience and zest, and, best of all, was a passionate and expert hand at croquet. Everyone loved him, and when we went to London for the coronation it was nice to meet his distinguished father and mother and the sister who later came to San Francisco when her husband, Baron Muzi-Falconi, was Italian Consul there. Hugh and Esme, the younger brother and sister, were as yet unmarried.

One day on the ranch Jimmy observed me reading and asked about the book. I assured him he wouldn't like it.

"It's called *Drums along the Mohawk,* Jimmy, and it sets forth the completely disgraceful actions of King George's soldiers in the late unpleasantness between our countries."

Jim leaned upon a mallet, considered this.

"I have no doubt that at the time it seemed sound," he observed mildly.

Had this fine man—a born diplomat, the king of impromptu theatricals, a racer of his own diminutive Siberian ponies at Pao Machang, an enthusiast at all games, a voracious reader of books—lived to fulfill his natural destiny, he might have rivaled in that field his famous father. But Jimmy after a few hours' illness was destined to die of exposure, during the Japanese occupation of Shanghai. This was before America entered the war; but the Japanese were making life difficult for all nationals in China, and Jim, driving home in a heavy rain at night, was waylaid, his car seized, and himself obliged to walk home to spend a restless, feverish night. It had been thought wiser for Bunga to remain at the hotel with friends; when she got home the next morning it was too late.

We were down at the ranch in the fateful August when war broke out in Europe. Now there was no excitement, romance, hopeful talk of "a war to end wars." The children who had been babies in Mount Holly were grown to draft ages now, and there was not one among the family groups that did not feel the menace of the war cloud.

Rosemary had been married for two years then, Jim was married, as were both Fred's boy and girl, two of Jim's three girls, and Frank. Bunga was at the ranch with her small Hugh. Alice's Kate was only a few months older. Bill Benét had come out to be at Kit's wedding, early in August, as he had come every summer after Elinor's death. Jim Barton's brother Hugh was there, and his blonde Danish wife, Rose-Marie. Joe's Kathy was to return to China with the Bartons for a visit. Almost all the cousins had gathered for the end of the season and the aftermath of a string of weddings. The weather was mild and balmy, fruit trees were heavy with pears and prunes and the first of the apples.

In the first breaking of the dark on August thirtieth Rosemary and Dick Dawson and I drove up to the hospital in Palo Alto, and it was only midmorning when I could go quietly in to ask the idly dreaming mother if she had seen her little boy.

"Oh yes," said Rosemary. "They brought him in. And he looked so like Edward G. Robinson that I almost pushed him off the bed!"

All that day we clung to the radios, listening to the incredible news. Late in the afternoon there was a cable for Cigi, from Jim Barton in Shanghai. "Tell Juggins I've cleared him here; he can go straight to England if he thinks it wise."

Cigi brought it up to the pool and read it to a ring of sober young faces.

"Juggins!" Hugh said. "He hasn't called me that since we were kids."

They were all young; they were all light of heart. But a shadow fell over the ranch then, never quite to be dissipated.

So it was war again. We were all more than twenty years older than we had been in the days of driving about Mount Holly, visiting the camps, prowling in Princeton's library, following the country roads under the summer stars. To remember the fun, the laughter, the drama of the big country house in New Jersey, when we were all under one roof, when we swam in the Rancocas, played hide-and-seek in and about the old barns and sheds in the dusk, pressed ruffled summer dresses and raised our hair over large "rats" to impress our service men, went to open-air movies with Chinese punks burning in our white shoes to discourage the mosquitoes —to remember all this was to remember Teresa, and an empty chair, a voice whose echoes never quite died away, a love and loyalty that had bound us all together in her eager clasp.

No, there was nothing good in this war.

We bore our agonies, as house after house was darkened and saddened, and the Spanish kitchen in the garden turned its talents to pigs' trotters and dried-apple pies. The glorious years of the ranch hospitalities suffered a sudden check; Cigi gathered coupons reluctantly from his guests and every pound of bacon was hoarded. All these details were unimportant, the restrictions on the use of the cars was unimportant, but the constant simmering sense of betrayal was not unimportant.

There was one warm summer evening when we had a young sailor on the porch, Mark's son, Second Lieutenant Conway Hartigan, U.S.N., the "grass-eater" of early theatricals in the barn at the ranch. He was just back from the South Seas. One of the maids had come to me with the puzzled comment that Lieutenant Hartigan had brought no bag with him. That meant nothing more than a suggestion that she hunt up some nightwear from one of the other boys, and perhaps a few toilet articles from a store I always kept handy. The luggage would undoubtedly be coming along; express deliveries were uncertain.

Cigi's music was over; the talk for a moment had stopped; the porch was quiet when I asked idly if there had been losses on the young officer's destroyer. For answer, in the warm dark, with the circle instantly quieted, he asked a question of his mother in turn. "Can you take it, Mom?"

Mark, from the dark, said unsteadily that she could take it; this wasn't her first sailor or her first war. Conway put his lean thin young hand across his eyes and said, "We lost our ship."

Lost. Two ships lost—for the destroyer was giving aid to the already stricken *Yorktown* when two torpedoes struck her in turn. Conway had been hours in the ocean water, too lamed by cold and shock to grasp the line thrown him, when the rescue ship came. More than two hundred men of the *Hamman*, his friends and associates, were drowned in the flaming oily waters. After the torpedoes struck, the *Hamman* was but ten minutes afloat. His own share of it won him the finest of the many ribbons he was someday to wear; his own sunny, courageous nature was unharmed. There was happiness ahead for him with his Fran, his home, his nursery full of small children.

But that night, up in the peaceful mountains under the redwoods, with the shadowy group of those of us who loved him sitting stunned at this sudden reality of horror and helplessness, this grief for the strong eager boys who had sailed away, impressed me once and for all with the sadness and waste of war. His experience was only one holocaust among countless others, but this was our boy, who had spent half the summers of his life with us on the ranch, and who might have sunk in the flash of guns and the foaming of oily water of Coral Sea, bringing the blinded world no step nearer to peace.

A nother young figure had been a member of our family for years; from her babyhood Frank Norris' little daughter had been very dear to her uncle and to me. "Billee" had been named Jeannette Williamson Norris, and had been adored by the gifted young novelist father who was destined to leave her fatherless so soon. In 1900 Frank was in the full flower of his rapid and astonishing success. He had married "Janny" Black, a San Francisco beauty, and they had gone to New York very much more securely established than we were to be nine years later, for Frank had had great recognition in San Francisco, writing a little sea classic of a man's experience being shanghaied, and his love for the mighty-armed, simple great Norwegian girl who, as a sea captain's daughter, managed her ship with the skill of a man, her great gold braids swinging around her shoulders. *Blix*, which had himself and Janny as main figures, with Chinatown and Seal Rocks and the Marion County hillsides as the background of their love affair, followed *Moran of the Lady Letty*. These two had been serialized in a local weekly, and Frank was the darling of the city's writers of the day, who were trying, aspiring, having as much fun talking about what they were going to do as if it were already done.

Frank and Janny had an apartment down on Washington Square, and there Billee was born, a beautiful little girl who was about four when I first met her, after Frank's death, with an oddly composed little face and enormous dark eyes. Frank and Janny had brought her to San Francisco to plan a trip to the South Seas, for their closest friends were Robert Louis Stevenson's widow, "Tamatai," her daughter "Teuila" (Mrs. Strong), and Teuila's young son, Austin Strong. Lloyd Osbourne, the son of Tamatai's first marriage, was also in the group whose home was Samoa. They were returning to Samoa, and Frank wanted to sail off in his own boat to the enchanted isles.

Appendicitis and talk of the vermiform appendix was all-popular then, and Janny had fallen victim to the current malady, having a most satisfactory recovery from surgery, returning home the tenth day, and all ready for the fascinating business of selecting what must be taken on the trip. Billee was to be left with her mother's mother, Mrs. Black.

Then it was Frank's turn for odd, sudden pains, the scare, and his doctor's decision that if there was any trouble with the appendix it had better be settled before they sailed. And so in high spirits and still talking of main sheets and spinnaker booms, he entered the hospital, submitted to surgery, survived in great spirits, and entertained his mother and brother in his own brilliant way when they called a day or two later. "All ashore that's going ashore!" he said, in good-by.

"We left him about four," Cigi said, telling me of it long afterward, "and when we got back to the hotel there was a message that we had better call the hospital.

I will never forget Mother's face. She knew. They'd told her ten years before that Lester was well on his way to recovery an hour before he died. 'Frank is going,' she said to me quietly. He died that night, at thirty-two."

After that Billee lived sometimes with her mother, sometimes with Teuila and Tamatai, who moved to San Francisco in 1901. With them were Austin Strong, Lloyd Osbourne and his wife, and Lloyd's two small boys, occupying the unusual and beautiful house they built on one of the city's hills. They were but half a block away from our first flat on Hyde Street and Teresa almost immediately was given the freedom of the house because she knew all the occupants through the bookshop; she immensely admired Mrs. Stevenson, a square-built, sturdy woman with her richly curled hair hanging on her shoulders. Not much remained of the beauty that Stevenson had married, but she was animated, magnetic, forceful. Tamatai dressed in native Samoan fashion, flowing robes of silk and loose trousers; and when I came to know her I never saw her sit on anything but the floor. Teuila, like her mother, had a dark, almost swarthy skin, bright prominent eyes, and both had voices that were strong and harsh, for women. My island fairies, "small and dark, the naiads of my cattle park," Stevenson called them, "for even lace, when lace they wear, shows on their golden breasts more fair." Later the lovely San Francisco house, built on a hilly corner that commanded all of the city and Bay, was a Carmelite convent, and it is now much-coveted apartments.

Little Billee was adored by all these people, but her

childhood was broken up by terms in boarding schools, and it was in a Canadian school, at about fourteen, that she contracted the serious illness from which she never quite recovered. She was brought to California for surgery, and when we moved to the ranch she had been for a year or two in a sanitarium in Belmont, supposedly stricken with tuberculosis. A long ranch summer and a trip with us to New York quite set her up, and she became the rather languid but extremely attractive little beauty who kept a string of admirers coming and going, and married at nineteen one of her own social group in San Francisco. New York she disdained. "Everyone tells me how popular my father was, and it bores me," she would say, and to a famous explorer she said, "Please don't tell me about the North Pole. I've just seen *Nanook of the North* and I haven't got warm yet." Asked her favorite book character, she answered, "Osma of Oz," and challenged in a game to select one of Shakespeare's heroines, she mentioned "Mercurochrome."

Billee and the fine man she married were regular members of the ranch group; Jerry never missed a weekend, and Billee stayed through the summer, drifting about, always a picture in oriental silks, and loving the warmth and laziness of the ranch days. She had a keen wit and a deeply affectionate nature, but these were not enough to save her as the nervous illnesses went on—the suffocation in any closed place, be it concert hall or railway train, the icy hands and helpless trembling that she could not control. Hers might have been a very different life, for she had inherited her Norris grandmother's thespian gift in a great degree, and in all the ranch theatricals, charades, and impersonations she displayed a natural easy talent that there was no mistaking.

But life grew wearisome after a while, the attacks of pain and weakness more frequent, and one night Billee scribbled a few letters, loving, apologetic letters, and reached for the bottle of sleeping tablets that was never far from her bedside. We were left, Jerry, Cigi, and I, we three who had heard her laughing only the day before, in the place next to Cigi that she always occupied at the long table, to wonder what we had done, what we hadn't done, to have her plan this, as she must have planned it. It was part of the same loss when the beloved big man who was her husband followed her not long afterward.

It was part, too, of the sobering changes that came with the long drag of the war; these were necessarily quiet years, the cousins busy with their own babies, of whom there were eventually a round two score. Twenty-two babies were my absorbing interest at this time, and weekly luncheons at the house of one young mother or another kept us all in touch. It became the fashion to hoard coupons for these occasions, so that the hostess could have some small take-home gift at everyone's place: a package of cigarettes, a dozen eggs, a box of gingerbread, or that treasure above all others, a pound of coffee. And where there are small children there is always an indeterminable amount of pride, and much laughter, so that Kate, Hugh, Nell, Dan, Dick, Cigi, David, Bill, Taffy, Cam, Judy, Stephanie, Denny,

Maggie, Jimmy, Markie, Peter, Julia, Andy, George, Timmy, and Jarry carried us through the bad time pretty well.

But a certain old mariner never recovered from the shock of the news that the radio ticked out on December 7, 1941. On that Sunday Happy, retired as a Rear Admiral then, was with Mark driving into Washington from their Maryland farm, Larkins Hundred. The *Oklahoma* had been Happy's last command, and the shock of visualizing her lying wrecked and helpless, with the sea breaking in and over her, and her hundreds of strong young dead gone with her, was in effect a deathblow, although Happy lived for another year. He lived to see Conway graduated at Annapolis and to hear the first reports of his career. Mark and the widowed Bunga with her small boy were with him when the end came, in Palo Alto, California. In that very week the Navy had sent him Conway's first decoration, to send on to his son, and by chance some of the boys from the *Oklahoma* were at hand to give him a guard of honor before his body was taken to Arlington for burial. His grave is marked with a plain monument engraved with his name and the essential dates, and underneath them, cut in relief in the white stone, is the Congressional Medal of Honor.

His loss was a loss to family happiness and to family celebration wherever he came and went; never was a nickname more appropriately bestowed. From 1908 when Cigi and I chaperoned the teen-age Mark on a visit to a ship in San Francisco Harbor, and my Merry

Widow hat caught tight in a gunner's tube, and had to be removed from above, his face always lighted up when he saw us, and his impromptu plans for lunch, dinner, dancing, midnight supper were instantaneous. His popularity was as universal as that of any human being I ever knew; complete strangers warm up still when "Hap" is being remembered: "I was on his ship . . . He was teaching at the Academy when I was there . . . They were in Peiping . . . Shanghai . . ."

Buying the Maryland farm had been a real adventure to Mark and Happy; they had only a few years there, but they were good years. The two-hundred-and-fifty-year-old brick mansion stood on a rise above its own acres of tobacco and forest. It was in a bad state of neglect, but the foundations were sound, and on the garden that sloped down to the creek there were remains of beautiful flowers, peonies, roses, and lilacs, blackberry vines, grapes and fruit trees.

Inside, Mark's digging and scraping uncovered colonial wallpapers, walnut panels, and diagonal corner cupboards whose shelves were lined with mysterious blue. Larkins Hundred became a show place. The comfortable wide old staircase turned into two staircases at the first landing; the ceilings were of the lofty type of a long-lost era. Mark, Happy, Cigi, and I spent long happy days toiling among the overgrown shrubbery, heaping weeds for small boys to carry away and incidentally unearthing a graveyard, where faithful old retainers had been laid in the days of faithful old retainers. Mark now developed a theory of reincarnation.

"If there is such a thing," she mused, resting, hot and panting, on a rake, "I was a slave here, two hundred years ago, and my one great desire was to be like the Missus. Now I am back again and I am the Missus, and working like a slave."

Even the winter they were blizzard-bound was thrilling to the Hartigans, a glimpse of what the old farm had been when it was new. Four days without water, heat, plumbing, light, telephone, or radio were educational, and yet the house rose to the crisis as no modern house could. Every room had a fireplace, a fine old range still stood in the kitchen, the well was not frozen, the chickens and the cows knew their duty, there was a massive woodpile, and other conveniences, which, though primitive, had served our finely bred ancestors well, served their descendants still.

"Every little while someone would say, 'What does the radio say about the weather?' or 'Try to get Cigi on the telephone,'" Mark told me when on the fourth day Cigi and I abandoned our car down the road and floundered up the long lane to find out how things were going. "You simply can't drop two hundred years and get used to it right away!"

When she had first gone to adjust insurance upon buying the farm, the agent, poising his sharp pencil over the blank form, had asked if she or her husband knew anything of tobacco farming. No. Is he at present employed? Mark said meekly yes, he was a Rear Admiral in the Navy, and negotiations moved forward with no further hitch.

Cigi and I went to New York in June of 1944. It was one of twenty—or thirty—such trips. We loved the few days in the train, when we played poker patience and did a lot of resting; we liked dinners in the dark world that flashed by the diner's windows; flames lurching to the skies and falling again above the factory towns; steep mountain flanks rising on both sides, rain pocking the swollen rivers, tumbleweeds rolling against cattle fences. It was always new. This trip seemed like all the others; life never stops to say, "This is the last."

The day New York was shouting over the landing of our troops in Brittany was the last day of my old life. When we came back from an evening together to hear Hildegarde, whom he knew and loved, Cigi complained of a bad headache, and in the morning was bewildered, not himself. Two months in a New York hospital ended with a slow trip home—it was wartime, accommodations could not be had—and there followed a long year that all our love, all our efforts, all that science could do, could not make comfortable. In July 1945 the end came very quietly. A great cold came over the world, and some inner part of me, my heart perhaps, has never been quite warm since.

Before the second war the college-free younger crowd had migrated almost in a body to New York, there to try their fortunes in writing scenarios, whodunits, newspaper articles, magazine fiction. This gave the senior Benéts an opportunity to see again the trio of Teresa's children whom they had so loved and guarded in their smaller years. Mother Bun and Laura, whose poetry was beginning to be noted, as was everything both brothers wrote, gladly absorbed all the young people's spare moments; Stephen and his Rosemary were living in New York, and Billy was established with his fourth wife, the sane and steady and gifted Marjorie Flack, in a real home where his children were always welcome. This third stepmother had already won a genuine affection from both daughters and son.

Fred's David and Jim Benét had gone to Spain with the Lincoln Battalion, and were back in New York full of such thanks and honors as their defeated side could give them, Jim's Josephine was there studying dress designing, Rosemary working on a radio program, Kit in Sarah Lawrence College, Joe's Joey working with a broadcasting company. Joey's sister Kathy was keeping house for him, at seventeen, Fred's Babs with *Good Housekeeping,* Fred's David free-lancing on radio scripts. Bunga and Conway came up from Washington and the Naval Academy at Annapolis for occasional visits, and the cousins' group that gathered in our hotel rooms was an animated reminder of younger days on the ranch.

At this time, and indeed until his death, William Rose Benét was a member of the staff of the *Saturday Review of Literature* and editor of the weekly column called "The Phoenix Nest." Several books of his poems were published as the years went by, and his verse-narrative, *The Dust Which Is God,* won the 1942 Pulitzer prize. Our adopted son Bill had finished his job of publicity and entertainment work in Morganthau's office and was busy with newspaper assignments.

But gradually the members of the younger group drifted back to the Coast, to marriages, to the establishment of a dozen homes up and down the San Francisco peninsula or across the Golden Gate Bridge in Marin.

In the years between the wars I had made myself a modest reputation as a speaker, having an unfailing feeling for the lost, the unpopular, cause. When California had passed a law for enforcement of the prohibition amendment in the twenties I took this up with passionate fervor. "Passion" is the word for the women who are devoted to this ideal of a world without alcoholic excess, and I found myself quite carried away by the speaking campaigns they laid out for me, up and down the state, and the simple and touching ardor with which the women of the small towns received the message.

To imply that almost my entire circle of friends looked askance at these activities is understatement. No one liked the idea, Cigi included; it seemed faintly ridiculous, dowdy, simple-minded. I received broadsides by mail and was dropped from various dinner lists. "Harry says he simply won't have her at his table," one friend said. The violence of it amazed me; some of the furious female defenders of the flowing bowl were some who had suffered most grievously from its effects.

Perhaps the most surprising twist was given when I was asked to express my views in one of the most exclusive homes of the East Bay. We had been to one football lunch at this house years before, and had seen a bar that would not disgrace a tavern in Las Vegas set up across one end of the drawing room. But there was no bar on the day I spoke: the hostess explained, rather apologetically, that many of her friends had merely wanted to know what defensible position we "spigot bigots" could possibly take, and she had asked me quite simply to explain my strange behavior. I sensed scorn and, what was worse, amusement, in their attitude, and knew that I had not my fervent friends of the out-of-town campaigning to face. But faced they must be, with my sentimental tales of children frightened, women struggling with bills, abuse, ruin, men debased.

But at the last moment, when the sables and diamonds and French hats had settled down, when it was about my time to rise, the hostess, who had been welcoming late arrivals in the hall, drew me aside and whispered, "My dear, we have another dry speaker, who is simply splendid. Will you take the other side, like a darling?"

I loved campaigning. I loved the small towns, the mild little hotels where I could rest and read detective magazines before going to the mild little dinners in mild little homes; I loved the school or town hall, with the faithful gathered there, lamenting that there wasn't a bigger crowd, and perhaps ejaculating an occasional "Praise God!" as I talked. Some stern New England reformer had mixed the missionary spirit into my Irish blood, and it seethed in response.

My second crusade began when I joined the Women's International League for Peace and Freedom in Philadelphia, under the leadership of the great Jane Addams. Later I was made president by William Randolph Hearst of the Mothers of America, an organization dedicated only to the ideal of peace and adequate home defense. Beside myself, there were three women, all with sons, at the head of Mothers of America: a Jew, a prominent Catholic, and an equally prominent leader in Protestant circles. Our membership, through the medium of the Hearst papers, which carried a simple pledge, was spread all over the Union and counted more than a million members when the first bombs fell on Pearl Harbor. Our inspired meetings, our eager crowds, our hopes fell forever with the bombs.

For some thirty years I spoke from a hundred platforms of the simple achievement of world peace. It is now more than forty years since Jane Addams gathered together some scores of women who eagerly believed that it could be accomplished.

It was sensible. It was economical. It saved pain.

War was wasteful of life, youth, wealth, resources, and amicable international relationships. It was flatly against the codes of all religions—Hebrew, Catholic, and all the offshoots and branches of Christ's law.

Men all agreed to this, and wrote endless books about it. Presidents, kings, emperors were all for peace. Clovis was. Napoleon was, Hitler was, and Aguinaldo was.

Magazines published pages of war costs. One pictured a lovely home, balconied, tree-shaded, garden-surrounded, with a big car at the door. Every man in this country could have that home, ten thousand a year —twenty thousand today—two children in college, travel, books, vacations, security for his loved ones, himself, for what one war cost. That was written of the 1914–18 war.

But I make no more peace speeches. I don't urge women any more to write the President, their senators, their congressmen.

They never can get at the very few men who make wars—a few in Germany, in Italy, in Downing Street, in Washington. Just a few. Their own wives aren't informed of what's going to happen in Hiroshima, Pearl Harbor, Balaclava.

The wives would stand aghast in the bathroom door, mouths full of soapsuds, toothbrushes gesturing.

"John Halliday, are you telling me that this fiendish thing that may destroy the entire world is absolutely going to be dropped upon harmless women and children? Who says so? Who voted for that?"

John might mumble that, gosh, when you invented a thing like that, gee whiz, why did women try to get up a rumpus? The fellers were talking about it, that was all.

"Well, they can stop talking about it," says Mary. "I'm

going to call Betty Pierpont, her brother's running for the legislature, and Lou Carraway, who just inherited all that money, and when you see the fellers you tell them we're a decent, humane people and we don't want any of that on our record! And I'll get Elsie to write one of her 'Dig This, Girls,' columns about it."

So men don't tell the girls, or the boys who might tell the girls. And when the murderous bombs drop it's too late. The deed that will live in infamy was accomplished weeks before, signed, sealed, and delivered. Just a few men know. Now the girls have got to button up their lips, and do nurses' aide service, and stand in line for coffee, and call once at the base hospital, where bewildered, magnificent young men are blundering about in shabby wrappers, watching T.V., listening to the radio, staring at the sky. Call only once. We can't stand it twice.

Many will remain there for fifty more years. For these were the physical, moral, and mental pick of the nation. They were strong. They might have been the doctors, architects, poets, preachers, builders, husbands, and fathers of tomorrow. They are nothing now. Oh well, we'll get along without them.

Like my war talks, and those of all Jane Addams' loyal followers, it's no use. For the aforementioned small group of men—the men who know—have built up a machine so large now that the only possible excuse for them will be to have a third and most terrible war, and wipe out half humanity, and so silence investigators and questioners. New great hospitals are already going up for the wounded. New uniforms for our teen-agers are already running through the mills. New bases are breaking out like asparagus sprouts—no, more like hideous cancer cells—all over Europe. New commissions, new jobs are being invented to meet the needs of a spiraling personnel. America has erected scores of splendid homes for these people abroad.

For the women—this falls largely on the women—stern thrift is advised, to avoid inflation. The aforementioned few men have reveled for years in the delight of spending other persons' money, thousands, millions, billions of it.

But upon the women at home strict economy is imposed. Character building, self-denial, the courage to do without. Meanwhile Germany flourishes on American help. Yet German war prisoners, men and women, a few years ago, were subjected in surgeries to cruelties beyond the belief of mankind. Foreign matters were introduced into their bodies, excruciating suffering was endured under the watchful, undisturbed eyes of scientists and nurses who never gave one instant's relief to their writhing, pleading fellow men.

Thousands of our young men, trusting in America to protect them when she could—and she could have protected them then—were strangled, burned, drowned in the waters of Pearl Harbor. But the little Emperor could share a day of rejoicing over Pearl Harbor's victory, and walks the streets of Tokyo still.

He was one of those fortunate few men who knew,

in Downing Street, the Kremlin, Washington, Tokyo. Nothing could touch him.

If Dr. Kinsey's books, read by me only in excerpts and by request, had not somewhat nauseated me, I would have found them funny. I forget how many man-hours of investigation it took him and his covey of helpers to discover that the human male is somewhat more subject to sex impulses than the female. The shock threw him so entirely off base that he was presently quoting enormous numbers of women as having confessed to him, or to the aforementioned associates, that they had been sexually at fault, by common social standards, either before or during marriage. This emboldened the doctor to predict just what average of wives, at the moment in good standing, would eventually fall.

The doctor is not cited here in mere amused contempt. I want to place my own considered theory of the main causes of human behavior beside his, Freud's, and those of Freud's whole school.

The abiding genesis of the way we act is based in jealousy. Jealousy and sex frequently intermingle, but jealousy comes first, starts earlier, lasts longer. I have seen it in babes of three months and in centenarians of a hundred and one.

The babe, his brother thirteen months older, and his heavy, dirty, forlorn young mother sat on the steps of one of the humbler churches of Mexico City. The mother was nursing both boys, and begging. Water is scarce in Mexico City, and the poor—and there are many very poor persons there—feel the lack.

The elder boy was contentedly breakfasting, but the younger, with a small dark face twisted with hate, had so squirmed across the maternal bosom that he could put an occasional scratch upon his brother's face or land a slap on his jaw.

The centenarian was an old crone into whose deaf ears I shouted in a hospital, held by her clawing hand. To cheer her I told her I had talked to a woman in the big ward who was a hundred and four years old.

"That's Betsy Kinncaid," shrilled the aged sufferer. "She ain't a hundred yet. Her and her son got up that story. . . ."

And so on.

I wonder if, deep within the decorated and portly breasts of the Few Men Who Know, jealousy doesn't hold an unrecognized place?

Jealousy of those young fresh sailors, with white caps on their blond heads, those square-shouldered, sun-browned G.I.'s, those magnificent marines, every one of them looking like a government poster promising trades, skills, professions, travel to the adventure-hungry boys. And finally the flying corps, gloriously free, spurning the dull roadways that never change their plodding course, masters of earth, sky, and sea. Would it be so surprising if age, with its ulcers and baldness and store teeth, found them "expendable"?

Sex, say the aforementioned authorities, takes many strange forms and disguises. Jealousy takes more. For every case of sexual obsession that runs through chills, fevers, hate, love, trembling wakeful night hours, stupid, bewildered daytime hours, there are three of jealousy.

So I don't talk peace any more. It's about as effective as curling the hair of a child hanging over a murderous volcano, or reciting Hodgson's famous poem to a bull just loosed into the arena.

Speaking of bullfighting—or, rather, the "running of the bulls," for nobody in any Latin country calls it a fight—it is interesting to consider the aversion, the delicate sensibilities and sympathies with which many persons regard it.

The bull has had three years of care and ease when he enters the ring. He has some dozen moments of amazement, pain, bewilderment, and fury, and also he has a chance to win, and sometimes does win, before his swift and painless death on the sand. There is comforting reason to believe that, like a human being, he is swept beyond all sensation of pain in the heat and anger of the conflict.

The aforementioned sufferers from sensibilities and sympathies might well pause to consider the situation of thousands of our finest boys in base hospitals. They don't die in twelve minutes; they have not even the bulls' chances. Innocent, gullible, gallant, they may live for half a century of headache and nerves and mental confusion.

If we could only send the bulls to war, and let the

boys fight it out quickly and cleanly in the ring, to the sound of music and handclapping and shouts of "Olé!"

My sister and I went wholeheartedly into the campaign to win Wendell Willkie the presidency. This was carried on on a high level; planes were met by impressive limousines, hotel reservations were for diplomatic suites, banquets were small but select. Often the candidate was with us, magnetic, eager, turning his rapt attention this way and that as is the custom with the leading man in these enthralling circumstances. To me this was intoxication. Our way was cleared across crowded sidewalks, we were rushed through packed lobbies, we were escorted to seats on high platforms, and while the welcoming applause broke out camera bulbs flickered in every direction; I could never get enough of it. Indeed, I did not get much after all, which was perhaps why it never lost its bloom. For some weeks I had a daily half hour of radio talk for this lost cause; more than once Clare Boothe Luce shared the time with me, and we began a friendship that was to ripen some years later.

Another lost cause was America First. To those of us who were charter members it meant exactly that: America first. We like the Monroe Doctrine. We like to belong to the hemisphere that respects boundaries and keeps the peace.

For America First there was once again the flurry of movement, enthusiasm, conferences. One glorious great meeting was at Madison Square Garden when mounted police kept the street crowds in order, and Senator Taft, Charles Lindbergh, and I had for audience a packed house. Another inspiring evening was in the New York home of an enthusiast named Webster, when Alice Longworth and her brother Archibald were in our fiery and hopeful ranks.

Exactly what happened to dim the simple patriot flame of America First I never quite grasped. Suddenly it was anathema; some lunatic fringe had probably considered it subversive. Years later I wondered if that ugly suspicion might have been the cause of a most uncomfortable experience I had in the early days of widowhood in California.

It began with the appearance of my name upon the cover of a weekly magazine, published in Hollywood, which supposedly gave the very last word in gossip about movie and radio stars. The cover carried a simple statement of my communist activities; for some months after its original appearance other statements of the same nature were made. I was accused of running a communist cell in a neighboring California town, Stalin's pet name for me was given as his "little red dolly," and when it was known that I was to speak at a Press Club dinner the editor of the Hollywood magazine stated definitely that I would be prevented, I would not be allowed to masquerade as an honest American citizen. Finally another headline broke the news that the

Vatican had taken up the matter and I was to be excommunicated.

Not only this, but every week this editor had a half-hour broadcast, and on no Sunday night did he miss a reference to my treacherous interests. It was a rather sad and lonely time in my life, and to listen to this voice, so full of hate and resentment, and so despitefully using my name, was singularly depressing.

I made no answer. This was thought a mistake by some of the people near to me, and over and over again the press of various California cities begged me to say only a few dignified words branding this man as a liar and libelist. But as his strange persecution grew into months rather than weeks his awareness of the shakiness of his position began to be observed; he faltered a little, he would like to have a good talk with Kathleen Norris, he would gladly correct any mistaken statements he had made.

Two men representing themselves as from the F.B.I., presently came to see me, and asked me to make a full statement that they could use against him. Later I ascertained that they were not from the F.B.I. at all; they may have been sent from my strange persecutor himself. An outburst of anger and abuse from me might have been just what he wanted. In any case I did not see them.

The Press Club dinner is an annual affair known as the "Late Watch." Its charter members now are few, for they must have been actually working on newspapers at the time of the earthquake in April 1906. We who remain are extremely proud of our distinction, and always make this a great occasion. In the face of the threats three or four of the Late Watchers telephoned and asked me if I was going to risk it, and suggested an escort. Coblentz, the grand old editor of the Hearst chain, was one, John Francis Neylan, a tall, raw, city-room cub in my early newspaper days, an eminent lawyer now, was another, and George Creel a third. But my son Frank settled the matter by growling that he would take me down. "One of those dopes might take a pop at you, Ma," he said in his Chesterfieldian way, "and I don't want anybody saying, 'Where the hell was her son?'"

We walked placidly up and down the sidewalk for a while before going in, the evening was balmy and bright, and several policemen, unsolicited but welcome, walked with us. After a while two boys parked an open small car across the street, a car bearing a banner with a strange device employing my name. One of the policemen went over in leisurely fashion some time later and suggested that they remove the banner, which they did, observing youthfully that their time was up anyway at nine o'clock. So possibly they were paid for their effort. Nothing else happened.

Just the same, the whole long experience was most uncomfortable, for there were always hotheads about, anonymous warnings arrived daily, and embarrassments were plentiful as it was. On one occasion a large audience seated in a hot amphitheater and comprising all the dignitaries of a fashionable suburb was asked to wait while the agitated president of the club called Senator Richard Nixon in Washington to ask the authorities there if it was advisable to allow me to speak. Mr. Nixon said it was entirely advisable. She then begged me to open my talk with "a full explanation of this most distressing rumor." But that I would not do. Eventually I was allowed to talk, an hour late; the temperature stood close to three figures. The talk fell flat.

Finally my name died out of the attack, and that of an East Bay schoolteacher took its place. But here there was a good sharp retaliation; this lady was valiantly defended by the great educational organization to which she belonged, and the calumniating editor went to San Quentin.

But even today delicate probing and timid inquiry occasionally meet me; in places as far distant as Virginia Beach and Tombstone, Arizona, much-folded, sodden magazine clippings are brought forth and once again the old libel comes to light.

For memberships in lesser groups I seem to have had a predilection, active in some, nominal in others. They range from the great peace society of the Women's International League and the Red Cross to the Shakespearian movement in Ashland, Oregon, and the Women's Republican Club of California. Literary societies, church guilds, countless missions, convents, monasteries, boys' homes, the W.C.T.U. and the S.P.C.A., museums, symphonies, KLIM and CARE, women's clubs, "Jackie," which finds homes for foster children, "Enchanted Hills" for the blind, and any organization that includes in its objective the peace of the world—I join them all.

Age has its immense compensations; among them perhaps the most important is that a great many things over which one agonized, things one desired with a desperate longing, are no longer glamorous. Age can be a time of peace, independence, realizations, enjoyments amounting at moments to bliss. Age can be a time when time is not. One is alive, one has plans for the day, one has dogs, a garden, the ocean at the end of the garden, one knows what, and what not, to eat. There are still books, and the unrolling of the world's marvelous story through pictures, music, poetry.

And of course, spread as last essential elements over all, one may have family love and faith.

All these things in lesser or greater measure have, to be sure, been attainable all along the road. But not in such peace and perfection.

My own adjustment to the change from a constant, all-absorbing companionship was helped by interest in politics. To a woman born in 1880 politics are not a natural preoccupation. It was my own grandmother who warned my mother, with a dark look at me, then aged about twelve, "If you aren't careful, Jo, that girl will grow up strong-minded." These ladies took no interest in the elections of Cleveland or McKinley. They glanced in scornful amusement at the struggles of the great suffrage leaders, Aunt Kitty's old view of politics still prevailing: noisy men in the back rooms of saloons, smoking, spitting, and defaming the opposing party. But somehow my sensitive sex bears up with commendable fortitude under these disadvantages.

Highlights in these last years were two political campaigns in which I played a modest but extremely enthusiastic part. It was an old friend, Adela Rogers St. John, who came up from her busy typewriter in Hollywood to fire San Francisco women with interest in a young congressman who had entered the senatorial race. Of Richard Nixon I had never heard but I liked his politics, and later I did identify him with the Hiss affair. If the appeal of mere speechmaking intoxicated me, speechmaking combined with politics proved twice as thrilling, and again there were the audiences, the meetings, the conferences, the splendid persons who immediately became one's bosom companions.

It was a grim November day when the end of that campaign came; I was in San Francisco, restless because of the issue that was so seriously in doubt, not wanting to see anyone, not ready to believe that it was over, that there could be no more fighting.

A Republican candidate in California must cancel out one million registered Democratic votes before he can start even, and although to meet this candidate—as has been proven many times since—is to be won at once by the force, simplicity, and earnestness of his personality, yet he had heavy competition and until the polls opened the betting was against him.

At about five I went into uptown headquarters and saw George Creel, and we went out for a rather gloomy supper; then he went back and I walked down Market Street in the early evening to the queer, dreary, big rooms that were the headquarters of the various campaign committees. And immediately the atmosphere became all-enveloping, and I was in for the most fascinat- ing five hours of my career as a campaigner.

My first thought upon finding the right rooms in a large, dark, Market Street building was that no one else was interested; I was almost alone.

Then a few men, anxiously murmuring among themselves, came in, and two boys brought in a large blackboard marked off into forty-eight squares, duly divided by the cryptic abbreviations "Dem" and "Rep," and under the words were the figures of former senatorial elections—not hope-inspiring. A few businesslike girls brought in some covered tubs of soft drinks and began making sandwiches, glad of my help and experience, but not optimistic. "Not a prayer," they answered my query.

But still the temperature of the room improved; strange folk came in, mechanics in work clothes, thin women, talkative campaigners, some of whom I knew, a great many men. Radios talked in corners, a T.V. reeled off pictures of other political doings, and the two boys aforementioned began to climb up and down ladders set against the chart with chalk in their hands. Bedlam set in.

Our buttering and spreading finished, we disposed of the cuttings and lined more empty tubs with stacks of sandwiches; these were flanked by larger tubs filled with bottles of pop and beer, packed in ice. A glorious sense of community interest and effort pervaded the group; it was not confident, not yet, but such harmony is worth while even in failure.

It is unfortunate that the words "communism" and "communistic" have been monopolized by the Russians, who found them ready-made and appropriated them to fit something harsh and unnatural. But to us the term "community house" has no sinister significance; convents are "communities," and we daily mention with hope our union after death with the Communion of Saints. The greatest of the Sacraments is Communion.

Community living on spiritual and intellectual grounds has been the ideal since More's *Utopia* and Ripley's Brook Farm. It is infinitely more satisfying to the human heart than are our separated units of twos and threes. A hundred years ago a score of English writers were immortalizing the households in which parents and children—Mrs. Gladstone and her sister had twenty-one between them—grandmother, grandfather, aunts, cousins, a governess or two, tutors and servants, visiting relatives and guests and the servants' servants, all made up small, busy, occupied communities where prayers and manners, lessons and languages, culinary cares and the graces and the arts were intermingled to round out a picture that endures still as something very near the ideal of human living. A fine Chinese family maintains the same dignity and decorum, or did, by strange irony, until "communism" came in. It was a safer world for the children, and for young marriages and for old age, that world of Trollope and Charlotte Yonge and the Kingsleys and George Moore, and an easier world than even electric can openers and instant mashed potato have made of our world today.

Grandma's room, the attic, the windmill, teatime and Sunday church bells, brothers and sisters of all sizes and ages were a good setting in which the awakening heart and mind might grow; law was law, duty duty, and authority commanded respect as well as affection. These are lost words today.

But something of it remains where simple women in simple towns gather to further the interests of the Red Cross, the W.C.T.U., the country and church clubs. The plain, fine faces, the eagerness to help with plans, with loans of card tables and silver, ice cream freezers, tickets, prizes, pies, cakes, raffles, the constant talk of sons and daughters, from baby days right up to college, make one feel that perhaps the community of saints is not so far to seek.

Ten o'clock, eleven o'clock. At eleven o'clock I said, slightly hoarse, to an imposing-looking neighbor who had been writing down figures for the last hour, "He hasn't once gone back!"

"No, I think he's in," said the stranger matter-offactly, "but it's trickles, still. The big vote from the south hasn't been counted. But I think he's in."

And with these thrilling words I sank back into an enormous leather chair and contented myself with watching the miracle take place.

Two years later Mark and I went to the Republican Convention in Chicago, where I was to do a few articles for the Bell Newspaper Syndicate, with which I had been working for more than twenty-five years, writing brief articles in the interests of women, and in answer to their letters, for the Sunday pages of various newspapers.

And once again the campaign caught me in its heady atmosphere; the sense of common aims and interests with hundreds of eager, excited people, meals hastily and indifferently eaten, plans fresh every moment, rumors and counterrumors thick on the air, and of course stimulating encounters with the great, whose names on posters and blowing banners, whose pictures on buttons and medals and front pages were the reason for the whole great show.

Chicago in the summer of 1952 was aboil with politics. Perhaps it is always aboil with one thing or another. Mark and I gloried in it. Two of the big hotels had turned great parlors into candidates' headquarters where Cokes and T.V.s and the distribution of trophies went on all day, in an atmosphere of lights, noise, music, and the occasional appearance of the headliners. Limousines were always at the door to rush one to the distant auditorium, which still smelled faintly of cattle and straw bedding, and, once there, the glorious hysteria of the press box took complete possession and everyone knew exactly what was going to happen and in the same breath assured one that sensational explosions were likely to come off this afternoon.

Taft was our choice and we were mightily encouraged by the feeling at campaign headquarters. I was having tea with Mrs. Taft, ironically enough, in the splendid Presidential Suite in one of the hotels, when somehow knowledge that the end had come, the fight was over, possessed the little group of some half dozen of us, with no message having been received, no unfavorable report made. It simply was there. Taft had lost. A quiet look from the mother to one of his sons, a serious nod in answer, and it was time for me to make an unostentatious departure, meditating on the lifelong ambitions of one of our great statesmen, ended forever that afternoon.

Strangely enough, for I have been a churchwoman all my life, I was at a loss for words, after almost half a century of using them and abusing them uninterruptedly, when I was asked by Edward R. Murrow to contribute to his symposium collected from many sources under the heading *This I Believe*. I accepted his invitation with some pride and sat down to write what sounded, at first hearing, like the simplest assignment in the world.

Family Gathering

My first effort was impersonal, brief, and said nothing
that is not contained in the Nicene Creed. In succeeding
efforts I tried to break it down, represent myself as
sometimes having been a backslider, as a wistful pilgrim
at last finding the path. But it didn't sound convincing,
largely, perhaps, because it wasn't true. My mother and
father were practical Catholics. The word "practical" in
this usage means that they lived up to the tenets, ritual,
and canons of their special brand of faith. Their children were early impressed with the importance of asking, in their prayers, for perseverance. Apparently my
young and wandering, and often somewhat bored,
prayers were answered. To believe in Christ is a miracle
that transcends all those of the evangelists put together.

My Church satisfies me. If it did not make me in-
wardly happy I would distrust it. Faith, in whatever
form it takes, ought to bring deep inner happiness and
a living consciousness that the kingdom of heaven is
within you. If that religion or creed or cult exacts certain tiresome restrictions and observances, why, these
are a small price to pay for security. Fish on Fridays,
Mass on Sundays, Confession, do not fit always into one's
plans, but obedience is but the guineas' stamp; the gold
glows under the outer sign.

Every Christmas I write an editorial for the syndicate
that distributes these articles to many a small-town
newspaper across the Union. And every Christmas I repeat the story of the one life that was actually lived in
human form to bring the words "God" and "Father"
into union, and the one voice whose teaching has never

303

been refuted or equaled or denied. Two thousand years after that life ended, in a land thousands of miles away, that name and that voice still hold so high a place that no other name is mentioned for a long, long time after that of Jesus Christ. And when another name is bracketed with His, it must be that of a follower, a leader and preacher like Himself, one who preached in His name. If for one day every year those who profess to believe in Him could keep His law—such a simple law, of forgiveness, and service, and sharing coats, and overcoming evil with good—the world would be saved. But that has never been, not even for a day.

After floundering about trying to make an intelligent and moderately interesting analysis of my religious experiences, I had to write Mr. Murrow regretfully that I could not fulfill the contract and return to him the very impressive documents that had accompanied his request for it. It could be of no interest to anyone to know that I had all my life been a Roman Catholic, sometimes devout, sometimes less devout, but never disturbed by fluctuations to any other form of belief, and for the most part extremely grateful for the privilege of belonging by birth, then habit, then conviction, to the organization that can honestly claim that it is one, apostolic, catholic with a small as well as large C, and universal.

The ranch has now been for some years a boys' vacation club, and the trails that we cut up over the mountainside and the big trees and the pool are enjoyed by swarming scores of long-legged, freckled youngsters who consume hamburgers by the solid pound, and whose annual destruction of property, attacks of poison oak, loss of bathing suits, and generous distribution of pop bottles on every bit of ledge or fence averages, per capita, those of our own boys. The Palo Alto house, once a show place, with its mellowed plaster walls, cloister, gardens, and tile roofs, is also an institution; it changed hands several times, and some years ago was turned into a club, the Newman Club of Stanford University. From the first, this institution has flourished amazingly, numbering now some three hundred members.

In connection with this club an event took place that was of great importance to the members and gave Palo Alto one more point of tourist and pilgrim interest.

Clare Boothe Luce desired to place some memorial to her loved and lost daughter in the college Ann was attending at the time of the accident that cost her her life. Clare's first plan was to build on the college grounds a little music hall, where beautiful records magnificently reproduced might add one more note to Stanford's curriculum. Or perhaps this was the second plan, the first being a chair in philosophy—probably exclusively

305

Catholic philosophy, for Clare is the last person in the world to admit that there is any other. For reasons I never fully understood college authorities found difficulties with both offers, no meeting of minds could be arranged, and there was a lull in the proceedings.

Then it occurred to me that a chapel on the grounds of the Newman Club might please this twice-baffled benefactor, and Clare seized upon this idea with her own characteristic enthusiasm and speed. Almost before we knew it she was personally superintending the erection of the Chapel of St. Ann, and a unique and much-discussed building it is. The wood of the pews is soft to the touch, the lighting is equally mellowed; the western windows are alternated with the almost life-size murals of the Stations of the Cross. A Madonna, especially made in Italy entirely of tiny protruding glass oblongs, looks with pain-haunted eyes from Our Lady's corner, and the magnificent thirty-foot-tall windows are painted in a medley of forms and faces, large and small, with the irradiation of certain sacred heads so brilliant as almost to seem to leave the glass and penetrate the atmosphere of the church. A famous French artist, André Girard, painted the murals and the windows as a work of love as well as art, and they show it. The undergraduates who pack the pews, and the faithful who never miss the early Mass in summer heat or winter dark, keep alive the Chapel of St. Ann, a heart-touching memorial among the myriad statues and buildings of the world by which we try to hold the beloved dead.

On a certain November Monday, I think in 1956, Frank telephoned me with every indication of urgency, to ask me to speak in Berkeley for United Charities. I suggested that in the college town there were fifty good speakers but he pleaded that a patient of his was stuck, as chairwoman, to find a speaker and he was accordingly pledged to find her one, and "Oh, for heaven's sake, say yes, and get this darned thing off my mind." I finally agreed and asked Walter McLellan to go with me on the thirty-five-mile trip, for my present driver could get lost even in Palo Alto; and Alameda County is famous for misleading signs, byways, and misinformed gas-station advisers.

Walter pleaded that he had promised to take his wife to a movie that Wednesday night. I asked him to bring Doretta to the charity affair and make the movie another night, and he agreed. My aunt's nurse urged me to wear a new lace dress, which I refused to do, claiming that it was not for me to display an expensive garment at this particular type of meeting. "You could have had your hair set," she said reproachfully at parting.

We were somewhat short of time, Walter nervous, Doretta saying nothing, myself reassuring. "They'll have to wait for me. I'm the speaker."

At ten minutes to six, in hot sunlight, we reached Berkeley's imposing high school, set like a Doric temple of creamy brick at the top of flights of steps. It was

307

swarming with people going in. My hopes of successful fund raising rose. We were met by a slightly nervous man who rushed us down the aisle of a great crowded auditorium to second-row seats.

"How long shall I talk?" I whispered to him. And then, seeing cameras and men on the stage, I said to my companions complacently, "Oh, good. We'll get some publicity on this. And look, there are big signs, *This Is Your Life*. That comes on at ten tonight! Could we stick around? We can go out for some dinner and come back for the live show. It's always been too late for us. I've never seen it."

"We could," Walter agreed, strangling. And the next moment a spotlight, in the hands of a man in the aisle, was touching the faces of various women in the audience with a pleasant "It could be you, but it isn't," and had alighted upon me.

What followed was for fifteen minutes a complete blur to a woman conscious of mussy hair, a ten-year-old dress, and utter unpreparedness. The signs for the cosmetic show had aroused no suspicion, for it never came on until ten and my supposed charity appeal was to be all over by seven o'clock. The emotion increased by the moment as Ralph Edwards set the tremendous machinery of *This Is Your Life* in motion. My three brothers in turn added their voices to the story as they came rushing out of the wings, and finally Mark, half laughing and half crying, came out in her turn. She had been secreted in a Berkeley hotel for two days, for rehearsals, warned not to telephone even her oldest friends for fear of a betrayal.

Old friends, one summoned from Canada, appeared, each making a contribution to the tale of younger days, and finally Frank, his tall, lovely Alice, their children, Teresa's children, Teresa's grandchildren, my grandchildren, and even the smallest of the Kathleens, who had made me a proud great-grandmother six months earlier, even while paralyzing me with the fact of being the mother of a grandfather. The beloved figures kept pouring forth, and so did my laughter—and my tears.

Well, then we all had a glorious dinner together and Mr. Edwards congratulated Mark upon the ease with which the performance had gone. Everyone had appeared for rehearsals, mastered lines, taken direction with professional promptitude.

"It is only fair to tell you, Ralph," said Mark, "that you have fallen into a nest of hams. It's a great deal easier to get us on than to get us off."

As is customary, I received really valuable gifts for this impromptu appearance, among them a heavy gold bracelet dangling with mementos, which has served since as an infallible conversation piece, not to say teething ring. Among the more than twenty souvenirs were tiny representations of my first book, our first home in Port Washington, a typewriter studded with jewels, a baby's shoe, a California bear and a redwood, even the dolls that Joe used to pack around when we were respectively three and four, shouting, as the wild-game hunters did in the streets, "Wi' game, wi' game!" But I cannot finish the story of this real honor that was paid me without recording that late at night, alone in my quiet, big room with its doors opened wide to the old garden, I felt the tears coming and for an hour could only see in review the young years that had been brought before me and the faces I had loved long since and lost awhile.

Aunt Mary had been apprised of what was going on, and when Mark and I got home she was all animation about the show, the family, and the bracelet. She studied the bracelet fondly for days. We determined not to miss *This Is Your Life* again, late though it came to us. And the very next week we were waiting for it.

This week it was different. A very sad man and his chirpy little wife held the stage. Whether he had been the inmate of a mental institution or merely a bad nervous case was not clear, but during the half hour he hardly raised his eyes from the floor, and his story was as sad as his face. His sisters appeared to greet him, his doctors, nurses, psychiatrist, clergyman, and each added to the note of encouragement of which he stood so obviously in need.

"That was the year you and your wife decided to try living apart," said Ralph Edwards, drawing him out. "And wasn't that the year you lost your son? . . ."

Aunt Mary had taken all of this she could stand. As the program finished in the darkened T.V. room her voice clove the silence.

"What in the name of God," she demanded, "are they going to put on his bracelet?"

Family Gathering

Aunt Mary. After her exciting younger years—they
lasted in full strength until she was fifty—she married a
fine and faithful man a few years older, English-born,
but a friend of her brothers in their young school years
in San Francisco, the perfect type of the county squires
of Victorian fiction: broad, dignified, inexhaustibly gentle and understanding. They lived quietly, shuttling
back and forth between San Francisco and New York
for some years, then settled in our Western city, cele-
brating a silver wedding and even ten years more.

As a wife, Aunt Mary became fanatically correct and
gloried in that proud estate, and was presently full of
kindly monitorial suggestions for those of us who had
borne the burden and the heat of the day for some years.
Her one absorbing interest outside of Edmund's comfort and her own small apartment was music, and she
feasted upon concerts, operas, symphonies as long as
Cigi and I attended them, and even afterward she and
I had regular seats and never missed good music.

One night, in the years when we had a box for opera
nights, I went up to her kitchen to pick her up. Over
her evening gown a big apron was firmly pinned, and
the dishes were about finished when I arrived.

"Oh, you have a hat on!" she said, seeing an inconspicuous strip of wired lace on my hair. "I haven't—wait a
minute."

And she disengaged a small square Chinese bag,
heavy with brocade, from a chair, caught a curl of osprey
feathers from an old bandbox filled with millinery junk,
combined the two with a safety pin, pulled the bag

firmly down over the beautiful silver of her hair, and was all ready to face the critical eyes of the opera crowd, as handsome as any woman there.

"Dishes and dusting!" she said ruefully in the car. "When my one ambition in life was to be a *grande dame!*"

But if anyone ever was that, she was. I told her so. She was always pretty, with very pretty hands, always wearing a good many rings, and draped with chains and earrings. But as her husband grew blind, heavy, and helpless we persuaded them to move to a country rest home. She was furious and miserable there from the first.

One day, quite against her doctors' orders, she quickly and quietly packed their bags, called a cab, and escaped back to the city, triumphing at our alarmed faces, as Mark and I hurried after her, and rejoicing that she and her man were alone, and she could get him his favorite dinner. Her familiar Spanish maid was installed and Tia Maria had won the day.

It was a brief day. A few weeks later, when Lupe had gone away for a two-day holiday, Mary fell on a newly waxed floor, and the gallant old man, then more than eighty-five, hurrying to her assistance, fell too, and it was a long twenty-four hours before help came. They lived on a top floor, the tenants below were out of town, and it was only when Sunday's milk and newspapers had stood for a night and a day that the housemaid discovered the tragedy. The lock of the door, bolted and double bolted, had to be broken down when Frank got there, and he and I had to handle the dazed and enfeebled pair. But Mary was not too broken to observe in a whisper that landlords ought to go on a round of inspection at regular intervals. Any reference to this endless night and day was brushed off by her afterward. "You and Frank made a great deal of it," she would observe dryly. "I do wish people would stop fussing over us!"

She lived for some seven years but never walked again without assistance. Restored to the rest home, she began to treat the whole affair as unnecessary.

"The moment doctors feel that a person can pay," she would say in high scorn, "then the operation must be right away, not a minute to spare! Sticking needles into my ear to tell me that my blood had so many hobgoblins in it!"

"You were pretty sick," one might modestly offer, remembering peritonitis, a broken hip, a fever that raged for days, and the last solemn rites of the Church.

"I never considered myself so," the *grande dame* would say in cold, unconcerned dignity.

When her blind, patient old partner died, Aunt Mary left the rest home and came to live with me. The third member of our trio was a certain kind and capable Ethel Cummings, nurse, confederate, friend, who was with us for more than five years. Mary was well enough then, and almost until the end, to get herself up magnificently, and be escorted to social affairs, luncheons in Woodside or San Mateo, receptions in San Francisco, and many of the debutante parties that were springing up among the younger generation, the cousins' cousins. It was now that she lost her heart to a certain good-looking man of about forty, a friend's son. His elegant European accent, his clothing, his negligently easy manner, all charmed her. He sent her flowers and completed his conquest.

At about this time my brother Joe gave a reception at the Bohemian Club for his daughter Kathy and her husband, Robert Parrish, Hollywood movie director, and the cast that under Robert's direction had been shooting a movie in Africa. Mary not only accepted her own invitation but informed me quietly that she had asked her boy friend to attend. That her host didn't know him mattered no whit.

The occasion came, and Mary was installed on a sort of throne in the Red Room, her velvet gown yoked in rose point, her sables negligently draped over one shoulder. And in due time her guest arrived, duly kissed her hand, and asked—if he might present his wife. He had been married only a few hours earlier.

My aunt took this staggering announcement with her native gallantry, and the happy couple could have seen nothing amiss. But an hour or two later, driving home, I observed that she was unenthusiastic, subdued, and said sympathetically that it must have been something of a shock.

"No, no, dear," said the *grande dame* in a dignified, resigned voice. "But I had hoped to make the circuit of the room on his arm." Even as Victoria at Windsor Castle.

Among the things that I am glad to remember is my gift to her of a drowsy, loving, Pekingese baby dog, easily seated on my palm. She became Peekaboo's besotted slave in a matter of moments, and her eyes filled with tears and her voice trembled when, with quiet assurance, he settled himself against her shoulder for the night. To the end of her life he was her first consideration; at one time she expressed concern that he must grow up in a household of women. "Poor little fellow, it's not fair to him," she said. I could see no way of remedying this situation.

While she could still walk fairly well we went to Los Angeles for a family wedding. We stayed at a large hotel, which always gave her great pleasure.

On the second morning I returned from early Mass to find her at the bedroom window.

"Great excitement down here," she said blandly, "the hotel seems to be on fire."

After one look at the confusion of engines and hoses, onlookers and fire fighters below in the side street, I suggested that we move out immediately, and sure enough the halls, when we hurried through them, were wreathed with faint, first streamers of smoke. The elevator was maddeningly slow, and when it stopped it was filled with firemen, who looked out, gave a few ringing shouts to confederates out of sight, and went on up, observing casually, "Better walk down, madam. And keep moving, too."

This we did, my aunt in a pleasant dream.

"Never have I seen such stunning fellows!" she said, slightly emphasizing the first word. "With their helmets and their hatchets!"

The story flags; grows quieter. The big house in Palo Alto, with its garden kitchen, the sprawling acres under the redwoods at the ranch, the blue and silver Christmas trees in the library are memories only. The twice-yearly ordeal of selecting new gowns and new hats is ended. The silver porridge bowl that I sent Fred's daughter, the first-born of the young cousins, has forty-four companion bowls now, and the tale is far from complete. So that in one important way the years have been filled with reminders that childhood is eternally the same, the small imperious voices have the ring they had in the days of the Medes and the Persians; methods may improve, nurseries may become safer, but new dangers, new obligations spring up to fill parenthood with the same agonies of fear, ecstasies of delight.

The croup, colic, fits, and brain fever, which made childhood in the nineties terrifying, have given way to loftier disorders: polio, muscular dystrophy, cerebral meningitis. Crossed eyes and harelips have practically vanished from view, with the buckteeth and freckles, the overweight and awkwardness that made girlhood one long purgatory. But the teens still have their trials. Personally I wish that science had been a little earlier with the introduction of the process of slinging a small baby over one's shoulder, halfway through a meal, and delivering that rabbit punch that is death on colic; also, it would have been easier on the mothers of forty years ago if Dr. Holt, the authority of the day on baby care, had not held out for meals on the minute: six, twelve, six. The unfortunate infants of the period were walked, shrieking with hunger, for perhaps fifty minutes or an hour, and were often too tired after this exercise of lungs and temper to want to eat at all.

Most merciful of all the bans lifted in these years is that ban that forbade any pain-relieving drug to childhood. Small boys with broken arms, boils, and concussions were allowed to writhe and cry it out; small girls wailed for hours with earache and the ever popular hip disease. Soothing syrups were out; aspirins weren't in.

But today's older mothers are wrong when they claim that even without household servants the young wives of today have an easier time than the days they knew as young wives. There are much higher standards for mothers. Children's teeth, tonsils, posture, eyes all must be kept under strict supervision; a child of three must be rated for good citizenship, capacity for getting along with his fellows, co-operation, even if he is lucky enough to escape weekly sessions with his psychoanalyst. Between his appointments, his engagements, his education, and his amusements, Mother's car rushes in and out of the garage forty times a day.

And yet there's no life in the world so rich as a life that is spent with children, and no memories so wonderful as the everyday miracles that go on wherever they are. Preparing for an outing, how they rush through the supermarket, picking out everything impracticable and indigestible upon which they can lay their hands.

How they swarm and shriek in the shallow waters of beaches, how hot and wet their adorable little faces are, stuck with sharp oak leaves and yellow manzanita dust, as they reach the picnic table at the top of Deer Hill!

Christmas, with the library floor deep in ruined expensive wrapping papers and tangled ribbons. With conscientious parents seated on the floor with pencils and paper, trying to list the givers as fast as the excited hands tear open the gifts. Candy has been mashed on best dresses, more than one toy has been broken, the key to the engine has been lost, somebody is crying, the fire has died down, and the holy day is moving solemnly toward its close over the stripped trees and the bare garden outside, before the uproar subsides.

"Rosemary," says one mother, her hands full of little wraps, in the confusion of the big hallways, "I was thinking that, another Christmas, it might be wiser . . ."

All so good, so filling, this living in the inexhaustible stream of childhood! Always so thrilling, that wait in the impersonal hospital sitting room, that swift raising of heads and stoppage of breath as a new little wail is added to the sum total of the "weeping and wailing in this valley of tears," as the prayer has it.

What fads and follies have had their day, during the long years, and disappeared from sight and memory! Who remembers the old German Dr. Knapp, who felt that all the ills of the world could be cured by barefoot walking, and the great Coué with his "Day by day, in every way, I am getting better and better"? Fletcher, with his regimen of forty-two chews to each mouthful, and mud packs that were recommended by every woman's magazine, where are they now? It was little dancing Irene Castle, with her Dutch cap and her bobbed hair, who really made a lasting effect upon her generation. David Copperfield suits, high-waisted, deep-collared, tortured our little boys. Their mothers could not go out without immaculate spats. Everyone played mahjong indoors and miniature golf outdoors; one hot Sunday I counted sixty-three miniature golf courses between New York City and Oyster Bay. Chatelaine bags, feather boas, Kewpie dolls—all gone.

And the kings and queens, too, with their castles, their palaces, their armies, their caskets of treasure, their stables filled with blooded horses, their carefully graded heirs apparent and heirs presumptive, grand dukes and grand duchesses. Why should our particular half century be the time destined to see them topple, one by one? They had gone on for so many hundreds of years with their thrones and crowns, the attributes of royalty, the indisputable power of majesty that seemed so secure! Why was it for us to see the downfall of the empires of China, Austria, Germany, Russia, and the kingdoms of Hungary, Italy, Portugal, Spain, Rumania?

All gone. The battles for the royal line that have rolled and thundered since Charlemagne and Attila are over; the thrones will never be filled again.

New York, my New York, is gone too. The young years of trying and failing, trying and succeeding are over. Teresa is long gone, and Steve, the loved younger brother of *John Brown's Body*, is gone too. Steve died untimely, after a long struggle with crippling arthritis. The three children he left behind him are themselves the parents of nine youngsters now, and Rosemary Carr Benét, as a proud grandmother, with Laura, his sister, herself a writer of half a dozen successful literary biographies, and as many books of poems, carry on Steve's memory in poems and memorial talks and articles that mean that it will not soon be lost. William Rose Benét and his wife, the Marjorie Flack of a dozen nursery classics, came West only a year or two before Bill's sudden death and were met at the airport by his son, James Benét, special writer on a San Francisco newspaper, and by Rosemary Benét Dawson, Kathleen Benét Fry, and the ten grandchildren in a shining row, plainly marked with names for rapid identification. Bill had finished his great work, the classic *Reader's Encyclopedia*, a few years earlier.

To list other absentees would fill another formidable volume. Theodore Roosevelt, Jr., who won all hearts at the ranch, and my specially appointed younger brother, Nelson Doubleday, Charley Towne, Mary Roberts Rinehart, and fifty more would contribute to the general air of loneliness and change that envelops me in the familiar neighborhoods now.

But lovely Ellen Doubleday, also with grandmotherly interests, lives in a smaller but still storybook house down at Oyster Bay, and still takes a poignant interest in croquet. Richard Leonard, still the lone holder of the Rover Emeritus medal, and his beautiful Elizabeth, now absorbed in the problems presented by three outsize sons, live up in Larchmont; Bruce Barton and his wonderful and courageous daughter Betsey, John Wheeler and "Tee" are other old friends without a glimpse of whom no Eastern visit is complete. And there is still one other old friend, with whom our friendship began in the days of the First World War, on the beautiful wooded slopes behind Stanford University, and who has long lived in the heart of New York. We were in the rambling Hopi Indian type of house where Lou Henry Hoover and her sons and husband made their California home on the night when the thirty-first President of the United States was elected. We shared with some fifty chance-gathered friends the tremendous excitement of that night, and I was privileged to be with a much smaller group on the soberer night four years later when so different a story was told. Only three women were huddled over a library fire as the news came in that the fight was lost: Charlotte Kellogg, wife of Vernon Kellogg, the scientist, myself, and the ever gallant wife of the President whose term had still a few months to run.

Many millions of his friends have also shared the slow, hard years of misrepresentation and injustice that followed for him, have seen that persecution borne with quiet equanimity, his service to America pursued with a serenity that does credit to his Quaker forebears, have seen the tide turn, brimming over into that triumph of power and popularity that means light at eventide. That I may call him, and all of these, my friends makes me feel a need to praise Allah, with Kipling, "that he hath not terminated all the delights."

Mark and I separately, instinctively, have shortened sail, worn our rue with a difference, moved into smaller quarters that were not thick with memories. It did not effect a whole cure, but it helped, and after a while we could begin to build up new memories, of holiday excursions, grandchildren's visits, of long stays with each other, of happy times in Palo Alto, Santa Cruz, Washington, and in La Querencia, the new summer cottage on the dunes of Virginia's long ocean beach at Sandbridge.

Other memories would include many a stirring moment when a steamer's dry brief whistle means "All ashore who are going ashore," many a steward's kindly voice assuring us, "There'll be no dressing. Sailing night, miss. Thank you, miss"; many an inspection of hotel rooms where bags are warily dropped, where one says gratefully, "Yes, this is very nice," and is restrained only by sheer strength of character from adding loudly, "Please get out. We can open the windows and the bathroom door ourselves; you just go away. Can't you see that we're dead tired, and hungry, frozen, damp, dirty, and that we need lots of things before we have to know that there's a beauty parlor on the second floor?" All part of the joy of travel!

Then there was the crowded amphitheater in Mexico City, when with Fred and Enid, his second wife, we watched Lacuna, just back from retirement, conquer a seventh bull, and Christmas high up in Caracas, when we walked under blazing stars to midnight Mass, across the high plateau upon which this strangest of all cities lies. This was when Mark's Conway and his Frances were stationed there for three very full years.

Ordering curries in the decorous old English hotels that are strewn in a line between Hong Kong and Trieste, and winding up the meal with a basket of great black figs, finding long plated serving spoons in the Caledonia Market and little carved wooden saints on the Lungarno, or leaning on a solid stone parapet in Perugia —a parapet, incidentally, that has been solid since St. Teresa's day—while the sun set lazily over the Umbrian hills in autumn, or watching *Henry VIII* at the Old Vic —remembering these brings something inexhaustible and vital to Wordsworth's bliss of solitude.

Even though gone from the actual picture, always in my heart is the tall figure in a brown topcoat, with the long cigarette holder, the tickets, checks, theater passes, plans, urgencies. And gone from my life in the quiet late afternoons is the sound of a slamming door and the familiar voice ringing through the hotel suite, or the Sierra camp, or the home rooms: "Katy? Katy! My God, I thought you were out!"

The study in which I am writing is high up in an old building on the highest of San Francisco's seven times seven hills, those heights that were sand dunes when Joe and Lizzie and I toiled over them seventy years ago. Tuckertown, a huddle of small cottages, was somewhere in this neighborhood then, and the Children's Hospital, now well built into the surrounding city, and a few loose planks to form a walk here and there. From my southeast windows I can see the Bay, and the arch of Golden Gate Bridge, and the dear familiar silhouette of Tamalpais mountain for a background against a dove-gray sky. Fog is stealing in, and presently the horns begin, and the city, sloping down away from me in graded tiers of roofs and windows, then rising up to steepness again between me and the faraway water front, turns a hazy cream-pink in the last long hour of daylight. There are November roses in the long row of gardens, and most of the trees that line the streets are in full leaf.

My own city. She has outgrown her gold-rush days, her covered-wagon days, her Barbary Coast era, and the days when Chinatown was a tottering nest of dark, steep, oily stairways, pigtailed heads, and black alleys where strange tong wars found cover. Gone are the sailing vessels from the Bay, gone the great ashy gaps the earthquake left; the horsecars and the gas lamps in the streets are no more.

Family Gathering

And Lotta's fountain and the Grand Opera House and the Tivoli, where we applauded Tetrazzini in *Carmen* from thirty-five-cent seats, and thrilled at Modjeska in *Magda*. It was to the half-ruined city after the earthquake that Maude Adams came in *Quality Street* and *L'Aiglon* and glorious Ethel Barrymore in *Cousin Kate*. My first real play, after Elsie Leslie in *Little Lord Fauntleroy* and Hoyt's *Milk White Flag*, was Mrs. Kendal in *The Ironmaster*, and many a year went by before any actress or any play equaled that in my enraptured heart.

Through Polk Street, once again a shopping street, where McTeague hung his great gold tooth, and down the Hyde Street hill walks the ghost of little Aunt Kitty, threading the markets with the ever present necessity of keeping six young appetites satisfied on a thousand a year; gallant little Teresa, in her gray corduroy and her braids, is beside me again, on the way to early Mass. Joe turns from the pages of the *Scientific American* to face the fireside group in the dining-sitting room: "Nervous? What on earth should we be nervous about?"

Fred, at fifteen, deep in Lorimer's *Letters of a Self-made Merchant to His Son*, laughs abruptly. "Nothing," he answers reassuringly. Mark and Jim are building block houses through which to walk the chessmen as characters in a never ending play; Mark's protagonists always travel to far places and oriental ports, as she was one day to do, but Jim's viewpoint is a little different.

"I don't think we'll ever like any place better than this, do you, Katy? Let's stay this way."

Night has fallen as I stand at the window. Over the descending strip of city that stretches down to the Bay lies the shadow of the Golden Gate Bridge, and beyond that the oaks and redwoods of the Mill Valley hills. Jim and his vital, magnetic Sally have a home hanging like a bird's nest on one of the long spurs of Tamalpais, the mountain that was the background of childhood for all of us. Farther down, on the edge of the Pacific in a canyon that stretches high up to the wooded ridge, is the old sea captain's house, where Fred's lovely and cultured Enid, whom he met when both of them had been widowed for some years, keeps in order the orchards and gardens, the quail and the intrusive deer, the big dog and big fireplaces, the famous Shakespeare collection, and incidentally Fred himself. Fred's children and grandchildren live farther up the valley, as do some of Jim's.

Joe lives only a short four blocks away from me, with his French-born Germaine, who has not only won the city's heart as a loyal American but won a decoration from her own native government for her services to France as well. As for my own son, one of the busiest of San Francisco's busy doctors, he and his Alice live a few hundred yards away, in a big house that is always swarming with children and grandchildren; now sheltering a Navy wife waiting for orders, now a New York woman hanging on reports from a beloved invalid in the nearby hospital, and now mothering a teen-ager in a teen-ager's chronic state of disorientation and despair between school shifts. Ruling over the kitchen, as he has for more than twenty years, is Chinese Kayo, diminutive, but loved as a member of the family, and far upstairs his even smaller wife is busy establishing a nationwide business for a certain type of oriental art.

Margaret, the small "Mark" of the long ago dreams of camel rides, diplomacy, an apartment on the Ile de la Cité, an old house in Georgetown, races at Pao Machang and Havana and Newmarket, journeys on camelback and Nile steamers, embassy dinners and picnics at Santa Teresa, has had them all. Her old dreams and mine have been only too generously realized, and yet no waking fact, in broad daylight, ever quite meets the dream.

Six o'clock on a December afternoon. The hills of the city, sinking to the long dip of Pacific Avenue below my windows, rising to the heights of Telegraph Hill and Nob Hill and Twin Peaks, are spiderwebbed with lights in the early dark. Through a thin fog that is blowing in from the Gate they gleam softly, like one of the old Maxfield Parrish pictures we used to love so long ago. The moon, rising over Berkeley's Campanile, has silhouetted San Francisco's profile of hills and bay shores with living silver.